FAMINE ECHOES

FAMINE ECHOES

Cathal Póirtéir

GILL & MACMILLAN

Gill & Macmillan Ltd
Goldenbridge
Dublin 8
with associated companies throughout the world
© Cathal Póirtéir 1995
0 7171 2314 6
Index compiled by Helen Litton
Print origination by *Deirdre's Desktop*
Printed by ColourBooks Ltd, Dublin

A catalogue record is available for this book from the British Library.

5   4

I gcuimhne

For my father, Charlie Porter, who died while I was researching
the material for this book, and for my mother, Mary.
Thanks for sharing your memories.

Contents

1

Folk Memory and the Famine

❖❖❖

The Great Irish Famine of the late 1840s and early 1850s was the biggest social catastrophe in Irish history. One million people died of starvation and disease in five years and people fleeing the Famine made up a considerable part of the two million who fled the country in the ten years after the Famine began. Three million of the pre-Famine population of eight million were dead or gone in a few years and those who survived and stayed in Ireland soon found themselves in a totally changed society.

The landless potato-dependent poor, labourers and small cottiers, were wiped out. The system of land ownership and use was totally changed and modernised by the disappearance of the rundale system and so-called clachán settlements, as well as by a huge increase in pasture lands and livestock numbers. The class structures were transformed, and political, cultural and linguistic moulds were broken and reshaped into those which we now recognise as forming the basis for modern Ireland. The Great Irish Famine of the 1840s was to be the last major famine in Europe and a watershed in Irish social and economic history.

The extremes of nationalist and revisionist histories of the Famine stretch, on the one hand, from theories of British governmental genocide of the Irish, to the belief, on the other hand, that everything that the British could have done to save lives during the catastrophe was done, and that the number of people who died of starvation and disease was both unavoidable and exaggerated.

Much recent research has come up with findings relatively free from either of those ideological strait-jackets and a more complex and deeper understanding of the circumstances surrounding the disaster is becoming available to a wider readership.

Rather than fail to do justice to the work of those scholars by attempting to give too brief a summing-up of their work on the history of the Famine, at the end of the book I have drawn up a short bibliography of recent and readily available books to provide context for the range and relevance of the folklore of the Famine.

The unravelling, explaining and analysing of the various interacting factors which led to the Famine, and the reaction to it, is part of the ongoing task facing historians, economists and others. This work includes a constant search for new or underused sources of information about the Famine and the application of new models and research techniques to analyse and assess the value of the material. This re-evaluation and interpretation of the Famine is constantly changing in its conclusions or emphasis, as evidence and perceptions are challenged and changed by new research.

Perhaps the 150th anniversary of the Famine period may provide an opportunity for furthering debate about the historiography of the Famine. As part of that process, this book, and the radio programmes on which it is based, is an effort to look in detail at the folk history of the Famine and provide a comprehensive overview of it for those interested in getting a fuller picture of the terrible events.

Working as a broadcaster, with a background in folklore studies, I often feel that the folk memories of the oral tradition are one of the most accessible, yet undervalued and underused sources for understanding the Great Irish Famine and its consequences.

The folk memory of the Famine has been accorded little attention by historians and there may be many reasons for this omission. The use of folklore as an historical source has been rare in Ireland and in the English-speaking world. Traditionally the majority of historians here, though not elsewhere, have tended to focus only on the evaluation of data in contemporary documents.

There is no shortage of contemporary written sources for studies of the Great Irish Famine. Indeed there is a wealth of official documentation from government and its various agencies, from travellers, journalists and diarists, from charities and churches. So great is the possible harvest of contemporary documentary evidence that, perhaps, it is not surprising that folklore and folk memory are among the areas which have been forgotten, disregarded, or put on the long finger, as attention has focused on other more orthodox areas of research.

In some lesser developed countries, where the written records are considered to be biased or lacking in their coverage of native history, folklore has been used to complement or fill the gaps in written sources. Perhaps the ready availability of a wide range of written sources for the Famine period in Ireland explains why historians have, by and large, ignored the folk record. There may be other reasons, however, for the general neglect of oral history as one of the sources for information on the Famine and other aspects of Irish history.

Anyone coming in search of material about the common people, and what they themselves had to say about what happened, will discover an incredible gap in the documentary knowledge of the Famine period.

While there is a vast amount of written evidence, little or none of it comes from the perspective of the ordinary people. The communities who suffered worst during the Famine were, by and large, not those which had the opportunity of leaving a written testament of what had happened to their district and their people. Most of those who died were from Irish-speaking communities. Equally in English-language communities, many of those who disappeared were illiterate. We rarely have their own words, in either language, to describe their experience of famine.

To have no record of the voices of many of those most badly affected by the hunger, diseases and deaths caused by the Famine is a notable gap indeed in our record of those terrible events. The perspective of those who saw their districts depopulated by death, eviction and emigration is not the one which is to the fore in official documentation of the period. On those rare occasions where official documents afford us a passing opportunity to hear the voice of those who suffered most, we find them translated and filtered by the perspectives of the writers who recorded them for us.

One reason which has been advanced by economic historian Cormac Ó Gráda for so little attention having been given to the folk memories and oral traditions about the Famine is the fact that much of the source material is in the Irish language. He argues that many of the researchers in the field have been simply unable to deal with material in Irish. While it is true that a lot of the best material recorded from the oral tradition is in Irish, there is also a rich, parallel and interlinked tradition in the English language. A lack of understanding of the Irish language is hardly an excuse applicable to the equal neglect of the English-language folk material. Perhaps some other explanation is needed.

There appears to be a perception that the vivid accounts afforded by a folk history of the Famine would be emotive and therefore unacceptable to many historians. There has indeed been a fashion in Irish historical studies to make accounts of the Famine, and other events, as detached and unemotional as possible, with the avowed aim of giving a more scientific and balanced analysis of events. This is partly due to an effort to play down emotive areas which had been, or could be, open to exploitation by nationalist propagandists. It was, and is, often considered safer to avoid those elements which risk the arousal of emotions and passions.

For a broadcaster, a folklorist or non-academic reader of history, in search of a human and gripping account of the great hunger, it seems odd that some of the most vivid and graphic accounts of a narrative should be ignored, avoided or sanitised to provide a more clinically detached and politically acceptable version of history. Some revisionist concerns are understandable in the context of the often highly-charged debates surrounding Irish historical facts and fictions. However, it should also be noted that other historians feel that the glossing over of the human suffering of famine has been a disservice to both the victims of the calamity and to the writing of history itself.

The reluctance of many historians to engage with the evidence of folklore seems to be based on the false premise that the folklore of the Famine, by dint of its nature as folklore, carries a nationalist interpretation of the causes, events and effects of the calamity. A close examination of the folk material might well disappoint the nationalist propagandist as much as it might pleasantly surprise the revisionist. Perhaps this volume will serve as an introduction for all concerned.

There are, however, a few popular images which seem to crop up when the folk record is dismissed by historians and others. Yet, having examined the folklore of the Famine in detail, the most common of these images seem much more prominent now than they were in the context of that genuine folklore recorded with diligence and understanding by the expert scholars and field-workers of the Irish Folklore Commission some fifty or sixty years ago. These modern impressions of what the folk memory of the Famine actually consisted of seem to be as pervasive as they are erroneous and unrepresentative of the tradition as a whole.

Today's populist images of the callousness and meanness of the British government, in the person of Queen Victoria and her fabled fiver, or of food-laden ships exporting much-needed food from Ireland during the height of the distress, rarely play a part in the thousands of traditions that were passed on orally within the post-Famine communities themselves.

There are, however, strongly attested traditions about many facets of the story of the Great Irish Famine and it is on these that I have focused. They include vivid pictures of the social conditions in which the ordinary people lived before the blight struck at the end of the summer of 1845. Among other things, we learn how they built their houses and how they existed before disaster struck (Chapter 2: Before the Bad Times).

There are many descriptions of the sudden and disastrous arrival of the blight and the decimation of the potato which followed. In an effort to understand the reasons for this disaster, the folk mind explained it as a type of divine intervention. It was widely felt that the blight was a punishment from God for people's previous abuse of abundant crops of potatoes immediately before the Famine (Chapter 3: Abundance Abused and the Blight).

There are strong memories of the types of alternative food that the poor and hungry sought out when their main source of food was largely destroyed. The ingenuity and desperation of the people are clear in the stories recalled of dependence on the blood of animals, herbs and weeds, the scouring of the seashore and the devouring of the flesh of animals not normally eaten. The introduction and growing importance of other crops, such as turnips and cabbage, also lodged in the folk memory (Chapter 4: Turnips, Blood, Herbs and Fish).

The general absence of the potato and the scarcity of replacement foods, combined with the lack of money, inevitably led to widespread theft of foodstuffs. Stealing food is recalled in a number of stories which, at times, praise and excuse the thief because of force of circumstance. But the levels of deprivation are also reflected in tales of violence and murder, both of the victim and of the thief, if caught. Both poor and better-off took many and varied precautions to safeguard their stores of food against their neighbours and others. Yet, there are also examples of great understanding and kindness in the face of adversity where the basic honesty and dire necessity of the thief is recognised, sometimes even by the person from whom the food was being stolen (Chapter 5: 'No Sin and You Starving').

Undoubtedly among the saddest and most harrowing of the memories carried in tradition concern those who died of starvation (Chapter 6: Mouths Stained Green) or disease (Chapter 7: 'The Fever, God Bless Us'). The pathetic attempts of families and individuals to stay alive left a strong impression on the minds of those who survived the horrors of the Famine. Stories abound about bodies of young and old being found along the road, outside houses and farms, in the poorhouses and fever hospitals. Among the most heart-rending pictures are those of people attempting to feed the starving only to see them die, their weakened bodies unable to cope with the sudden intake of food.

The terrible deaths of the hungry were at least equalled by the horrors of death from myriad famine-related diseases such as relapsing fever, typhus, cholera, and dysentery. The understandable fear of contagion from those already suffering from disease led to many measures being taken for self-preservation by those lucky enough to have escaped the ravages of disease. This often led to a lonely death in their homes for the families affected by disease, shunned by their fearful neighbours. Nevertheless, the names of many of those who tried to help the victims of disease in make-shift 'fever huts' were still fondly recalled in their neigbourhoods a hundred years later. Some of these were traditional healers who pitted their skills against the famine fevers, others were simply neighbours who bravely tried to minister to the sick and dying. Many of the helpers died in their attempts to help others.

Another element of the period which has remained strong in the folk memory is the horror of the poorhouse. The stigma of having entered the poorhouse was often cast up at those who managed to survive these disease-ridden refuges. Some of the recollections of the poorhouses are stark and depressing. Many of those who worked in them are depicted as cruel and heartless and the conditions are constantly remembered as being harsh and inhuman. What help the poorhouses provided to the army of destitute people, who crowded into them despite the stigma, seems to have been largely forgotten (Chapter 8: The Paupers and the Poorhouse).

Often, even the relief food which kept so many alive during the worst of the hunger is mentioned with disdain and distaste. The use of Indian meal had been limited or totally unknown before it was introduced by the government as a relief food. Many failed to cook it properly and suffered the consequences. As well as the dislike of the 'yellow male', the distribution of it was often seen as being marked by corruption, injustice and cruelty. The distributors of the meal were often accused of favouring themselves, their friends and cronies, while cheating or ignoring others in desperate need. Many of the images which come to us through the oral tradition paint vivid and detailed pictures of the physical distribution of the meal from depots and boilers. Tales of unfair treatment are matched by other stories of the distributors being outwitted and cheated in turn by local people who had quickly learned to play the system to their advantage (Chapter 9: Boilers, Stirabout and 'Yellow Male').

Relief food was also distributed as a means of payment on

some public works set up to relieve distress. In other cases cash payment was made on these schemes. The stewards and supervisors of these public works are often remembered for their harshness, but sometimes also for their achievements in road building. The works themselves are seen as having been of varying benefit to the people of each area in the long term. Many are depicted as having been worthless to all but the landlord, and sometimes not even to him. Yet men and women flocked to these public works and there are hundreds of accounts of the conditions workers lived in and the kind of payment they got (Chapter 10: New Lines and 'Male Roads').

One of the bitter man-made legacies of the Famine period is the one left by the attempts of some evangelical Protestant groups to proselytise. They became known as 'soupers', for their efforts to gain converts from Catholicism by offering food and other comforts in return. While many religious organisations and individuals are remembered for their unconditional charity, including the Society of Friends and many Church of Ireland clergy, the stigma of souperism lasted into the twentieth century. There is much bitterness, and some humour, in the accounts of proselytising which have been passed on in tradition (Chapter 11: 'Soupers', 'Jumpers' and 'Cat Breacs').

The burial of the one million who died during the Famine has left its mark on the landscape as well as on the minds of the people of Ireland. Graveyards, famine pits, ditches, fields and the ruins of dwelling houses all hold the remains of those who died. There are chilling stories of the incredible efforts made to see to it that family and friends got a proper burial in a consecrated graveyard. Often it was impossible for the survivors to bring their dead to a graveyard and many makeshift burial places were made to cope with the huge numbers who died. Many were buried without coffins. Others were wrapped in a simple sheet in a straw covering. Coffins with sliding bottoms were employed in many places so that they could be reused when the body had been dropped into the single or mass graves. Sometimes houses were tumbled on whole families who had died of fever because their neighbours were too frightened, or too weak, to carry their diseased remains to the graveyard. Horrible pictures remain of unburied corpses being eaten by animals (Chapter 12: The Bottomless Coffin and the Famine Pit).

The Famine and its aftermath swept away not only the cottier and labouring class but also, to a large extent, the landlord. The Irish landlord was often castigated by the British government, as well as by ordinary Irish people, for being responsible for the state of Ireland at the time of the Famine. The images which traditional accounts give us of landlords are of the good, the bad and the ugly. Landlords who made efforts to help their tenants in distress are recalled with fondness and thanks, but the majority of memories centre on the heartlessness of the landlord class. Landlords were perceived as callous in their demands for rent from people who were in dire straits. They were seen as abusing relief measures to benefit themselves and their favourites, and popular imagination interpreted their final demise as being a divine retribution for their cruelty (Chapter 13: Landlords, Grain and Government).

The greatest odium seems to have been reserved for those members of the community who acted as agents for the landlords. They were often seen as having turned on their own, so that they and their families might benefit from the suffering of others. They were cursed and reviled by the people for what they did, on behalf of the landlords or on their own behalf. They shared this communal dislike with other members of the community who were seen to prosper by grabbing the land of those who died or emigrated, either by buying it below its value, or by taking it in lieu of unpaid debts, run up with shopkeepers and gombeen men who supplied food on credit during the period of distress (Chapter 14: Agents, Grabbers and Gombeen Men).

Mass evictions, during and after the Famine, have remained one of the most strongly resented and often retold results of the period. The deserted and tumbled dwellings of the landscape often continued to carry the names of those who had been evicted, and those who had evicted them, many years after both were dead and gone. Individual evictions and the fate of the homeless are often remembered in great and telling detail (Chapter 15: 'A Terrible Levelling of Houses').

Emigration had been a fact of Irish life for years before the Great Famine, but the scale of panic emigration caused by the returning blight and grinding hardship of the Famine often led to a portrayal of the Famine as being the beginning of emigration *en masse*. The Famine did, however, see a switch in the areas of greatest emigration, from north and east to south and west. Final destinations also changed, with the United States of America becoming the main hope of a new and better life.

We have accounts of the preparations people made before heading for the ports. There are memories of the hardships of life on board and what awaited the emigrants on the other side. Emigration, 'free' or otherwise, engendered mixed emotions. On the one hand, there was the relief of escaping hunger and death and the hope of a new life overseas. On the other hand, there was a fear of the unknown perils of the voyage, and bitterness, resentment and loneliness at having to leave family and friends behind (Chapter 16: The Coffin Ships and the Going Away).

Finally, we have the folktales, legends, anecdotes and folk poetry which encapsulated community experience and belief in stable and recognisable traditional forms. Some of these stories were widely told and believed all over the country. Many of them reflect a belief that goodness was rewarded and meanness punished. Some of them tell of miracles, others of curses, yet others afford a glimpse of humour in the face of adversity. This body of tradition was a product of the society in which it existed. It offered people an opportunity to deal with the harsh realities which surrounded them in forms which seemed to make the disaster more easily understood and remembered. These narratives also functioned in other ways by expressing the wishes of the community as to how they would have preferred communal life and values to be (Chapter 17: Of Curses, Kindness and Miraculous Food).

One of the difficulties in dealing with the reliability of oral tradition is to recognise and separate the genuine historical material from other material which functions at another level. Even where we have accounts of historical events passed on with great accuracy, the gap in the time from the actual happening to the time of collection poses certain difficulties. Where verifiable historical detail has become imbedded in accounts, the task of evaluating the accuracy of events is easier, but we must remain aware of the possibility that the passage of time may cause distortion.

The enormity of the Famine has led some historians to focus on it as the beginning of certain trends in Irish society. However, many of these trends can be traced to pre-Famine times and the events of the Famine are now seen as having accelerated and accentuated them. This may also be the case with the folk memory of the period. Accounts of all aspects of the Famine, like emigration, eviction and souperism, for example, had also occurred before and after the Famine itself. Because of the historical similarity in the incidents that happened in these related time layers, it would be surprising if, on occasions, some chronological compression did not occur. Some of the accounts given as happening during the Famine may, therefore, have happened some time before or after the Great Famine itself, but the thematic similarity in the incidents, remembered and recounted over a period of a hundred years, will have linked them to the more concentrated focus of lore concerning the Great Famine of the 1840s. The neat chronological demarcations afforded to scholars by hindsight and the written record are not the prime concern of the folk record. That caveat should not lead to the richness and accuracy of much of the oral tradition being undervalued.

The transmission of lore can be seen as happening in a number of ways. Within a traditional community, folk material can be transmitted through that community in 'parallel', to the contemporary members of that community, or 'vertically' to the children who form the next generation of that tradition. The constancy and accuracy of tradition can often be ascribed to the corrective mechanism implicit in that double axis. Where elements of tradition were in danger of being changed in transmission, the awareness of that tradition by other members of the 'parallel' community saw to it that the 'vertical' tradition also adhered to the known facts and forms of tradition.

The incredible memory of practised traditional storytellers in

Ireland has been commented on by many authorities. Many of them made conscious and successful efforts to maintain the integrity of their traditions. One study of this phenomenon, in which I studied the craft of Micí Sheáin Néill, a renowned storyteller from the Rannafast Gaeltacht in Co. Donegal, demonstrated his ability to render word for word retellings of traditional stories, even though there was almost 50 years between his various recorded versions of these long and involved folktales.

Undoubtedly there were huge variations between the ability of specialist storytellers and the efforts made by those passive tradition-bearers who would not normally have functioned as storytellers. They only did so when pressed to in the absence of those who were held in high regard as storytellers by traditional communities. But the passing on of local historical lore was not seen as being the preserve of the specialists alone. Differing types of folklore were valued and passed on for differing reasons.

Even where these traditions seem to depart from historical fact, they may maintain a functional value as examples to reinforce the cultural norms or ideals of the community, of how it was felt that, for example, kindness would be rewarded and lack of kindness punished. Many of these formalised narratives predate the Great Famine of the 1840s; some of them can be identified in international oral tradition, while others have only a localised currency.

Part of the work carried out by scholars is the task of sifting through all the various forms that the lore has taken in the tradition, so that the particular properties and functions of each genre can be established and more fully appreciated.

Although we cannot now totally recapture the experiences of the ordinary people of Famine Ireland, it is surely incumbent on us to make every effort to listen to what we still can hear of those silenced voices, in all the forms or genres available to us.

I feel that the echoes of those silenced voices which we have in folk memory are the nearest we can get to the experience of the poor of the 1840s and 1850s. Survivors, as well as victims, suffered hunger, lost loved ones and neighbours, suffered the ignominy of the poorhouses and the dangers of the fever. Many of those who lived to tell the tale had witnessed the dying days of individuals, families and communities who would otherwise have lived and perished without mention in official records.

Some of the tradition-bearers recorded by the expert collectors of the Irish Folklore Commission were people whose own families had been evicted, people who had buried the dead, received charity, worked on relief schemes and existed on relief food. Others were those who benefited from the Famine as their families increased their holdings by getting the land of those who died or emigrated.

Many of these survivors of the Great Irish Famine lived into this century with a store of personal and communal memories of the bad times. Not everyone had the same story to tell. The memories and the telling of them varied from person to person and from place to place, depending on individual circumstances and experience. Undoubtedly many memories and stories of the horrors of the Famine were suppressed consciously and unconsciously for a variety of reasons. Other elements were simply forgotten or reshaped with the passage of time.

While we are not fortunate enough to have a written record from the ordinary people of the period, we are exceedingly fortunate in having a very rich and detailed source in the folk memory which was collected and preserved within one hundred years of the Famine.

The material in this sampling of the English language folk memories of the Great Irish Famine was collected in two ways (see Appendixes I and II). About half of it is the result of a questionnaire circulated by the Irish Folklore Commission in 1945, and the other half was collected from 1935 on by the Commission's full-time and part-time collectors, who were later incorporated into the Department of Irish Folklore in University College Dublin. Indeed, it is evidence of the persistence of the oral tradition in Ireland that 150 years after the Famine, field-workers are still able to collect material from the living tradition.

Most of the material quoted comes from the children and grandchildren of the people who were eye-witnesses to the Famine.

The collectors who worked for the Commission were experts

in the lore and traditional learning of the areas in which they worked and lived. They sought out those individuals who had gained a reputation as masters of 'seanchas' or traditional lore in a given area and carefully recorded their words for posterity. They knew the storytellers, the community and the shared folklore which was their communal property.

We are forever in the debt of such expert folklore collectors as Tadhg Ó Murchú and Seosamh Ó Dálaigh in Kerry, Seán Ó Cróinín in West Cork, James G. Delaney in the Midlands, Michael J. Murphy in the north-east, Michael Corduff in Mayo, Seán Ó hEochaidh in Donegal and many others who worked so diligently all over the Irish countryside.

The full-time and part-time collectors of the Irish Folklore Commission recorded their material in a number of ways over the years. The earliest collections were carried out with pen and paper only. The collectors painstakingly wrote down verbatim each and every word of the storytellers, singers and other bearers of tradition. Later came the use of wax cylinder recordings made on portable Ediphone machines, which allowed the informants to tell their tales with little or no need for constant repetitions to facilitate the collector, who could then go home with the recording to transcribe every word of the recorded voice from the cylinder to the page. Sadly the Irish Folklore Commission was under-funded and very few of the wax cylinders could be kept for posterity. In fact, what happened was that following transcription, by which time their value as sound records had been greatly degraded, the cylinders were returned to the Folklore Commission in Dublin, pared and sent back to the collectors for re-use. Apart from some exceptional Ediphone recordings now safely archived in the Department of Irish Folklore in University College Dublin, the only reflection we now have of these early recordings is the careful transcriptions made by the collectors and sent to the archivist Seán Ó Súilleabháin, who organised their classification, binding and safe storage in the archive.

Sound recording proper began with the occasional use of mobile recording units which cut disks in situ, and developed during the 1950s with the ready availability of cumbersome, but portable, tape-recorders. The difficult and time-consuming work of transcription continued but, from that period on, the original sound recordings made by the collectors could also be kept and safely stored in the archive.

Another method of collecting, which was used on many occasions by the Irish Folklore Commission, was the use of questionnaires. Hundreds of these were sent around the country to school teachers, local historians and other individuals who knew their locality and its traditions well. A series of questions was devised for each of these questionnaires. The collector then made inquiries in his or her own area for information on the various queries about customs, beliefs, practices, local lore, legends and traditions of all sorts.

A questionnaire on the Great Irish Famine was distributed all over the country to mark the 100th anniversary of the Famine in 1945. The resulting answers came to thousands of pages of manuscript which are now held in the Department of Irish Folklore in UCD.

The one major study of Famine folklore carried out before the 1990s refers only to the material gleaned from the replies to the questionnaire and makes no specific mention of the excellent and copious material in the general manuscript collection. This is Dr Roger McHugh's chapter on 'The Famine in Irish Oral Tradition' in *The Great Famine: Studies in Irish History*.

There had also been a major collection carried out through the national schools in 1937–38. With the co-operation of the Department of Education, teachers throughout the 26 counties (to which the experience was confined on account of the Northern Ireland Department of Education's failure to participate) encouraged and guided schoolchildren who were given the task of making a collection of folklore from their family and neighbours. There was a wonderful response to this scheme and, apart altogether from the high intrinsic value of the material collected in areas where full-time or part-time collectors had not yet had an opportunity to do their own collecting work, it alerted the staff of the Irish Folklore Commission to the strength of various aspects of folk tradition around the country. It also highlighted individuals and areas particularly rich in certain types of lore and created a large network of valuable contacts, many of whom were of assistance in developing the Questionnaire system and providing answers to the Famine Questionnaire which was undertaken seven years after the Schools' Collection. The results of the Schools' Collection includes thousands of references to the folklore of the Famine.

The thousands of pages of manuscript material collected by the Irish Folklore Commission, and preserved for further generations, gives us a rare opportunity to learn about the Great Famine from the perspective of the people whose voice is usually lost with the passage of time. It comes to us in their words, with their memories and choice of images strongly linked to local places, individuals and events. These are the words of men and women who grew up surrounded by the physical and psychological legacy of the Famine. They echo what they heard from their parents and neighbours who experienced the reality of it.

It is not the type of statistical material you will find in official documents. It is not a definitive overview or an analysis of the catastrophe in context. It is more a series of memories, personal narratives and interpretations of the events from the perspective of ordinary, often illiterate people. Those individuals in London and Dublin who played such a prominent part in the official history of the Famine do not appear in the folk history. The names which do appear are those of family and neighbours, local agents, landlords and clergy. The folk history is strongly tied to the locality in which it is found, with the obvious advantages and disadvantages which that carries. It does not provide us with figures to analyse, with details of administrative policy or the debates which surrounded its formation. The context given is almost entirely local. We have to go to other sources to fill in the historical context of the events described if we are to attempt to quantify them.

The picture which folklore gives us is broken and fragmentary, but that in itself is no reason to undervalue it. These thousands upon thousands of shattered pieces of memory can still form part of the mosaic of our understanding. We must rely on other research to sketch the outlines of these pictures into which the fragments of folklore can be fitted. The varieties of shape, colour and texture of the traditional folk material can give us a fuller, deeper and more varied picture than would otherwise be possible.

Not only can the folk material offer us an opportunity to view the events of the Famine from a perspective rarely afforded us by other sources, it also paints a picture of what was believed to have happened by the generations who lived directly after the tragedy.

Where the reality of historical happenings in a particular area can be established by local studies, this may or may not be in harmony with the accounts collected by folklorists in these areas a hundred years after the events. To compare and contrast the versions of history provided by oral and written sources is part of the process which is necessary to properly debate the trustworthiness of oral tradition as an historical source.

It is hoped that, by making a representative selection of the folklore of the Famine available in this book and the radio series which accompanies it, local historians will have the opportunity to review the oral traditions of their own area within the context of their other sources. Whatever the final results of such comparisons may be, there is another element of the folk history worthy of note.

Even in the cases where the oral tradition and other historical approaches part company on the actual events of the Famine, the oral tradition still holds an importance of its own which has rarely been studied or remarked upon by historians. If the folk record, as we have it, is an accurate description of the way in which ordinary people in the generation after the Famine viewed and understood the events which so changed their own lives and the history of their country, then the dynamic created by those beliefs has an importance of its own.

The accounts collected by the Irish Folklore Commission in Ireland in the 1930s and 1940s from people born in the last half of the nineteenth century is unlikely to be vastly different from the memories passed on to, and by, their departed neighbours in America, Australia, Britain and the other destinations of the post-Famine diaspora. At this remove it is impossible to establish how much the folklore of the Famine interacted with other versions and interpretations of Famine history, but the oral traditions which ordinary people had heard, at home and abroad, surely formed part of their own understanding of the history of Ireland during the Great Famine.

A methodology has been worked out in some other countries so that the folk material can be used as source material by historians and others. As yet, in Ireland, no generally acceptable methodology, based on the particular characteristics of the Irish oral tradition, has been arrived at between folklorists and historians. While this work now seems to have started here, adjustments are necessary to fine tune imported models to suit Irish conditions. Until such a customised system of evaluation is accepted here, I hope that this sampling of the English-language folklore of the Famine will demonstrate the richness of detail available in it.

I have also prepared a similar collection of the Irish-language folklore of the Famine for broadcast by RTÉ Radio 1 and Raidio na Gaeltachta, and for publication by Coiscéim as *Glórtha ón Ghorta*.

My intention in both works is not to analyse the material in any detail or in a scholarly fashion, but to give an idea of the variety of experience recorded in oral history and the very human way in which the Great Famine of the 1840s was remembered one hundred years after the event.

All the material I have used comes from the Main Manuscript Collection of the Department of Irish Folklore in University College Dublin, including the Questionnaire material. Footnotes comprise the abbreviation IFC followed by volume number, separated by a colon from the page numbers. Dates, when included, are those given to the collector by the informant when available. As the texts have been heavily edited, reference numbers refer to the total contribution of the individual informant or collector as the case may be. Lack of time and space did not allow me to investigate further some four or five thousand other references to the Famine in the Schools' Collection, and the material quoted in this volume is just a fraction of the material available in the sources used. I hope my selection gives a representative sample of the tradition to those who might otherwise be unaware of its range and richness.

Finally, I wish to thank Professor Bo Almqvist, Head of the Department of Irish Folklore, University College Dublin, for his permission to quote from the manuscript collection there.

Gabhaim buíochas fosta leis an Ollamh Cormac Ó Gráda agus leis an Ollamh Séamus Ó Catháin a chuir comhairle orm faoi ghnéithe eagsúla den ábhar. Tá mé féin freagrach as aon locht atá ar an saothar.

❧❧

2

Before the Bad Times

❧❧

In the hundred years before the coming of the potato blight to Ireland, the use of the potato had spread rapidly and saw other produce, such as butter, grain and meat, gradually disappear from the tables of the poor and become confined to the tables of the better-off or to the export market. Oats had become a cash crop in most of the country as dependence on the potato grew.

The cottier system expanded to the point where one-third of the population was living in one-roomed cabins and the labourers existed on what was basically a potato wage, providing the farmers with cheap labour. On the eve of the Famine there were two to three million cottiers, labourers and their families, many of them living in clustered settlements on previously unpopulated hillsides and poor marginal land, where the spade and lazy-bed cultivation allowed a perilous existence on a diet dominated by the potato. The land was held under the conacre system and the cottiers could be evicted at will by farmers.

The population explosion had seen rapid growth from one million to over eight million people in 250 years, half of that growth taking place in the 75 years before the Famine.

In 1836 the Poor Inquiry Commission reported that about two and a half million people in Ireland were living in such poverty that relief measures would be needed to help the huge number of landless and destitute in one of the most densely populated countries in Europe.

As the population grew, holdings continued to be sub-divided and on the eve of the Famine most Irish farms were small: half of them were less than five acres and in the west of Ireland only a quarter of the farm holdings were five acres or more.

❧❧

Before the Bad Times

Seán Ó Domhnaill, b.1873, Scairt na nGleobhrán, Ballylooby,
Cahir, Co. Tipperary

The typical local farmer held no more than ten Irish acres. Many held much smaller places. However, owing to this poverty he found it difficult to till his wheat, oats or potato plot. He often got help from his neighbours, a fact which gave rise to the now well-known word 'meitheal' [communal work party].

His standard of living was very low; he and his family depended mostly on the potato crop for their sustenance. His corn crops were sold to pay the enacting landlords, the Jellicos, Wallpoles, Jacksons and Waterparks. Of course the population generally was then double what it is now.[1]

❧❧

Laurence Mc Intyre, b.1865, Kilcrossduff, Shercock, Co. Cavan

The people were living in very poor circumstances before the Famine. From 30 to 35 shillings an acre was the rent paid to the landlords for farms in this neighbourhood. The farms were small. Some had four to five acres, very few had twenty acres, others had only two acres, a woman called Anne Collins had only one acre, there were people had an acre and a half, the average sized farm in this part would be about seven acres. The had no ploughs and they dug the land with loys, big old loy [láí, a type of spade]. They lived mostly on potatoes.[2]

❧❧

Seán Ó Duinnshléibhe, Glenville, Fermoy, Co. Cork

Wheat and black oats were grown by the farmers who limed their lands well, as is shown by the great many old kilns in the district. The limestone was quarried both at Kildinan and Ballyhooly to make plant food i.e. to release plant food.

At Kildinan was a flax-mill. The proprietors supplied seed to the farmers. This factory employed about 200 and gave the farmers and their hands useful employment at home preparing the flax for factory. The poor in this way had a means of earning some money for their support. Acres upon acres were grown in ridges, no one made drills in those times, as plenty men were available to attend the crop.[3]

⚜

William Doudigan (O'Dowd), b.1863, Redbray, Tullaghan,
Co. Leitrim

An old man near here, Phelim Maguire, said to be 106 years [born 1838], said swapping was a great go in his young days, that is when neighbours had surpluses of different kinds of crops, say one strong in hay, another in potatoes, they exchanged the surplus, balancing the superior quality of one with a greater quantity of the other. Say 10 cwt. of turf for 1 cwt. of hay.

Days in swap [meant] exchange of labour. One man giving another days at a set job, say building or roofing a house that had to be finished up quickly and he paid him back at some such similar work. This gave rise to 'on you' 'It's on me'. He has a day on me in the bog or at the haystack. I have to go to him or send a man in my place. A man counted as good as a horse, that is if a man came with his horse and cart, say carting hay for a day, I must give him two days single labour without horse.

In the case of fishing boats, with say a team or crew of five men, seven shares were made of the catch: one for each man, one for the boat and one for the tackle. The last two shares necessary, as one man might own boat and tackle.[4]

⚜

Barney Gargan, b.1860, Tierworker, Bailieboro, Co. Cavan

The population was very big before the Famine. There was a house on nearly every four acres of land around here, and some people had only two acres, and some had only one. The population was three or four times thicker before the Famine. If you cross Tierworker Mountain you will see where they set potatoes in ridges on it. The ridges are there still. You would wonder at anybody setting potatoes in such places where there is nothing but heather and long grass, but the place was so thickly populated at the time that they had to plant potatoes there.[5]

❦

Thomas O'Flynn, John Melody, Attymass, Ballina, Co. Mayo

They had few cattle or sheep as they had little place to keep them. Most families owned a cow and a calf only and those near the mountain owned a few sheep each. As many as could possibly manage it also kept a couple of sheep in addition to the cow and calf. The land supported the household for they lived on potatoes and, now and again, had oatmeal cakes and butter and milk.

The corn was sold to pay the rent and taxes. Flax was sown, a few quarts by each farmer, out of which they made their linens, and wool provided the heavier clothing which was also made locally.

Bed clothes were torn up and used as clothing. Men wore short knee breeches, long tailed coats, high hats, white linen shirts, long stockings and nailed boots. Women wore a cloak with a white linen head cloth.

Extensive use was made of credits. The district had its 'gombeen' men who charged four shillings for the loan of a pound for a year. The loans were taken out when the seed was sown, as there was then scarcely any potatoes left, and repayment was made in November. Certain days of the week were appointed for the loaning of money and again for repayment. Only quite recently the direct descendant of the most notorious gombeen man in the district died and left a fortune of over £30,000. These were Catholics. Two families of Protestant gombeen men disappeared about 60 years ago.

Shopkeepers gave credits in the same way and repayment was made in November or before Christmas. The custom has survived in the seed and manure business still, and even when some farmers can pay cash, they put off settling their accounts until November and lose cash discounts by doing so.

Wages were small 6d. to 10d. per day and long hours were worked.[6]

&

Seán Ó Duinnshleibhe, Glenville, Fermoy, Co. Cork

At those times the labourers settled with a farmer for a year. Lady Day [25 March] was the day when the labour year commenced, and on that day could be seen families moving from one house to another with loads of furniture and their belongings. There was a habit among some families of moving every year from one district to another for better prerequisites, for the pay was much the same everywhere, about 2/6 a week.

Owing to big population the farmer had many willing hands to work for their diet alone. The head of the family was paid the agreed wage and the rest of the family were helpers. In return these people got a gobal of butter at Christmas and Easter, and the wife or daughters would be supplied with a jug of sour milk once or twice a week for drinking or baking.

The women also prepared light for their homes. They made pádóig [páideog: tallow candle] from melted tallow or rush lights or mould candles. The turf fire gave light when the candle was not there in winter, or when they wanted to spare the candle for knitting and sewing. They used splinters of bogdeal for ordinary purposes of lighting such as suppertime. An instrument was made by the local blacksmith for holding the splinter. It was called an coinnleoir iarainn [iron candlestick] or trilseán [a lamp or torch].

The worst feature to notice in those days was the houses were small, often badly roofed in winter, and insanitary conditions both within and abroad.

The farmers' houses were much bigger and much better kept.

There were three rooms on the floor: the kitchen in the centre, large accommodations, but the manure was again stored in front and back. Seldom a flowerpot was seen at the front door. The houses were well lighted and at least one room was lofted. In many of the farmers' houses there were half-lofts in the kitchen, having a bed in each for a workman.

The farmers as a whole were contented although too many were depending on them Their only enemy was the landlord or his agent for, when the gale-day came about, the rent was demanded and in some cases there was distress and afterwards evictions. Only about a dozen could be described at the time as 'independent' farmers, the others may be described as 'struggling'.

Poor families were the subjects of their master, who may himself be stracaling [strachailt, struggling] along or, as they say, 'pulling the devil by the tail', and struggled along together. It was only for a year after all, if the workman was not satisfied he would look for a new master before Lady's Day. Or the farmer would give him notice to quit. This seemed common in the South for labourers, as already mentioned, were on the go to a new destination. It was always an understanding that a labourer's family should help wherever they settled. If the landlord or bailiffs came to take possession of a farm, the whole community of farmers and labourers would unite to protect the farmer and defend his property, whether he was worthy or not, as was done at the time of the Land League later.

Farmers gave help to one another when work was stressing. A meitheal [co-operative labour group] would gather to perform his work. When a poor man had potatoes to dig a meitheal would gather on a Sunday morning and clear the potatoes.

The farmer's wife was helped by the labourer's family at milking and churning, as a reward she would give a half-stone of flour occasionally, or a little butter.

On account of this great population about 1842 or '43, early marriages were common. Young people met at Mallow crossroads on Sundays for a dance, and on summer evenings they chatted and sang at outdoor meetings in the neighbourhood. At winter they had meetings within, that is scoireachta [festive house gathering], where the news of the day was discussed and revision of songs and stories took place.

Finally money was scarce and hard to get. The farmer received little for the produce of his land, and the upkeep of workers also rested on him. He in return was unable to repay much to the labourer. Two shillings or 2/6 a week or rather per year about six pounds.[7]

❧

William Torrens, b.1872, Lisminton, Ballintra, Co. Donegal heard accounts of the Famine period from his father, William Torrens, 1828–1912

The houses were low and thatched, some having only one room divided from the living apartment or kitchen by a thick stone wall. The better class farmers had two rooms to their cottages besides the kitchen, which in this case generally occupied a central position, and sometimes in the back side-wall of the kitchen near the fire a place for a bed was built out in which some of the older people lay for the comfort and warmth. This spot was called an 'out-shot'.

The floors of all apartments were just earth, which kept cold and damp during the long periods of rain in the winter time or in times of deep snow when the clay became absolutely sticky by the snow dragged in on the feet. The windows were small and often not capable of being opened to let in the fresh air, but missing panes from the sashes sometimes did this to a certain degree.

There were seldom any ceilings on either rooms or kitchen, nothing but the scraws which lay on the roof timbers under the thatch. Hazel or sallow rods called 'scollops' were driven u-shaped into the scraws to hold on the thatch. This has always been the method of fastening the straw on roofs in this district.

In other parts of Donegal, notably around Killybegs, Kilcar, Glencolumcille and the west coast generally, the thatch was at that time, and is mostly yet, held on with straw ropes placed about nine inches apart and fastened to iron pins or bits of iron of all shapes driven in along the side walls. The latter method did not look so neat as the straw held on with scollops, nor did the job last as long.

The habit of keeping cattle and fowl and sometimes pigs in the dwellings was not practised to the same extent in this district as in other parts along the western seaboard, which up to a much later day than the Famine years, adhered to this primitive and unhygienic custom.[8]

⁂

Seán Ó Duinnshléibhe, Glenville, Fermoy, Co. Cork

In this area most of the people were very poor as may be judged by the very large number of houses which have disappeared and from the nature of the localities where they were built. The houses of the poor were of a standard plan built by handymen. They were one-roomed and thatched. The walls were of stone and mud, one door and two small windows, usually one pane of glass inserted in the masonry. The room was divided in two by means of a dresser and cupboard, the division between the two acted as a doorway to the sleeping apartment. The sleeping accommodation was small, just enough room for two taister beds with the window on the end wall to give a little light between the beds. If the window was in the front, the sheeting at the back of one bed should be removed to admit light through the bed to the room.

The taister was used as a canopy to prevent dust or cobwebs from falling on the slumberers. It was also used for comfort, for the Irish in those times would not be happy if they hadn't plenty of bedclothes, which included double sheets, feather pillows and bolsters foot and head, home-made quilt, two blankets, all laid on a feather tick, and all covered with a cotton bedspread.

At those times the roofs of labourers' houses were bad and in wet weather the rain would come down, hence taisters were used, with a pan on top to take the drop.

Generally three or four people slept in these beds, heads and points. If sufficient space was not in one room, a bed was placed near the fire and under the kitchen window for the old couple. This bed had no taister, so as to admit light. Often a coop full of hens was used in the division of the house or the lower part of the dresser was a coop for fowl.

In front of the door was a footpath made of flat stones and beyond that was the dunghill. The yard was surrounded with a stone fence on which was planted some elder cuttings (for luck) and some whitethorn. Beyond the fence was the kitchen or cabbage garden.[9]

❧❧

Ned Buckley, Knocknagree, Co. Cork

In those days the habitations of the poor were very miserable. They lived in every kind of hovel. In a broad bounds ditch between two farms it was usual, with their consent, for a poor working man to scoop the earth from the centre of the ditch leaving the shell at the sides stand in the shape of walls that could be roofed over with sticks and heath, and scraws of tough mountain land laid down on the roofing and thatch over with rushes. If those old side walls were inclined to fall in, they were propped inside with old bog-deal sticks or maybe an old kind of bed up against one side would keep it from falling in, and if there was a bulge on the outside it could be propped with a crockels of bogdeal that would be made by the hatchet nearly flat on both sides. Often several crockles of bogwood would be placed up against the walls of such houses as these so that one wouldn't see anything but bogdeal. Now those props, as well as keeping the house standing, were very handy for tying the sugauns to. The sugauns were ropes made out of hay which were thrown across the roof of the bothan [bothán: hut or hovel], from a foot to two foot apart and the end of each rope could be tied to the crockel supporting the hovel so that if a storm arose the wind could not carry the thatch without carrying the whole lot together. There used to be a hole in the roof over the fire for carrying the smoke and the door used to be plain boards with boccawns [bacán: jamb] and hinges attached to a stout bogoak stick that was sunk in the ground and the earth about it packed well. In the door were two hinges, ring-shaped at the end, and those rings were fit to receive the boccawns on the framestick. The door could be taken off and put on very easily and in summer it used to be off all day.

Another way they had of building was to seek a sheltered corner of a field and cut away the ditches where they met and let the sides stand until they had sliced out sufficient room for a home. They'd stand two bogsticks for the door and fill up any space left with dry stonework or square mountain rods cut for the purpose. Some men of those days were very clever at building such homes and the right men were in great demand for making such homes. No wind could penetrate through those walls and they were mentioned as being very warm and cosy, if not airy.

There used to be mud-wall houses which farmers made themselves in those days and fine safe comfortable homes they were. They used to dig up mud or earth and wet it with water and mix it with shovels and spades. Sometimes when they'd have a great pile of mud sufficiently mixed and wet, they used to drive ten or twelve heifers over it and slosh them around it so that their legs would mix it and make it tough as could be. When mixed tough enough they'd shovel it on the walls, two or three feet thick. They'd leave no space for windows or doors. One man used to stand and have an armful of rushes and he would trample the mud in the proper breadth of the wall and, where it was too soft, he'd throw on a fistful of rushes and trample it away. Where it used to bulge out or in too much, it used to be cut away with the sides of a shovel used as a slasher. In this way they used to work until the broad wall was the required height, eight or nine feet, and when it was finished it used to be slashed smooth with the sides of the shovels and left stand for a few days until the required hardness came on it. Then the space for the windows and doors were cut out of the solid mass and frames put in for the windows and doors. A 'wall plate' timber was placed on the walls and the house roofed. No wall could be as windproof and as airtight as a well-made mud wall and, if the mud is of the right quality and if it be kept dry, it will live for ever and show no signs of decay for centuries.[10]

⟡

J. O'Kane, Dromore National School, Dromore West, Co. Sligo

They lived from hand to mouth and therefore any failure in crops, their only food supply, meant for the majority great privation. Generally there was no money laid by, there was little money in circulation, and there was no food stored up from which to draw in the event of crop failure.

The small farms were brought about by the father dividing a fairly economic farm among two, three or more sons. A son got married and he built a house on a corner of the farm and was given a few acres or a field or two to till. Another son got another patch and so the original farms were carved up without any new tenancies being created, unless the landlord, when he thought he could by doing so, increase his rental. Potatoes were the main food from August to Christmas for dinner, breakfast and supper.[11]

⟡

William Torrens, b.1872, Lisminton, Ballintra, Co. Donegal

The poor people of Drumholm Parish in pre-famine years made such use of potatoes that they cooked them for breakfast, dinner and supper. Buttermilk and salt usually accompanied them in the absence of fish, which were not to be had at all times, though undoubtedly more plentiful in the district in those days than they are now.

The usual way of eating potatoes in these poor homes was out of a large basket made of unpeeled rods, into which the pot of potatoes was dumped on the doorstep and the water allowed to drain off. 'Teeming the spuds' this was called. The potatoes were left in the basket which was set down in the middle of the kitchen floor. The people of the house then sat round in a circle on stools, with some salt on another stool near the basket, and noggins of buttermilk which they balanced in their laps or set down on the earthen floor. No knives or forks were used. The potatoes were boiled in their jackets and peeled with the left or the right thumbnail, according to the hand which the person engaged was most accustomed to use. The nail was kept at a certain length for this purpose, and so expert were the people at peeling potatoes in this way that nobody with a knife and fork could divest a potato of its jacket half so quickly.

A meal of salt, buttermilk and potatoes was called 'dip-at-the-stool', a term fairly expressive of the performance of dipping the potato in the salt which reposed on the stool.

If a large fish, on occasions, took the place of the buttermilk and salt, it was unceremoniously dumped in upon the potatoes in the basket and everybody took a piece off with their fingers and thumb as the dinner or supper went on.

Some had oaten meal for a few winter months, depending on the time when the local corn mills would be able to handle the grain. The old-time quern for grinding the oats at home was still in use in some remote parts of this parish, and meal was made by this primitive method as required for use.

Butter was fairly plentiful and cheap.[12]

⚜

William Doudigan (O'Dowd), b.1863, Redbray, Tullaghan,
Co. Leitrim

Large potatoes even though put in the bottom of [the] pot when being boiled might not be boiled through and were put in gríosach [embers] with red coals on top and left toasting until finish up when they were eaten as an after course, these large potatoes were called toasties and the burned peel or skin pucán. Champ or poundies (toasties mashed up in a porringer with a boiled egg and butter) – great feeding for children, especially when recovering from sickness.

Boiled potatoes left over from the dinner were often used up in making potato cake (griddle bread, slim cake, fleatar). Boxty bread of raw potatoes.

Boiled potatoes were eaten to the supper in the harvest time with buttermilk and raw onions and were counted very healthy. When the oatmeal was ground in late fall, oatmeal porridge and milk was the supper and, as a rule, the first course to the breakfast, followed by oat cake, new milk and butter. Occasionally, say after churning, porridge was made on buttermilk and some of the fresh butter melted in it, by means of the hot porridge. The porridge was then supped, each spoonful being dipped in the well of melted butter. Milk was supplied in bowls to each one so that, should a spoonful of hot porridge become a burning question, a sup of the milk relieved the situation. A gag used to be 'What goes nearest the heart? A spoonful of hot stirabout.'

Samhain, a jelly-like porridge made from slow boiling the juice of seedy oatmeal previously barmed for a week or ten days. It was generally made for the first time in the season around Oíche Shamhna [Halloween] when the oatmeal was ground, hence name. It was also a great novelty for men engaged in heavy manual work, cutting turf or mowing. It was supposed to be the foremost cure for a bad stomach, as 'twas pleasant to take, easily digested and had great sustaining properties. Hare's soup was also counted good and very nourishing, but best of all was salmon broth, the water in which salmon was boiled.

When milk was scarce in the winter season or immediately before the calving time, the milky juice of oatmeal called 'Bull's Milk' was drunk instead with potatoes.

Boulagín (veal). As there was little or no demand for bull calves around 100 years ago [1840s] they were generally slaughtered when three weeks old and the flesh used as food, generally boiled. It made fine kitchen with potatoes and cold hungry children coming home from school relished it. (So old James Harte of Scaurdon, Manorhamilton, told me, who, if he were alive, would have been about 100.)

Fowl, generally roasted in summer and boiled in winter (soup for cold weather) a great go for Sunday's dinner, always meat of some kind on Sunday if at all possible, as the family circle [was] generally complete (men folk often working away during the week), and friends often visiting on Sunday, so the women folk liked to make the best show possible.

Colcannon (bruitín) made in old times as a special dish for Halloween. The mashed potatoes flavoured with sliced onions, blended with hot milk, pepper and salt, and thoroughly pounded and served hot on dishes with wells of butter just like the oatmeal porridge. Bruitín was of course a great face-saver for the bean a' tí for fast-day dinners when neither fish nor eggs could be got.[13]

❖

Pádraig Pléimionn, Killarney, Co. Kerry

It was the custom to build houses along public roads in many places and the young men used to marry early and work for the neighbouring middleman and large farmers while occupying such houses. Such had, of course, large families and they were the principal sufferers. They used to get 'sure ground' to set potatoes from the farmers and others and, as they and their families lived principally on potatoes, this was a great advantage till the blast came.[14]

❖

3

Abundance Abused and the Blight

❧❧

When the previously unknown fungus, *Phytophthora infestans*, arrived in Ireland in the late summer of 1845, the scene was set for several years of devastation of the potato crop and the poor people who depended totally on it. This unpredictable ecological disaster struck at the sole food of the majority of the country's poor. Until the blight struck, potatoes had been eaten morning, noon and night, at an incredible seven to fifteen pounds per person per day.

A third or more of the crop was destroyed in 1845; three-quarters in 1846 and 1847 and one-third in 1848. Between 1845 and 1849 the crop failed three years out of four and the failure to sow a new crop added to the problem of food shortage due to disease. The blight appeared in varying degrees for six years and was remarkable in its longevity and geographical spread.

Although the government set up a Scientific Commission in 1845 to investigate the blight, an antidote was not discovered until 1882, almost forty years after the first loss of the potato crop to the blight.

❧❧

P. Foley, b.1890, a farmer, Knockananna, Co. Wicklow

Everybody was remarking to each other how dark the sky was. The old people all said they never saw such a coloured sky before. The wise or rather 'learned' people all said it was an eclipse of the sun. It was the topic of conversation with everybody. By night a thick blue fog had descended on the countryside and visibility was very poor.

The people went to bed in fear and dread that some great calamity was about to befall them. Next morning when they awoke and went out, to their consternation their lovely potato plants, which were in such bloom and showed such a promise of beautiful crops the day before, were all covered over with black spots and the leaves and stalks hanging down as if dead.

The potato blight had appeared for the first time in Ireland. The awful smell and stench of the blight was everywhere.[1]

❖❖❖

Eamonn Mac Dhuírnín, b.1878, retired national teacher, Creeslough, Co. Donegal

Early in 1845, to all appearances, there was going to be a fine crop as the potatoes grew well and were far advanced for the time of year. However in the latter days of June a dense fog came in from the sea and lasted three or four days. When the fog cleared away the potato stalks withered away in a couple of nights. The fields became black and, in a week's time, not a stalk remained. Ever since the year of the Famine is known here locally as Bliain na Sceidan [the year of the small potatoes].[2]

❖❖❖

Conchubhair and Solomon Ó Néill, b.1860s, farmers, Cratloe, Co. Clare

In the autumn of that fatal 1845 the crop was dug out as usual, nothing to arouse suspicion had been noticed during the growing and digging periods. The crop was pitted in the customary way, but later when taken from the heaps and boiled it was first observed that there was something wrong. The woman of the house used to be blamed for putting the potatoes to boil without washing, for that was the appearance they presented on the table. But very soon the people found out that it was not for want of washing that the potatoes looked dirty, still they did not know what was wrong.[3]

❧❧

Séamas R. Ó Domhnaill, b.1888, school teacher, Meenbanad,
The Rosses, Co. Donegal

I remember well hearing an old teacher, many years dead, tell of
his going on a pilgrimage on the old side-car to Lough Derg. The
day he and his fellow pilgrims entered the island the potato crop
was in full bloom, on the third day the whole crop was stricken,
leaves and stalks blackened and an air of pestilence, corruption
and stench pervaded the air.[4]

❧❧

Michael Corduff, Rossport, Ballina, Co. Mayo

About the year 1846 a number of Rossport people, young and
middle-aged, were proceeding one Summer's evening in the
month of July to a wake in the townland of Kilgalligan. They
were traversing the fields of the townland of Cornboy when their
attention was attracted by a very strange smell which they had
never felt before. It pervaded the night air and they wondered
what it meant or what was its cause. That night at the
wakehouse the strange smell was the topical subject of those
present. Nearly everyone had experiences of it on his or her way
and all were puzzled. One old man who was present said.
'Whatever it is, it is certainly not a good thing. I'm afraid that it
is only the prelude to some great calamity, perhaps disease, and in
all probability there will be a story told about it in a day farther
away than this.' I am giving the literal translation of the words in
Irish of the old seer. Next morning on their way home the
revelation was obvious. The whole potato crop was withered and
burnt to the ground in one night.

It is said of an old woman of Rossport who on returning to the
house after paying the usual morning visit to the crops
exclaimed, 'Oh the devil polluted all the potatoes last night.
There is not a stalk standing.' There was consternation and woe

among the people owing to the sudden calamity.[5]

⋅⟨§⟩⋅

*Mrs Kate O'Carroll, b.1877, native of Mullingar, Co. Westmeath,
living in Bailieboro, Co. Cavan*

The first year of the Famine there was hardly a potato and very
little oats. The two crops failed. My grandmother said there came
something like a 'drought'. The stalks of the potatoes were burned,
and nothing would grow. There wasn't a blade of grass in the fields
for an animal to eat. It all withered. My grandmother would go out
in the morning and get the fowl dead in the yard. Next morning
she'd go out and get a cow dead, and on the following morning
she'd go out and get another cow and a couple of sheep lying dead.
The sheep and cattle died, and this went on until the people were
paupers. The people died in hundreds around Mullingar.[6]

⋅⟨§⟩⋅

Mrs G. Kirby, Stradbally, Co. Laois, in 1945

Several reasons are given as to the cause of the blight. Most people
think it was a punishment from God for the careless manner in
which they treated the crops the years previous when there was a
very plentiful supply of potatoes. They were left in the ground by
some people and not dug out, and they threw them on the
headlands or in the ditches and left them to rot. Another reason
given is the continuous planting of the same kind of seed year
after year.

I heard contradictory statements as to the use of guano as a
manure at the time. Guano had not been long introduced as an
artificial manure and the people did not know how to apply it
properly to the land. If it came in contact with the seed it had an
injurious affect on it and a liberal supply of it was supposed to rot
the potatoes.

Another version was that it was only well-to-do farmers who

could afford to purchase the guano and many of these people saved their potatoes, while the poor farmers, who had no artificial manure, lost their crops.

The general opinion is that the blight was caused in 1846 on account of all the rotten potatoes that were left on the land from the previous years, as the germs of the disease remained in the soil and affected the growing crops in the years 1846. Then in 1847, when the potatoes were being planted in the spring, the seed was so scarce people only cut the bare bud and kept the rest of the potato for food. The seed was so weak the crop was a complete failure in 1847.[7]

·᷏᳐᷇᷈·

Local farmers, Moate, Co. Westmeath

So plentiful were they [potatoes] in pre-famine years that it often happened that farmers filled them into sacks, took them into the markets at Moate, Athlone or Ballymahon, offered them for sale but nobody could be found to buy, so that on the return journey the farmers often emptied them into the ditch on the roadside for 'they weren't worth the sacks they were in'.

Afterwards it was said that the Famine was a just retribution from God for the great waste of food. A local saying which may refer to this is 'A wilful waste makes a woeful want'.[8]

·᷏᳐᷇᷈·

*John Murtagh, b.1878, a farmer, Clonelly, Dromard Parish,
Co. Longford*

They were too well-to-do before the Famine an auld man told me. I was only a gossun at the time and I used to be down with this auld man. He was 90 years of age when he died and he's dead now nearly 70 years. He was born sometime around 1798. He said that in the month of April 1846, the potatoes were taken and thrown in the gripes, because there were too many of them and the people couldn't use them all. They used not to feed so many cattle and pigs that time, and so had no way of using them all up.

This auld man told me of another man who had plenty of potatoes that year and he called into the blacksmith's forge one day and told that blacksmith that he had more potatoes than he could use. 'Call up to the house,' he says to the smith, 'and take what you want.'

'I couldn't go that far for them,' says the blacksmith, 'have them in the next time you're passing here.'

And the smith wasn't living more than a mile or two away. He didn't think it worth his while to go for the potatoes.

Every crop gave a wonderful yield before the Famine. It was the same with the oats as with the potatoes. There was a great yield. The yield was so great from the oats that they began to make poteen with it. They nearly quit working for the twelve days of Christmas. Every day was a holiday during that time and plenty of poteen drunk. They were too well off.

It was the same with the milk of the cows. The cows gave much more milk then than they do now.

The Lord said that as time would go on milk and honey would decrease. I remember in my young days how plentiful the bees' nests would be. You would find them in the meadows and you mowing. You couldn't take home all the honey that you'd meet.

There's another thing that you don't see nowadays, 'the honeyfall'. In my young days on a fine sunny day in June the honey would be falling on the bushes. The honey would fall from the clouds with the heat and the extra growth. The leaves of the bushes would take it and grass. You'd often hear the old people say that there was a fine honeyfall today. It was especially noticeable in the sycamore.

The year of the Famine the potatoes rotted in the ground when they were growing. There were two years of famine. It looked like the hand of God.[9]

FAMINE ECHOES

William (Bill) Powell, b.1869, a pensioner, Eniskeane, Co. Cork

The years 1845 and 1846 were the most plentiful years that had come within living memory before it, there was a bounteous harvest and a grand crop of potatoes, especially the year '46. Old people said it was God's will to have the Famine come, for people abused fine food when they had it plenty. I heard it for a fact that spuds were so plentiful that they were put on the fields for manure.

Well, it was God's will I suppose, the year following the potato crop was a complete failure with most people, The gardens in the low-lying lands were left without a leaf early in June. People didn't know what blight was that time, 'a failure' 'twas called, and any garden that did recover a little, the spuds that grew in them weren't fit for human food, they blackened and rotted.[10]

⁂

James Argue, b.1865, Galbolia, Bailieboro, Co. Cavan

The blight appeared first on the growing crop, and when the people went to dig the potatoes they found that the roots were spotted. The people did not pass much remarks on it in the first year because spots of a similar kind had been seen previously and didn't do any harm worth mentioning. The people were not alarmed and didn't take enough pains when they were picking the potatoes, they allowed too many spotted ones to get mixed up with the good tubers, with the result that the spotted ones smitted the others, and the most of the good ones went bad. They had very poor seed for the following spring and that was why a lot of them did not grow. The disease affected the whole district, it was all over, no man's crop escaped. Moory or boggy land was safer than any other class of land, the crop planted in it was not so badly affected, but it was not free from the disease. Potatoes planted in high up ground suffered most.[11]

Bean Uí Sheoighe, b.1873, a farmer's wife, Dawrosmore, Letter, Letterfrack, Co. Galway

The blight came before Saint John's Day. It came like a fog in the evening and appeared low on the water. Next day the potato stalks were black. As the people were digging the potatoes they were eating them. Anyone who had small potatoes left had to make pits under turf stacks in case people would take them. There is a poem that was common in those days:

> In the year '46 build your house of rotten sticks,
> In the year '47 pray to God in Heaven,
> In the year '48 build your coffin straight,
> In the year '49 build your house of stone and lime.[12]

❧❧

Michael Howard, b.1883, a farmer, Gladree, Belmullet, Co. Mayo

The year which was called Black Forty-Seven came with rain and snow and frost and the cold was fierce. The weather was so bad that they thought no crops or potatoes would grow. They put too much confidence in their prophecies. It was supposed to keep raining for three years.[13]

❧❧

Seán Ó Duinnshléibhe, Glenville, Fermoy, Co. Cork

The effect of the blight on the potato crop in the summer of '45 was that very little potatoes were lifted that year, and although being small, had to support the family to which they belonged. These were counted, a certain small number for each member of the family, so that when '46 came in, few had even the small potato to plant. The worst was to happen, the blight again appeared and so there were no potatoes planted in '47 (Black Forty-Seven) or in '48 in this district.

Miserable potatoes in '45–46. The smallest were picked and kept for seed in '46. The crop left was not half a crop and these had to be rationed in every home, only a few potatoes for a meal. Even the seed suffered, for some were eaten when the hunger pinch was felt.

In '46 the small potatoes were planted but the blight again appeared – then was heard the cries of the people lamenting at the sight of hunger.[14]

❧

Tuosist, Kenmare, Co. Kerry, from Seán Ó Súilleabháin, Irish Folklore Commission

There was a great crop of potatoes in the second year of the Famine 'for those who had potato seeds to plant the previous spring'. Varieties known at the time were Green Tops, White Rock and American Sailors. The Champion variety of potatoes was introduced into the parish later on, about the year 1879 or 1880.

At that time the potatoes were usually planted as late as the month of June, much later than at present. The last portion of the potato crop sown is usually the first to be affected by the blight as the stalks of that portion are the weakest. During the Famine, and prior to it, it was usual to plant potatoes in the same field for several years in succession. This made the land and crop weak, hence the bad effect of the blight when it came.[15]

❧

Máire Ní Gharaidh, An Grianán, Dromod, Co. Leitrim

In Bornacoola these little 'haws' were dug out of the ground and were used for seed the following year 1847. Barely one 'eye' was used in sowing each hole and the 'split' was so tiny it was scarcely visible. Yet every 'eye' bore fruit tenfold. There seemed to be nothing to store. It was when rooting for the seed that the little 'haws' were dug up and tried with undoubted success. It seemed to be just an experiment attended with unexpected success to go digging them out from low down in the clay later on in the season.[16]

❖❖

J. O'Kane, Dromore National School, Dromore West, Co. Sligo

Matthew Kennedy said that before the Famine the potato stalks were green until November, until they withered naturally. The first year of the failure, towards the end of May, he went out early one morning and the potato stalks of a whole field were quite black and drooping, as if a severe frost had hit them. These stalks were quite green and healthy the evening before, so that the whole damage was done in one night.

One man, Tony Gallagher [b.1865], told me that he quite often heard that the first night the blight came it blackened only a wide 'swipe' right across the field from side to side in some places and that in a few days afterwards the whole field was gone. All are agreed that the destruction was done in one night. The stalks never recovered.

Some of the small potatoes were kept for seed and planted next spring. The stalks came up as usual but they were 'struck' even earlier than the first year, and there was not even the póiríní [small potatoes] to be got, except one here and there, a few handfuls in a whole field [meaning about half an acre], and these little potatoes were soft and watery and not fit to eat. This failure was general. No field escaped in either these two years. But anybody who was optimistic enough, or determined enough not to be beaten, and who gathered the póiríní of the second years crop and set them the third year was rewarded beyond belief.

The second year's crop here was never dug and nothing was done with the land until it was ploughed or dug up for oats, barley or turnips in springtime following, but those who gathered the tiny potatoes, most not bigger than thimbles, and set them, never had a better return from good potatoes sown before the failure.

But those who did sow were few, and they were not those who were poorest.

By the way, I was told that before the Famine times, and I don't know if it continued afterwards, the potatoes were not sown in drills or ridges as now, but in 'lands'. A 'land' was a sort of ridge from 10 to 12 feet wide with a dyke or furrow at each side, and the potatoes were sown 'broadcast' on this and not in rows. The clay from the furrows was thrown up to cover them. The old people say that no matter how you sowed the potato before the Famine, you had a good plentiful crop.[17]

❦

William Torrens, b.1872, Lisminton, Ballintra, Co. Donegal

The blight in the Ballintra district first appeared in the summer of 1845 after a severe storm of thunder and lightning. On the following day it showed on the leaves in the form of brown spots about the size of a shilling and quickly spread until all the leaves had withered and decayed.

The 1845 crop was soon used up and there was consequently great want before the spring of 1846. Seed was scarce at any price and in order to try and recover some of the scant supply for food and also contribute towards the problem of having enough seed for the amount of land it was proposed to till, various plans were thought out to make the seed go at least twice as far as was ever known from previous experience.

One farmer had a labourer engaged for a day's setting of potatoes in the spring of 1846, and when the pair arrived in the field the labourer asked his employer where he had the seed, as there was no appearance of any near the place where they were about to begin work.

The farmer's only reply was that he reckoned he had as much seed out with him as would last them till dinner time, and thereupon proceeded to produce two capacious pockets of his old frieze coat. What the pockets held were potato buds gouged from their position in the potatoes, with a small disk-shaped portion of the potato itself adhering to the bud. The remaining portion of the potato was then kept for food.

The resulting crop, despite the unpromising appearance of the seed, showed fine promise in the early summer of 1846, but late in July the tops were cut completely away by the blight, leaving nothing but gaunt stalks which soon began to melt and fall flat on the ridges.[18]

❧❧

Martin Manning, b.1875, Carrowholly, Kilmeena, Westport, Co. Mayo

There was an abundant crop of potatoes that year (1846). They were dug and stored in the pits in the best of weather and it was only getting on for Christmas that they were noticed to be getting black or rotting in the pits. The people began to change them from pit to pit trying to save them (which they did in small quantities) until at last the day fell in and all was lost.

The people were advised by the clergy not to trust the potatoes any more but to sew turnips and grain crops which they did and the turnip became the staple food for a time. My father sowed about six stones of potatoes which he had saved the next year and that gave the best crop he ever had. But the people in general had not the seed because any they saved was eaten long before seed time.[19]

❧❧

Anna Bean Uí Cheamharcaigh, b.1864, Cnoc an Chaisleáin, and brought up in Druma Fhrighile, Ballycroy, Westport, Co. Mayo

During the Famine years people often dug ten ridges a day and got no potatoes. They used to dig the soil three times over to see if they could even get any poreen. The third year they were advised to sew potatoes but to put in turnips or cabbage. Some people noticed little stalks coming up on the soil that was dug three times over and they moulded them and had a wonderful crop. That was known as the 'toradh céadtach' [hundredfold crop]. They had great crops for a long time after.

A man was setting potatoes. The local priest chanced to pass the way. He had already advised them not to risk sowing any more potatoes but to put some other crop. He said to the man 'Ta tú ag cur na bhfataí agus nár fhásaidh siad.' [You're setting potatoes and they won't grow.]

'Is tú a dúirt is ní hé Dia', d'fhreagair an fear [You said it, not God, the man answered].

That was the third year and he had a great crop.[20]

⁂

Thomas O'Flynn, John Melody, Attymass, Ballina, Co. Mayo

Many farmers continued to sow potatoes year after year, that is the poreens which were little use as food but which were free from blight. The local clergy urged the people to discontinue the growing of the crop. Still, many kept up the experiment and finally met with success. It is said that the priest asked those people for some potatoes and was refused. From that stage on people took courage and began to set more and more.[21]

⁂

Thomas Kelly, Rockfleet, Carrowbeg, Westport, Co. Mayo.
b.1855, Rosturk, Co. Mayo

The potatoes failed for three years. The third year very little potatoes were set. The parish priest said there was no use in setting potatoes. Anyone who had 'bruscar' [bits] of poreens or even stalks in soil and set them, or allowed them to grow, had 'tons' of potatoes that year.[22]

⁂

Brigid Brennan, b.1863, Stradbally, Co. Laois

By digging the potatoes out when the blight first appeared people were able to save some of them. Those who left the potatoes in the ground until the usual time for digging them out thought, by sorting them and separating the black or diseased ones from the good ones, that they could save them in the pits, but they rotted in the pits no matter how carefully they tried to preserve them.

In the spring of 1848 the seed potatoes were very scarce and dear. I was told by an old woman that she heard her mother say no one could afford to sow potatoes that year, except people who had money in the bank, and could afford to pay high prices for the seed. She said her mother who was a widow, paid four pounds for two barrels of seed potatoes and she had to get a man she could trust to make a hole in the rick of hay to hide the potatoes.

She took them out in bucketfuls every day to cut the seed, and put them all back in the rick again at night and covered them, as if it became known that she had them, they'd be stolen for food. Her trusted man covered them with the plough and stayed up for some nights to watch them in the field.[23]

❧❧

Felix Kernan, b.1859, a farmer, Drumakill, Castleblayney,
Co. Monaghan

A native of this district saw a field of potato drills that had not been digged. He felt that if he digged he would find some sound potatoes for food. He dug from morning until evening and at the end of that time he could only pick two potatoes which he thought were quite sound. When he brought them home and cooked them they were no better than the others. They were black, uneatable.[24]

❧❧

William Doudigan (O'Dowd), b.1863, Redbray, Tullaghan,
Co. Leitrim

The blight first struck in these parts very suddenly, whole fields of potatoes being left as black as your shoe in four hours, just like after a bad night's frost in May, old people here say they heard from their fathers. The whole district here was affected, but moss land worse than clay and along the seafront not too bad.

Some farmers cut down the affected stalks and a ridge or two of those adjoining and removed the cut stalks to another place. Others cut down all the stalks near the ground. Others lit fires to purify the air but it seems to have been of little use as most of the big potatoes melted and there was nothing left only rotten ones and poiríns/póitíns/poithíns [three pronunciations for small potatoes in the north-west].

According to accounts generally in the north-west there was a bumper potato crop in 1845 and in 1846 all other crops were fine especially grain – wheat and oats – the potato alone failing. In 1847 some people who kept the poitíns, no bigger than thimbles, planted them, evenly splitting makes halves of those with two eyes. 'Twas even said in places where the póitíns were scarce that the eyes were scooped out and planted in lengths of quills an inch or so long. Other people said 'twas only a waste of time experimenting with póitíní, but those who did had a fair good crop as they planted in fresh ground, that is not the ground used in 1846. The blight doesn't seem to have done much harm in 1847, but was fairly bad in 1848 and 1853.[25]

❧

William Naddy, b.1863, Inistioge, Co. Kilkenny

The priest of the place was so terrified, and so much was he in dread of the black potatoes that he would not even allow the people to sow them as seed. Those who obeyed him had no potatoes the following year, whilst those who sowed the black potatoes had a fairly good crop, notwithstanding the type of seed sown.[26]

❧❧

Seán Rowley, a storyteller, Rossport, Co. Mayo

Long years ago I heard an old man named Manus Henry of Cornboy say that when he was a boy in the townland of Kilgalligan, he was one night present together with a number of the neighbours in the house of a man named Monaghan who was possessed of some education. At that time, which was about three years before the Famine, a man who was able to read and write was a rare specimen. Monaghan was reading a book *sotto voce* and some member of the company said to him, 'Why don't you tell us something from your book and not be keeping all the knowledge to yourself?' The reader thereupon closed the book and addressing the visitors said, 'Well, would you believe what I am just after reading? A day will come when a three-legged animal will descend from the air on the land of Ireland and in one night, with fire belching from its mouth, will burn and destroy the potato crop of the whole country.'

The assembled only laughed in ridicule and scorn and said the information was arrant nonsense and the mere imagination of some madman. No more was said about the subject at the time but the information was very forcibly recalled to us on the fateful night less than three years after when all the growing potatoes were burned to the ground. Then we remembered the story of the fire-spitting three-legged aerial serpent, as told by the man Monaghan of Kilgalligan.[27]

❧❧

4

Turnips, Blood, Herbs and Fish

❧❧

When the blight struck the potato, people tried to salvage what they could of the good parts of the diseased tubers, which were cut out to be eaten, boiled or made into boxty bread.

For the most part the option of alternative grains and cereals was not available, as those fortunate enough to have grown them used them as a cash crop. Neither did the very poor have livestock to support them, and what sheep or poultry they had were soon killed and eaten.

Although turnips and cabbage came into greater prominence in the absence of the potato, even where they were available they didn't have the nutritional requirements to keep the people healthy. In the absence of crops or the money to buy food, the masses of poverty-stricken people turned to foraging in an effort to get enough food to keep themselves alive. Hungry people searched the fields and ditches for edible weeds, herbs and nettles, or headed for the rivers and sea-shores in the hope of finding sustenance.

Though the sea offered a limited opportunity as a food resource, a number of factors prevented the majority of people exploiting this possibility to the full. Grinding poverty and the need for money to buy alternative foods, resulted in fishing nets being pawned. In addition, many small fishing boats were unable to set to sea in the bad weather and the once plentiful herring had moved further from the Irish coast.

While the sea-shore did give an opportunity for harvesting shellfish and seaweeds of various kinds, the sheer numbers of those in search of them saw rocks and beaches stripped bare and many, who had not previously eaten these seafoods, did not know how to harvest or cook them properly.

Inappropriate food, lack of cooking or eating food out of season caused both sickness and disease.

❧❧

John D. O'Leary, Lynedaowne, Rathmore, Co. Kerry

The year 1846 or 1847 (my father is not sure which year) was called Bliain an Bhrain – the Year of the Bran, which formed a big part of the people's diet, and some of those years were also called Bliain na dTurnapaí.[1]

❧❧

Seán Eddie Moynihan, b.1842, a farmer, Srón Darach,
Lios na gCeann, Glenflesk, Co. Kerry

I remember eight or nine of us to sit around a table of boiled swedes [turnips]. My mother used go to Killarney. They used come in from the west [Cromán] with baskets of cockles and mussels, and she used to bring them home and boil them in milk.

A poor middle-aged man wearing a loose frieze coat, I saw him coming into the house where I was born, and sticking a swede into the fire, and indeed he didn't leave it there very long when he took it out and ate it.[2]

❧❧

Thomas O'Flynn, John Melody, Attymass, Ballina, Co. Mayo

Wheat was not grown in large quantities in this parish and when grown, the grain was sold and the straw used for thatch. It appears that the straw was considered more valuable than the grain for it lasted much longer than oaten straw as thatch and it was for the purpose of getting the straw, more than for the value of the grain, that wheat was grown. It was said that wheat made the soil poor.

Oats was the main grain crop and it provided food for man and beast and, of course, paid the rent, taxes and the gombeen man. Oatmeal cakes were made in this way. A leaf of cabbage was placed on coals of fire, the oatmeal cake consisting of oatmeal and milk, or oatmeal and water, was placed on the leaf. Then another cabbage leaf was placed on top and coals were laid over this. The juice of the cabbage leaf penetrated the cake and made it more palatable. Cabbage was grown specially for this purpose and some rye was grown on light soils unfit to grow any other grain. It was used for bread and the straw was considered better than oat straw for thatch.[3]

❧❧

Gerald Fitzmaurice, improvements and drainage inspector, Knockrour, Scartaglen, Co. Kerry

Workmen (at 5d. and 6d. a day) coming to work for a local farmer, called to the cornfield on the way to the house, reaped down a barth of oats, brought it with them, 'scratched' it against the edge of a tub to knock out the grain, then shook it and lifted it up between their hands to winnow the chaff away. Then it was taken into the house, dried in a pot over the fire, ground in the 'curn', and mixed with milk and eaten for the breakfast.[4]

❧❧

J. O'Kane, Dromore National School, Dromore West, Co. Sligo

When there was no milk they had subhachán made from the seeds of the ground oats. This 'subhachán', 'cheerins' or 'sounds', as it was called in some places, was drunk with the potatoes oftener than milk by the poorer classes.

The middle classes could afford to have oatmeal porridge with milk or oatmeal and barley mixed made into porridge. The oaten meal was often eaten raw with milk. The meal was thrown into a bowl, the milk thrown over it and all mixed up and eaten. Flummery was a sort of dainty from boiled 'sounds' or 'subhachán'.

Re the oaten meal, the oats was dried on the kiln in the mill, the farmer bringing his own turf, or it was dried, before being brought to the mill, on a 'cliath' or 'ciseóg' [latticed frame, shallow basket] covered with straw. The latter, the oats dried on the ciseóg, was considered to make the best and the sweetest meal. When the meal was taken home after being ground it was sifted on a sheet on the kitchen floor. The cáithníní or seeds were kept to make the subhachán for the year and the meal was put in a bag and hung from a 'maide ceangal' [tie-beam] of the roof of the kitchen. There it was always dry.[5]

⚜

Michael Gildea, b.1872, Dromore, Ballintra, Co. Donegal

The 'skoddy' was made thus: a couple of turnips were sliced and put into a pot of boiling water. Some oatmeal was added and allowed to boil for some time. When it was cooked the mixture was like porridge. The turnips were supposed to give the oatmeal a sweet flavour.[6]

⚜

John Treanor, b.1870, a retired scutcher, Forkhill, Co. Armagh

The people had to live on brawlum. It was a handful of meal and a head of cabbage. It was yellow meal though, you know, and maybe a dumpling if they had a fistful of flour. It was made anont of the butcher [made without any meat]. There was no meat in them days.[7]

⚜

Seán Ó Duinnshleibhe, Glenville, Fermoy, Co. Cork

They had no food for the cattle save hay alone, but none for the hens. The hens did not lay for the want of food, and then they became less and less until there were none. They had been killed and eaten.

Livestock was very much reduced during the Famine period.

Some animals were killed for food by the farmers, some were sold where soup houses were established, and those farmers with their families, who went into exile, sold out their stock.[8]

❧❧

William Torrens, b.1872, Lisminton, Ballintra, Co. Donegal

During the height of the Famine they lived largely on turnips, of which there was an abundance grown by Mr Foster in the sandy soil surrounding them.

There was also a good supply of shellfish, such as cockles, mussels, 'brallions' and razor fish along the nearby seashore which they gathered frequently, and in the channel, a few hundred yards from where they lived, they often went 'tramping' for fluke. This meant going barefooted into the water where these flat fish were plentiful and, by putting a foot down on them as they swam lazily around, no difficulty was experienced in picking them out of the water and flinging them high and dry up on the strand. Many dozens of fluke, with a minimum of effort, could be secured this way in a short time.[9]

❧❧

J. O'Kane, Dromore National School, Dromore West, Co. Sligo

For dinner there was sometimes a salted herring or periwinkles or barnacs [bairneach: limpet] got at the sea and boiled. The water in which the barnacs were boiled, barnacs and a little salt added, were put in bowls or mugs and drunk and eaten with potatoes. Meat was only for very especial occasions for the majority.[10]

❧❧

Michael Corduff, Rossport, Ballina, Co. Mayo

The treasures of the sea came to the aid of this maritime population. Fresh fish, shellfish, edible seaweeds such as 'slouk', 'dilisk', 'tripead' and miscellaneous marine products were caught, gathered and cooked with a little meal or animal fat and so helped to sustain the people.

Wild seabirds and their eggs was another fruitful resource and raids for these were frequently made on the cliffs, men being lowered and hoisted by ropes in so doing.[11]

Seán Ó Beirne, Malin, Inishowen, Co. Donegal

They used all the usual foods to be found along the shore: dulse, sloak, famanach, wilks, barnacles, braillins, aghaus [awmucks: a kind of fish found on sandy beaches?], cockles etc. and dulaman. They of course used fish. This dulaman is a growth somewhat like carageen moss or as they call it here in Inishowen 'crothar' and is not edible until after the first severe frost in Winter. It is not left to bleech like carageen but can be cooked (boiled) immediately after being pulled. It has to be boiled for two or three hours.[12]

James Donnelly, b.1847, a farmer and fisherman, Roskeen, Coalisland, Co. Tyrone

During the Famine years there were bigger catches of fish than had ever been know up to then. At a point on the shore in the townland of Columcille (just beside Barnfoot Ferry) a fire was kept burning every day and people from districts further inland used to come for meals of roasted fish which were cooked by the people themselves on this fire.[13]

Tuosist, Kenmare, Co. Kerry, from Seán Ó Súilleabháin,
Irish Folklore Commission

People used shellfish a good deal as food prior to the Famine and
during the Famine years, as witness the dumps of shells near most
of the old houses. Fish was plentiful during the Famine years,
hake being the most common fish.[14]

❧❧

James Cormack, Rossport, Ballina, Co. Mayo

Among the expedients adopted by the coastal natives for the
provision of food were the capture and killing of seabirds and the
gathering of the eggs of sea fowl in the lofty cliffs and rocks,
which were the natural haunts and aviaries of the ocean poultry.
The rock islands known as the Stags of Broadhaven, and in Irish
as Stácaí Iorrais, were prolific venues for this purpose, and so
from time to time as weather permitted men essayed forth in
their hide curraghs to these places to capture and collect birds
and eggs of which there were various kinds, and while some were
preferable to others as food, yet all were acceptable and none was
rejected. All kinds of these fowl and their eggs, the latter were
obtainable only during the nesting season, were taken home and
cooked.[15]

❧❧

Liam Ó Danachair, Sunvale, Athea, Co. Limerick

Men out on the mountain used root out any potatoes they could
get. They would put them into a hole in the fence, and set fire to
the fence around them. When they were cooked they were
scooped out and eaten. The names of the potatoes at the time
were 'Leather Coats', and before them came 'Brown Bulls' and
'Black Bulls' . The 'Champion' came years later.[16]

❧❧

J. O'Kane, Dromore National School, Dromore West, Co. Sligo

By the way, did you ever hear of 'scadán caoch' [blind herring]? Well, 'scadán caoch' was nothing more or less than salt and water. A little salt was added to water in a shallow vessel and the potatoes were dipped in it. 'Scadán caoch' was kitchen for the potatoes when there was nothing else to be had.[17]

❧❧

Thomas O'Flynn, John Melody, Attymass, Ballina, Co. Mayo

Good portions of the potatoes were boiled and made into 'cally' or eaten whole. Partly rotten ones were scraped on a scraper so as to make pulp and this was converted into 'boxty'. The pulp was placed in a cloth and squeezed as dry as possible. This was then flattened out and baked on a tongs on the red coals or placed on the warm hearthstone. When one side was baked the cake was turned. The making of boxty continued down to about 40 years ago and was generally made of the partially rotten or frosted potatoes about the time of lifting the crop in about October and November.[18]

❧❧

Seán Mac Cuinneagáin, Scoil Mhín an Aodhaire, Carrick, Co. Donegal

Boxty was made of the rotten potatoes. The potatoes were grated and put in a tub. Water was poured until the tub was overflowing, when the rotten lighter stuff flowed away leaving the more solid stuff to sink. This method of making bread was followed in the later famines too.[19]

❧❧

Colm Ó Danachair, Áth an tSléibhe, Co. Limerick

They used go into the potato gardens and dig the ground already dug. When they had any few potatoes gathered they used take them into a farmer's house and put them down to boil with the family potatoes. They used put a few cabbage leaves in between the two sets of potatoes, and so there would be no mistakes one way or the other.[20]

❖

Mick and Mrs Kelly, b.1865 & 1877, Caddagh, Delvin,
Co. Westmeath

The Scotsdown was the name of the potato that failed. That was the potato in general use, at that time. The ordinary people had no early potatoes. The potato that was sent in relief was mostly the Champion. There used to be a rhyme describing a wordy battle supposed to have taken place between the Scotsdown and the Champion. Mrs Kelly remembered a bit of it.

'You dirty clown,' says the Scotsdown, 'how dare you me oppose.
'Twas I supported Ireland when you daren't show your nose.'

The Champion potatoes were mostly sent from Scotland. Another verse was as follows:

Out spoke the noble Champion, with courage stout and brave,
'Only I happened to sail over here, there'd be thousands in their grave.'[21]

❖

P. Foley, b.1890, a farmer, Knockananna, Co. Wicklow

In crossing the hills they often saw groups of men cornering cattle which they would bleed by cutting a vein in the neck of the beast and extracting a few pints of blood, or whatever amount they could safely take, without endangering too much the life of the animal. When they would have sufficient blood extracted from a beast, they would fix up the wound to prevent further bleeding by putting a pin through the skin across the incision in the vein, then clapping a few hairs from the animals tail around the pin to keep it in position. The men would carry the blood home in jars and other vessels slung across their shoulders, some of them having to travel many miles before reaching home.

When they would arrive their women folk would carefully salt the blood and some of it would be cooked by frying in a pan.[22]

❖❖

John Doyle, b.1900, a labourer, Rasheenmore,
who was reared at Craffle, Ballyteigue, Aughrim, Co. Wicklow

One Protestant who lived in Ballyteigue House grew turnips and mangels to feed the poor. Each family got two per day.

The people ate crabapples and holly-berries and the leaves of the crabtree. They climbed trees for nuts at Rednagh. The favourite was the oak nut. Many were so weak they fell out of the trees and were killed.

They fought and killed each other over the blackberries before they were ripe.

A favourite dish was to boil nettles, sorrels and dock leaves with a spoon of yellow meal on top, heat and then cut like a cake. They ate pig-nuts and other roots like a dock-root.

The river in Aughrim ran out of fish and they could be in for days without getting an eel. In the end they could get none at all. They collected grubs called mindios [?] in the bottom of the streams. They were different colours but mostly brown, short and about as thick as a pencil. The shells were taken off and the insides boiled. They were in shells like the bud of a beech tree.

Trees were climbed at night in search of crows and

woodquest's [woodpigeon] eggs and they would eat every bird of all descriptions that they could catch.

A landlord who was afraid that all the birds of the county would be exterminated paid a bounty of 2d for every live bird that was brought to him and he kept them and fed them until after the Famine.

The people around Aughrim had snares for killing mice. They skinned and ate them but never gutted them. One man saw a rat and a weasel fighting and tried to kill both of them but the weasel bit him and he was so weak that the poison from the bite killed him.

They boiled sloes in a pan and then fried them and ate them. They ate the blossoms off the bushes and sceacha. He heard of one family getting cancer of the stomach from eating grass.

His grandfather told him they killed frogs and fried them and ate them. When everything else got scarce they mowed down young furze and ground them and ate them.

People gathered a lot of bog berries to live on but many died from cramps after eating them. This happened whenever the foam was on the berries.

A man went into a house and found the owner dead and a rat eating the corpse. He killed the rat and brought it home and ate it.

A man went to look for honey in a wasp's nest and got some but he died from the stings that evening. He said he got backs [?] that wasps have eggs in and took these thinking they were honey. When he opened them they were full of young wasps which flew in his face and stung him.

A woman lived in a group of famine houses and she got so hungry that she killed the cat and ate it. She died of fever that the cat contracted from something it had eaten.

A man was going to bury his horse which had been killed by lightning but a few men bought it from him for 4d and brought it home and divided it amongst them.[23]

P. Lennon, b.1900, Crossbridge, Co. Wicklow

People ate sycamore seeds. There were two kinds of haws they used eat, but one kind was poisonous. Many died from eating the latter because they didn't know the difference.[24]

❖❖❖

Hugh Byrne, b.1915, Blindennis, Hacketstown, Co. Carlow

His father told him that a hungry man used to draw blood from the first thing he'd meet with. One man attacked a fox but he was so weak the fox snapped at him and took his arm off.

Half the population died from hunger and were buried in the ditches.[25]

❖❖❖

Jim Lawlor, b.1877, a labourer, Knocknaboley, Co. Wicklow

A family of O'Kanes in Rathbawn had two old women sick and the doctor ordered soup. All they could do was kill the dogs and make the soup of them.

When the Protestants mowed oats the Catholics went and picked the grain out of the falling sheaves and said that a stocking full of oaten meal was worth its weight in gold.

A cow owned by a farmer in Mullans died with cancer and the poor people, when they heard of it, dug her up and ate her.

The people ate snails. One family in Rathbawn who went around the country when snails would be plentiful and gather them and dry them and keep them for a whole year.

Children would go out into the woods and stay out night and day living on fraughans and some were so weak they could scarcely stand up. They also ate laurel berries.

The people mixed cattle blood, mushrooms and cabbage and baked it. They called it relish cakes. They also made wine from elder berries and in frosty weather they ate ice.[26]

❧

Jimmy Quinn, b.1869, a shoemaker, Dunnaval, Kilkeel, Co. Down

My mother lived in Dunnaval and I heard her tell that that time of the Famine there was a man out there had two pigs died with a thing was going that time called the cholera. They were pigs belonging to James Nickle (Nickleson). And when the pigs died he took them and buried them where he had the early priddies. It was a sort of a disease that took them away that time. And I heard my mother say that they hardly waited till night come till they went out and hoked up the pigs and destroyed whatever priddies was in it. And they took them home and ate them.

And so James Nickle, when he came to her of it, he come to them and he was in an angry state about it. He wasn't pleased. 'You aren't allowed till ate them,' says he. 'They died with the cholera.' But he done no more.

And they ate them, my mother sayed, and damned the bit harm it done them.[27]

❧

Seán Rowley, a storyteller, Rossport, Co. Mayo

During the Famine times many and varied were the means devised by people for procuring food. Around 1847 or so there lived on the coast of Leacht Murrough beyond Porturlin a man who was a famous cliff climber. In the immediate vicinity of his house there was a very high precipitous cliff where the Golden Eagle used to nest, and the man was in the habit of robbing the nest and selling the eggs to a gentleman near Belderig who sent them to England. This cliff climber left one egg in the nest which the eagle hatched and a bird came out. The old eagle would go off every day foraging for food for the young bird, and Martin, that was the man's name, would see it coming back with a fish, a hen or fowl of some kind, a kid or lamb or hare or something or other for the eaglet in the nest. These were speedily devoured by the young bird and the old bird would set off again on a similar mission. When Martin saw the parent bird flying away he would rush for the cliff, and any flesh which the young bird had not consumed, Martin would take it home, cook it and eat it. As the eaglet was growing bigger and stronger it more quickly devoured the food, and frequently there was little or nothing left for Martin. He thought of a plan and stitched up the rectum of the young eagle so that it could not evacuate its excreta, and therefore could eat but little or nothing while the poor bird was so constricted. The man would watch for the old bird coming with its prey and, as soon as ever it went off again, Martin ran for the eyrie and took away the spoil whole and entire, as the young eagle was sick and suffering and unable to touch the food. On the return of the old eagle, with a fresh capture of fish or flesh, he discovered the previous supply had disappeared and thought it was the young bird which was eating it. In order to keep the young eaglet well provided for he would go off again and again, and so would Martin keep coming and raiding the eyrie. Thus the work went on and, notwithstanding the old eagle's incessant efforts for the support of its offspring, the latter appeared to the parent to be only pining and languishing. After a while when Martin thought it time to relieve the young eagle, he would undo the constriction and the patient would soon recover its health, when Martin would again subject him to a similar operation as before.

The ceaseless purveying of food by the old bird and its equally ceaseless purloining by Martin was thus carried on, with periodical operations, and undoing of operations, on the young eagle, and continued until such time as the bird was able to leave the nest and fend for itself, and Martin had to resort to new stratagems for food.

Martin had some narrow escapes from being killed in the cliff by the old eagle.[28]

⁘

Michael Corduff, Rossport, Ballina, Co. Mayo

The natives had a profound knowledge of the food value of many wild plants and their roots such as 'briscarláin' [briosclán: silverweed] and the 'cuirdín fiáin' [wild carrot]. Youngsters sucked the juices of red clover and heather blossoms, while there was much wild honey and berries to be found among the heath. Then again, there was a good deal of game close at hand, hares, grouse, plover etc. Goats and their kids, of which there were large numbers at the time, were much in vogue for their flesh and milk.[29]

❧

Thomas O'Flynn, John Melody, Attymass, Ballina, Co. Mayo

Rabbits, hares and wild fowl were caught by having rights to hunt, the flesh was used and their soup, mixed with Indian meal, was considered excellent. Bull calves sold for half a crown and were not kept. They were slaughtered for food. Sheep provided most of the meat used and sheep stealing was common. Pigs were reared on a small scale and disappeared altogether when the potatoes failed. Goats were plentiful on the mountains and were practically wiped out for food during the Famine.[30]

❧

Mrs Fitzsimons, b.1875, Sheepstown, Delvin, Co. Westmeath

There was a Fr McCormack in Clonmellon and he was an invalid. He had a dog that use to bring him in food. When he would send the dog out for food the dog would bring him in parts of a dead person off the road, but Fr McCormack would send him back again with it and tell him that was not the kind of food he wanted. In this way he trained the dog to bring him in the right food. In this way he sent out the dog for food and he came back with a small bag of wheat that he had got in a farmer's barn.

There was a man named Fleming lived near Clonmellon during that time and he used to keep a great number of cats shut up in a shed. The children of the district would steal them. They would get into the shed by means of a hole in the wall, then they would bring them home and roast them and enjoy eating them.[31]

❧❧

Seán Ó Duinnshleibhe, Glenville, Fermoy, Co. Cork

In winter, men, women and children would be seen stalking through a turnip field where grew the turnips, to pick up any root of those vegetables left in the ground. In extreme hunger the children used eat grass.[32]

❧❧

Thomas O'Flynn, John Melody, Attymass, Ballina, Co. Mayo

Cabbage was the principle vegetable and as well as being used in the ordinary way was also used in the making of oatmeal cakes. Cabbage juice was regarded as excellent food and provided a substitute for milk when used with potatoes, oatmeal cakes and boxty. Cabbage and fat were boiled in a pot and the juice got in this way.

Turnips were grown and used as a vegetable and for juice in the same way as cabbage. Boxty was also made of grated turnips and they were used raw.

Capógs [copóg: dock] and nettles were boiled and mixed with Indian meal while boiling and provided food. Bráiste (bráisc) grew plentifully in the corn and even the poor from the towns used raid the cornfields to pull it for boiling with Indian meal for food. Other weeds were also used and grass was boiled and mixed with Indian meal and used like the nettles.

'Mangels' were used in the same way as turnips, used raw or boiled, and 'mangel' juice was also used in making cakes. The hearth oaten cake was called cáca teallaigh.

Onions were boiled with grass, capógs, fúarán and other weeds, even leaves of trees. Watercress was much used.[33]

❖❖

Seaghan Mac Cártha, b.1893, national teacher, An Bóthar Buí, Newmarket, Co. Cork

She lived on herbs and turnips during the period after her husband died. She ate caisearbhán [dandelions], samha [samhadh: sorrel, sour dock], nettles, turnips and anything she could find. Poor people could be seen crawling along the ditches looking for herbs, and their mouths were green from the leaves they were eating. Poor Máire's mouth was often green, but she lived through it all. She helped to nurse me and was a very decent soul. May the heavens be her bed.[34]

❖❖

Mrs Fitzsimons, b.1875, Sheepstown, Delvin, Co. Westmeath

The people used to gather the leaves of the dandelions and boil them. Then they strained the water off and made gruel by putting meal into the water. They used to make drinks from the holly berries too.[35]

❖❖

Liam Ó Danachair, Sunvale, Athea, Co. Limerick

A well-known figure in west Limerick some 50 years ago was Lord Mr George Roche, formerly Relieving Officer to Newcastle West Union. He tells how he was driving his pony one dusky evening to the west of the town. Passing a country churchyard he saw in the twilight a stooping figure moving amongst the graves. Thinking that somebody was taking old coffins as firewood or otherwise desecrating the dead, he stole in and placing a hand on her shoulder asked an emaciated woman sternly 'What are you doing here?'

'Oh Sir,' she said, 'my children are starving and the nettles grow so nicely here I pick them at night unnoticed.'[36]

❧❧

Mrs Mary Kettle, Cohaw, Cootehill, Co. Cavan

A man called Browne was telling me that his people lived near Drumgoon Bridge and they had a servant boy hired. They made potato-bread, that was bread made from a mixture of flour and boiled potatoes, and the boy wouldn't eat it. He left them, and the following year when the potato crop failed one of the Brownes saw him coming up to their dunghill and eating the skins of turnips that were thrown on it.[37]

❧❧

Michael Corduff, Rossport, Ballina, Co. Mayo

Owing to malnutrition with its lack of bodily resistance to disease, sickness and fevers became prevalent and the number of deaths was abnormal.[38]

❧❧

5

'No Sin and You Starving'

⊰⊱

During the Famine period there was a sharp rise in crime, as desperation to get food or the money to buy it saw the numbers of offences rise dramatically. Food riots occurred, sheep, cattle and crops were stolen and people and property were attacked. The greatest rise was in non-violent offences against property, which rose threefold during the Famine, although there was hardly any increase in offences against the person. According to the crime statistics, Irish crime rates remained high until 1849 after which they dropped sharply. This rise and fall in recorded crime seems to have coincided with the course of the Famine itself and the desperation for food which accompanied it.

Of course, much crime went undetected and remained unrecorded in official records. In others cases, it may have been dealt with locally without recourse to the law, which is not to say that it went unpunished.

People of all classes went to great lengths to prevent the theft of their own resources by those in search of food. Measures taken to prevent theft ranged from hiding the food, placing a person on watch (sometimes armed), and setting mantraps to catch or kill the thief.

⊰⊱

William Doudigan (O'Dowd), b.1863, Redbray, Tullaghan,
Co. Leitrim

Pat Healy, Mullaghmore, Co. Sligo, now over 90, and the only one around here who can speak Irish, having kept it up with his mother who could speak no English and lived to be over 100, told me a short time ago that all the potatoes around Malagh were killed except a few gardens. They had one which they dug and heaped out in the garden in front of the house and in view of it. They had other potatoes in the house which they used in the winter, but when they went to bring the potatoes into the house in the spring, as is still the custom in these parts, they had been all stolen, though the outward appearance of the heap remained undisturbed and the theft must have taken place by night. He says his father told him that they of the household cried in despair when they discovered the cruel wrong.[1]

⁂

Ned Buckley, Knocknagree, Rathmore, Duhallow, Co. Cork

'Twas a very usual habit for the poor travellers and people in Famine days to have a spoon in their pocket and when they go into a house where a pot of gruel would be boiling, to steal a spoon of hot gruel when the woman of the house would have her back to the fire or be gone outside for some purpose such as turf or water.

Every farmer in the Famine years who had a field of turnips had to mind it day and night from hungry people. Mick Connor Doon, [b.1900], told me how his grandfather was working for a farmer there and had to take his turn watching the turnips at night. One night a man came and pulled up two turnips. He left him alone till he was leaving the field, then he spoke to him and asked him why he came stealing turnips. He knew him well as a very honest man but never thought he was so badly off as that he should steal turnips for food. When the poor man told him his position and how badly of he was, he said to him 'Wait now and I'll give you a couple more of turnips and carry them with you.' ''Tis no good for you to give them to me,' replied the poor man, 'for I am so weak that I couldn't carry them, and 'tis as much as I can do to carry this two, and who knows what the help of God will do for us tomorrow.'[2]

⁂

Jim Lawlor, b.1877, a labourer, Knocknaboley, Co. Wicklow

One family got an ounce of turnips from a Protestant farmer and they brought in clay and sowed the turnips on the kitchen floor to make sure that they would not be stolen.[3]

❖

Felix Kernan, b.1859, a farmer, Drumakill, Castleblayney,
Co. Monaghan

Food stealing was naturally reverted to in Famine times. Crops or cattle were often taken by those who were in want. Those found at this were usually punished severely and man-traps were set to catch any who attempted to poach.[4]

❖

Bean Uí Artagáin, b.1878, a farmer, Knockanevin, Kilmallock,
Co. Cork

Food was taken by stealing calves or turnips but this was practised by only a few, and so long as the value of the food taken was not large no action was taken. There was a custom here up to a few years ago and was apparently a relic of the Famine days. When a beggar came to a door for help he was given a pint of meal or flour or the full of his two hands (ladhar) of potatoes, money was never given. He sold the meal at the first house for a penny and the meal was given to the hens.[5]

❖

Eamonn Mac Dhuírnín, b.1878, retired national teacher,
Creeslough, Co. Donegal

To supplement the meal supply cabbages, turnips etc. were availed of; also cockles, limpets and other shellfish, but the landlord showed his hand. He sent a man round armed with a gun to prevent the starving people from gathering the shellfish, saying that that was his property and that the people were trespassing. The watchman's name was William Duail, and well he carried out his orders.[6]

⋅⋅⋅

Pilib Ó Conaill, national teacher, Main Street, Kilfinane, Kilmallock, Co. Limerick, b.1878, Wilkinstown, Navan, Co. Meath

I heard my mother and others refer to an attack made on the meal carts bringing that 'English meal' away. The carts were guarded by two soldiers as well as the drivers. The attackers had scythes fixed to handles like pikes, others carried pitchforks. They were ordered to halt by the soldiers. They came. One or both soldiers fired, one in reality took aim, the other pretended to do so and stumbling the bullet passed over the attackers' heads. The other did not, but wounded a poor fellow in the abdomen. The attackers promptly cut some of the bags in two to make them more easy for quick transport and cleared off. The poor wounded chap was carried away but died later.[7]

⋅⋅⋅

J. Toole, b.1885, Tinahely, Co. Wicklow

His grandfather used to drive a car for the landlord and collect goods from the people to pay rent. One day when they were passing through Baltinglass with a load of meal, the people were driving thorns and things into the horse's sides, trying to get out the blood, even though there were guards to protect the car. Finally they attacked the car and the guards levelled some of them but, when they were fighting, a woman tore a hole in the back of the car and got away with a stone of meal.

On one journey from Woodenbridge to Baltinglass he saw six dead people for the three he saw alive.[8]

❧

Mrs Kavenagh, b.1865, Knocknaskeagh, Co. Wicklow

Her own grandfather went into a house of a well-to-do farmer in Slievenamoe and saw a leg of mutton boiling in a pot on the fire. His family were hungry so, despite being scalded, he took the meat out of the pot and brought it home.[9]

❧

Jim Lawlor, b.1877, a labourer, Knocknaboley, Co. Wicklow

There was a man in Ballycumber named Arthur Fox and one day a wagon load of meal and other things was going to the landlord. Fox stopped the wagon with a few others and killed the driver. He took the horses and killed them later on and ate them when the other food had run out. A lad at Byrnes of Sandyford used plough with two asses but he finally got so hungry that he killed one of the asses but he was caught and got eight years for doing it.[10]

❧

Thomas Whyte, b.1880, a farmer, Cappa, Inistioge, Co. Kilkenny

Attempts were made to obtain food but very strong measures were used to prevent it. In Sallybog a man was on duty with a gun to ensure that the turnips would not be stolen. A man was also employed by Green in Cappa, also armed with a gun to prevent the stealing of turnips. This measure was not successful as Green had the turnips stored in a large house. The poor people used to get a long stick with a spike on the end of it and try to get the turnips out of the house through narrow windows in the walls, known as spy-holes.[11]

❧

P. Foley, b.1890, a farmer, Knockananna, Co. Wicklow

Luke O'Toole and Richardson used to go at night to the farm of a Protestant named Ebb, of Mullans, and take the turnip scoops which would be left by the sheep. This became such a regular practice by Knochananna people that Ebb placed men on guard and they caught the two boys, but only after they had hidden their bag of scoops in a 'sceach' bush. They were tried and sentenced to three months in jail. On their release they were overjoyed to find their bag of scoops still intact and brought them home in triumph.[12]

Edward McGrane, b.1857, Ballintra, Co. Donegal

Cartmen who used to go weekly to Derry for supplies of different kinds, and travelled night and day, were afraid to go when the Famine was at its worst, as there was a danger of their being attacked on the way and robbed of anything which they had on their carts.

The wild Barnesmore Gap, some six miles from Donegal Town, had a bad name in this respect, which led to the establishment of a police station there.[13]

John Devoy, Stradbally, collected by Mairtín Breathnach, Inistioge,
Co. Kilkenny

A widow who lived about a mile from the town here had six sons. They were very badly off and one night they stole a sheep. They cut up the meat, put it into a tub and buried it under the hearth stone. Police came next day to search the house. One of them struck the hearthstone with the butt of his rifle and noticed that it produced a hollow sound. He drew the attention of the other constables to this and they lifted the hearth stone and found the meat in the tub. The six boys were arrested and the sentence was transportation. They were taken away and never heard of afterwards. Their poor old mother died in the poorhouse.[14]

⁂

Pádraig Ó Diomasaigh, b.1854, Lios a Londúin, Cill Conaidhrean, Co. Galway

They'd steal sheep, why wouldn't they? They had to put a bell on the sheep's neck. When the bell would ring out he'd [the steward] go then, and hunt them that would be stealing. I saw the little houses where the poor herd had to sleep out watching. And sure, 'twas no sin, and you starving, to steal whatever you could to eat.[15]

⁂

J. O'Kane, Dromore National School, Dromore West, Co. Sligo

A small farmer named Feeney, who lived on the border between Co. Sligo and Co. Leitrim came to a miller with a hundredweight of oats to grind into meal. The farmer asked the miller to grind half this amount for him and keep the other half-hundredweight to be ground at a later date. The miller said that it was not worth making halves of so small an amount and that it was as well to grind all together. The farmer agreed. That evening when the farmer was returning home with his meal, the 'return' from his hundredweight of oats, he was waylaid and killed and, of course, his meal taken. The miller was very upset for a time as he felt he, by his advice or persuasion, was partly responsible for the poor man's death.

John McHugh told me he often heard his grandfather tell this story.[16]

⁂

Seán Rowley, a storyteller, Rossport, Co. Mayo

This class of crime was fairly common among the people. Sheep were very much the subjects of theft, to be killed and eaten. It was said too that cows too were sometimes stolen and never seen again. These practices were committed by the natives themselves, but on occasions mass raids were made on the hills, cliffs and mountains by robber bands who used to come from distant parts of the country, said to come sometimes from Ulster, and drive away cattle and sheep and even horses *en masse*. Sometimes after a bloody fight the stock might be rescued, but other times they would be taken away completely by the marauders.[17]

❖

William (Bill) Powell, b.1869, a pensioner, Eniskeane, Co. Cork

The people that had spuds anyway plenty had a job to try and mind them. There was no chance of keeping them outside in a pit nor in an outhouse, for the starving people would face the soldiers to try and get them if they thought they were there, so it was inside at home in sacks or in their rooms they had to keep them.

And another job they had was to have their gardens from being rooted out. As soon as the stalks appeared above the ground there was a danger of they being rooted to find the sets or to dig out the new potatoes before they were half mature.

There was a Yeoman Captain lived in Palace Anne at that time. He was known as Captain Sam Beamish. I needn't say he was bad for 'twas in everyone's mouth, and 'twas his delight to see the people in the way they were.

It is an old saying why 'The devil's children has their father's luck'. So it was with Captain Sam. He had as fine a garden during them bad years as he had at any time, and he had his yeomen minding it.

But one day himself saw two men rooting out the new potatoes when they thought there was no one around. He came on them but they ran and hid themselves in a corn field close by. He called his men and picked out six Protestants to comb the cornfield and seize the men. His men went through it but found no one. He ordered them to search back again. They did the same with the same result. From his men then he picked out six Catholics and ordered them to search it. The Catholic men brought out the poor fellows in hiding, and I can't say but as I heard, the two poor men died in Cork Jail. So there it is, the Protestant men would save them and their own colour caught them.[18]

❖

Thomas O'Flynn, John Melody, Attymass, Ballina, Co. Mayo

People from the towns raided corn fields to pull bráiste [práiseach: wild cabbage] to cook and they also pulled up potato stalks and took away the potatoes adhering to same. This was a great loss to farmers. Others went into the potato fields in the spring when the crop was set and with sticks, in which a long nail was driven, they picked up the 'slits' or 'sets' and carried them off for food. Cabbages were stolen – also turnips. The stealing of corn was quite common.

Sheep stealing prevailed and continued long after the worst famine years. Farmers on the mountain sides suffered most. Robbers frequented caves and lived there on plunder. Many of those caves, connected with forts, are still pointed out as the haunts of robbers in those days.

Darby Dempsey (Diarmuid Mór of Coolcroney) was the most notorious robber of Famine times. He was born in Ballycong and was so strong that he used carry six hundredweight of slits [potato sets] out to the field together with a bucket and stíbhín [a stick for making holes to receive the sets]. He went to reside with relations in Byhalla near the Ox Mountains and got into the habit of sheep stealing. He was joined by a man called Mulderrig who later gave up his evil ways as the revenue men were on their track. Darby stole, not only for himself and his friend, but to assist the very poor.

Man-traps were set in potato fields etc. A hole about eight feet deep and about two feet wide was dug, filled with water and concealed with brambles and grass etc. People lay in wait and when the robber fell into the trap he was pounced upon and beaten to death with sticks. In some cases the trap held the water and the robber was drowned.

The prevalence of robbery in Famine years is given as a reason why tiny windows were used in old houses. Mantraps were set outside windows also.[19]

❦

Seán Ó Barclaigh, b.1907, a farmer, Barnatra, Ballina, Co. Mayo

People living along the sea coast had another means of obtaining food. They used go out with their small boats called curraghs and rob ships that were travelling from America to England and Scotland, some of them coming to Ireland. I suppose the ships at that time were not armed, same as they are done since, but the people used to be there, great multitudes, maybe ten or fifteen curraghs and each carrying four men, and I suppose the crew of the ship would take pity on them and give them any amount of meal they wanted, for it was mostly Indian meal that most of the ships used to carry at that time. And of course the weather was fine and the sea was calm, when they would go out to meet them ships, for them ships to pan within five or six miles of the headlands. Well, that went on for some time, but the poor unfortunate creatures got badly trapped at last. The British government got to know about this very soon and they sent out the patrol boats called Cutters. These boats were fully armed. They kept the Irish coast well watched with the result that some of those people were caught robbing the ships and they had no means of escape for their frail craft were not swift enough to escape on those boats that were driven by sail and they were made for having good speed in them. The little curragh rowed by little paddles were no equal to them. Those poor people were the ones got and got perhaps long terms in jail, so that would be the source of more death during the Famine years.[20]

⋯❧❧⋯

Martin Manning, b.1875, Carrowholly, Kilmeena, Westport,
Co. Mayo

In this part of the parish around Carrowholly the land was suitable for wheat and barley which, after selling enough to pay the rent, left a little over for food which they go milled at Knappogh, Westport Parish. Now the people who attended the mill should be sure to take it home with them at midday or it would be taken from them, and even then they should travel in considerable strength.[21]

⋯❧❧⋯

Pádraig Ó Díscín, Baile an Mhuilinn, Eadar Dhá Ghabhail,
Co. Galway

My father and mother both remembered clearly the years of the Famine.

It would appear that many were fairly comfortable during those years having a supply of oatmeal and these gave all the aid they could to the immediate neighbours. In this connection I have more than once heard my mother telling of an incident that happened in her own house. It appears they kept a kilncast, as they called it, in a disused room, sifting what they wanted now and again as required. In those days the country mills did not do this. One night her father heard the low sound one makes as they sift the meal with the sieve, or perhaps an accidental noise or thump of sieve got up, went to the room and found a poor neighbour sifting some meal.

'Céard a thug anseo thú?' ar seisean leis. [What brought you here?]

The poor person only answered: 'Maise, thug an mí-ádh.' [The bad luck.]

He then told how he got in. He watched a time when he found the household all out, went to the house and hid in the room. He had no sieve of his own and so was obliged to sift it there. He was sent away and not empty, neither was he blamed. Who could have the heart to blame him?[22]

⚜

Cáit Uí Bhraonain, b.1858, Kilbeggan, Co. Westmeath

The poor people used to steal sheep for food and anyone caught in the act was hanged. The man-traps were deep trenches covered with bracken. When people went to get food they often fell into these and broke some part of the body and often were unable to get out and died there with hunger, exhaustion and illness.[23]

⚜

*Mícheál Ó Beirne, national teacher,
Cor an tSilín, Bawnboy, Belturbet, Co. Cavan*

John King, Cornacloice, states that ducks and geese etc. were stolen and cooked by putting clay around them in the fire and when the owner came looking for his bird he could find no trace.[24]

⚜

*Mrs Brigid Butler, b.1895, a farmer, Grange, Newtown, Kilcock,
Co. Kildare*

If caught stealing food they were threatened with shooting or transportation to Van Diemen's Land. There were people named Chandler living in Capagh (Kilcock parish) who were caught stealing a bag of potatoes. One of the family was hanged out of a cart on Chandler's Hill and some of the family were transported.[25]

⚜

Tomás Ó Ceallaigh, b.1860, a farmer, Caherea, Ennis,
Co. Clare

A neighbouring farmer (Mr Thomas Cherry) told me that his grandfather had a little garden of turnips and one night captured another neighbour taking some of them. He asked why the poor man should come by night to take what he could gladly have by day, and the reply was that he was ashamed to let anyone know that he was in such want.[26]

⊰⊱

Mrs Gilmore, b.1867, Moyleroe, Delvin, Co. Westmeath

You would never see anyone in the daylight. The grown-ups would stay in their houses and their children would steal under cocks of hay or stooks of oats or rye. They would have little bags with them and into these they would gather grains of oats and hay seed, or grains of wheat or rye.

When night would come and they had their little bags full, they would steal back into their houses and boil the grains for supper. They would have nothing else until the next night when they would have collected some more grains.[27]

⊰⊱

Pádraig Sabhaois, Darmhagh, Co. Laois collected this account in
Moycullen, Co. Galway

To appease the pangs of hunger sheep were stolen from the fields and eaten. The people were told from the altar that they should always ask for food first but that in extreme need they need not hesitate to take it in the event of a refusal.

My grandmother told me that in '47 they had 53 sheep but before the year was out they had only three which they managed to keep by locking them in the barn at night.

The chief, if not in many case the only, article of diet available was Indian meal and twice a week military escorted people returning from Galway with food to a distance of four miles.[28]

❖❖

Francis McAleer, b.1868, Teebane East, Co. Tyrone

I heard them say that people died along the roads here. I heard my father tell it. They used to eat pressaugh [práiseach: wild cabbage, práiseach bhuí: charlock], they would steal it. I heard them tell of a feed of turnips down in Gorticashel (Rooskey Parish) and there was great pressaugh and turnips in it and it was a Protestant man owned it. They were stealing in for it. So he shouted to them to go ahead and take all they wanted. I heard them say that five of them died crossing the ditch.[29]

❖❖

Michael Corduff, Rossport, Ballina, Co. Mayo

The meal was imported by a ship which came regularly from Westport, but sometimes for some cause or other, the natives of Rossport and Kilgalligan seaboards would have to convey the meal in their own boats from Belmullet across Broad Haven Bay to be stored at the depots for cooking as required. Stories are told of how the crews of these boats, which were yawls, frequently pilfered quantities of the meal from the bags, unknown to the representative of the landlord who always accompanied them on these voyages to prevent stealing or theft. It was found at first, before the steward used to accompany them, that several bags were short of their appointed weight, and hence it was decided to place a trustworthy servant, a permanent employee of the landlord, in charge of the transport, for suspicion rested with the crews, that they were the offenders[30]

❖❖

Mrs Peter Reynolds, b.1871, Ballykilcline, Kilglass Parish,
Co. Roscommon

My father used to boast that he kept his family alive during the
Famine. His mother made a big pocket for him inside his coat
and he used to steal oatenmeal and put it in this big pocket and
bring it home and that's how he kept his family from starving and
he was only a very young lad at the time.[31]

❧❧

Michael Howard, b.1883, a farmer, Gladree, Belmullet, Co. Mayo

One day out on the west coast about one mile from the mainland
there passed a ship which seemed to be carrying a heavy load.
This ship was followed by three men in a small fishing boat.
When they overtook this liner they halted her and asked the
crew what this liner contained. So the man said it was carrying
six tons of Indian meal which they were bringing from India to
Cork. So those men robbed the ship and took off the most of the
meal and brought it to the shore where many poor people
awaited them who were in danger of death.

It was not long after, about two days, when the landlords of
Connaght came to hear about the men who did the robbery, so
those poor men were arrested and put into jail for two years. But
the meal was hid in the fields and covered with clay but there
was still a search sent out by the landlords for the meal and they
promised to prosecute the people who lived near the shore of
Scotchport when they would not tell where the Indian meal was.
But when the people who were near the place would get a
chance, they would go where the meal was hid and take some for
food. When the searchers had spent a week looking for the meal,
they had to surrender because they got no information from the
people of the village, and the rest of the meal was divided on
neighbours who were dying for the want of food.

Those young men who were put in jail died a few days after.[32]

❧❧

Barney Gargan, b.1860, Tierworker, Bailieboro, Co. Cavan

There was a poor man in County Meath and himself and his wife and family were starving. There was in the same locality a big farmer who had a lot of sheep. One night the poor man went out to steal one of the sheep, to bring it home and kill it and cook it. The owner of the sheep was at the back of the ditch and saw him. The poor man was very honest, it was starvation and want that tempted him, and, when he caught the sheep, he got sorry and said, 'Oh honesty, honesty, how will I part with you? But my wife and children are starving and what can I do?' The owner jumped from the back of the ditch and caught hold of the man and caught hold of the sheep and said 'Were you going to bring this sheep?' 'Oh I was,' said the poor man, 'My wife and children are starving.'

'You have the worst sheep in the field. I'll get you a better one.' The owner went and caught a fat sheep and gave it to him and said, 'Because you are an honest man and didn't want to part with honesty, I am giving you this sheep.'[33]

❧❧

Jim Carney, b.1861, Cill Da Lí, Kilworth, Co. Cork

There was a man that was well off, and he had sheep, and he used to be minding them. There was three brothers living near him and they were starving. They said they'd kill a sheep before they'd die. They went into the field, and the man was hidden in the ditch watching the sheep. One of the brothers said 'Leave 'em alone. We'll die dacent.' They turned back and they went home. The next morning there was a but of spuds went up to the house to them. The man heard what he said.[34]

❧❧

Mrs Fitzsimons, b.1875, Sheepstown, Delvin, Co. Westmeath

The men often used to steal the tails of the bullocks. They would wait till the landlord was gone to bed and then steal out and cut the tails off the bullocks. They would skin them and roast them.

There was a man in Ballyhealy during the Famine and he was the only man in Ballyhealy who had any cattle. He had four and the tails were cut off them. He did his best to find out who did it. At last the man who did it told Poynton and Poynton gave him one of the bullocks for telling the truth and admitting his guilt.[35]

❖

Thomas Flynn, b.1860, a farmer, Carntulla, Ballinaglera,
Carrick-on-Shannon, Co. Leitrim

The priest got some trouble from people who, by charm or other means, could take their neighbours' butter. So he visited the scene of operations and found out the means and words by which it was done. After restoring peace among the parties, and having got a pledge that such would not occur again, he returned home rhyming to himself the words used in taking the butter, in order that his housekeeper, Nabby, would hear all. He lived in Hollymount townland and kept one cow, so that when Nabby went to churn she could not move the dash. The churn was packed with butter and the priest had to go back and see who lost it.[36]

❖

6

Mouths Stained Green

❧❧

Direct starvation was not the major cause of death during the Famine period. A minority of the one million excess deaths was solely due to starvation and dropsy (hunger oedema, with its familiar signs of swelling of organs as a result of acute starvation), but general nutritional deficiency left people particularly vulnerable to a range of deadly diseases.

Purely nutritional diseases, which affected people in the absence of the nutritious potato, included widespread scurvy because of vitamin C deficiency. This caused anaemia, swollen and bleeding gums, swollen, painful and discoloured joints, bleeding beneath the skin and a purple discolouration. In infants it caused malformation of bones and teeth.

Lack of vitamin A caused xerophthalmia, which caused excessive dryness of the cornea and conjunctiva, damaged the sight and could finally end in blindness. This particularly affected children and was rife in the workhouses. Other dietary deficiency diseases included pellagra, due to a lack of nicotinic acid, which is characterised by a burning or itching, often followed by scaling of the skin, inflammation of the mouth, diarrhoea and mental impairment. Starvation and malnutrition also left people more vulnerable to typhus, relapsing fever and cholera.

❧❧

Mrs G. Kirby, Stradbally, Co. Laois, in 1945

The population was so dense, both in the town and the surrounding districts, it was impossible, when the potato crop failed, to obtain a sufficient supply of other foods for the needs of people who had been in the habit of living almost exclusively on potatoes, the food that seemed best suited to their constitutions.[1]

❧❧

Mrs Peter Reynolds, b.1871, Ballykilcline, Kilglass, Co. Roscommon

There was one whole family died of hunger in Ballykilcline and they were dead a whole week before they were found. The men that entered the house got weak and sick and had to be given whiskey[2]

❧❧

Kate Flood, b.1882, Cranally, Granard, Co. Longford

I heard me aunt say it was nothing to see a woman with six or seven childer come into a house that time looking for a bite to ate, and the woman of the house would give her a noggin of milk and stirabout made of oaten male. She'd feed the childer first, then herself and then on to the next house.[3]

❧❧

Patrick O'Donnell, b.1863, Cam, Mostrim Parish, Co. Longford

I always heard that them that had full and plenty were just as hungry as them that had nothing. The auld people always said that it wasn't want of food made the people hungry, but that hunger was in the air and everyone suffered. There was no cause for the Famine. It come from the will of God. The hunger was in everyone's heart.[4]

❧❧

Mrs Mary Kettle, Cohaw, Cootehill, Co. Cavan

One morning the time of the famine of 1846 and '47 my grandfather was going with a cow to the fair of Cootehill, and he saw a girl that was standing up against a gate that was along the road. The cow moved over to the gate, and when my grandfather went over to drive the cow away from it, he got a terrible shock when he found that the girl was dead. She died from hunger and cold. Her clothes were stiff with the frost.[5]

❧❧

Sarah Treacey, b.1868, Glenkeele, Glenelly, Co. Tyrone

There was thousands died with hunger. I mind my father telling that he was six years old at the time, and that's how he always counted his age. And he told that one time his mother sent him down to an old man that was lying dying with the hunger on the rock. She sent him with a wee small tinful of gruel made of nettles and the like. The man was dying with the hunger. He was lying outside on the rock, and the moans of him was awful.[6]

❧❧

Pádraig Sabhaois, Darmhagh, Co. Laois collected this account in Moycullen, Co. Galway

The Parish Priest, F. Kenny, who died in 1896 aged close to 90 years and who had charge of the parish long before the Famine, told me that on a certain Saturday on his way to the church to hear confessions he anointed 19 on the roadside dying of starvation.

On another occasion he pointed out to me a spot on the road just outside the church gate where he found a poor man sitting one Sunday morning. The man had a small loaf clutched in his hand and was making attempts to raise it to his mouth. He was so weakened from hunger and exhaustion that he had not sufficient strength to lift the bread to his mouth. Then he used to bend his head down, holding the loaf between his knees, to try to get a bite in that way but the result was that he simply toppled over. The priest then anointed him and he died there tearing the dough with his nails.

I have heard stories of unfortunate people who used to come to farm yards searching on the dung heaps for cabbage stalks that might have been thrown out.

One woman told me that they always gave food when they had it to these poor creatures but that in cases where they were too far gone in hunger they were sometimes afraid to give them anything to eat lest they would be overcome by the food and as she put it 'would die on the floor with them.'[7]

❧❧

Séamas Ó Móráin, Gliasc, Glenbeigh, Killarney, Co. Kerry, in 1937

There was a girl who had her hands worn from scraping the stones of the strand for food, such as sladdy and all sorts of shell fish, When she had the strand bare, she was found lying dead. She died of starvation. This girl lived in a place called Rhodes (west of Kells, about ten miles from Cahirsiveen).[8]

❧❧

Kathleen Hurley, Ballymoe, Co. Galway, in 1937

On many occasions, hours would be spent at the door of some charitable institution, soup school or a gentleman's house. Oftentimes after a long wait in the bitter cold the people would be sent away without a crumb of bread. There was no bread to be got for them. Everyone was coming short and they were afraid to satisfy their hunger or eat enough, thinking the day was not far off when they found they had nothing left to eat.

Those pitiful scenes remained fresh in my father's memory. People worn out with untold hardship, badly clad staggering for want of food, or any kind of nourishment, wending their way back to satisfy the hungry gnawing pang with a drink of hot water or a mouthful of fresh grass or herbs they gathered by the roadside.

My father said he saw people dead on the roadside, such

88

sights, their bodies all skin and bones, with bunches of green grass in their mouths, the green juice of the grass trickling down their chins and necks. Eating such foods brought on disease on the mouth and lips.[9]

⁘⧢⁘

Peter Clarke, b.1872, Usker, Bailieboro, Co. Cavan

Doctor Adams, of Lower Knockhide, was a young man out of college at the time of the Famine, he was after finishing his medical course, and he got an appointment in the west of Ireland. He told me it was most terrifying to drive along the road and see a corpse lying here and a corpse lying there, and some of them seemed as if they had been trying to get as near as possible to the cemetery. Both sides of the road were strewn with them. He said that they died from starvation.

When the Indian meal came out, some of them were so desperate from starvation that they didn't wait for it to be cooked properly, they ate it almost raw and that brought on intestine troubles that killed a lot of them that otherwise might have survived. They just grabbed it and swallowed it down almost raw.[10]

⁘⧢⁘

Hugh Clarke, b.1873, Bailieboro, Co. Cavan

My father was born in 1823 and he was a man in the Famine times. His father lived at 'The Monument' below Rockcorry. My father told me that one day during the Famine a man was passing on his way to Monaghan. My grandfather was feeding pigs with turnips, and the man stood and said to him, 'Would you give me some of them turnips?' My grandfather told him to eat away, and he came over and ate a feed of the turnips. He thanked my grandfather and went away, and when he was coming back he died of exhaustion on the side of the road. The inquest was held and, when the body was open, there was nothing in the stomach only the turnips that he got in the morning. When his clothes were searched there was over £100 in his possession. He was so much afraid to spend any of the money, in case he might need it later, that he starved the whole day in Monaghan.[11]

⚜

Dáithí Ó Ceanntabhail, national teacher, Croom, Co. Limerick

The deaths in my native place were many and horrible. The poor famine-stricken people were found by the wayside, emaciated corpses, partly green from eating docks and nettles and partly blue from the cholera and dysentery.[12]

⚜

John D. O'Leary, Lynedaowne, Rathmore, Kerry

When I was a small boy I heard an old man talk of the Famine period. He said his mother sent him out to invite in a man that she saw leaning against a wall in Millstreet town. When he spoke the man did not answer. When he touched him he was dead.

When my grandmother (d.1894) was going to mass at Rathmore she saw a man lying dead on a heap of stones on the roadside. A young girl named Cotter is said to have died rather than accept help from the Soupers.[13]

⚜

*Tomás Ó Ceallaigh, b.1860, a farmer, Caherea, Ennis,
Co. Clare*

There was a labouring man in Caherea, his name was Cusack. He was found lying up against a wall dead in the morning. There was another man in Decomade and his name was Tom Hadlock.

90

He was 18 years. He died of starvation. He was taken to Clondegad graveyard. They heard the noise in the coffin. They opened it and took him out and he lived to be an old man.[14]

❧❧

Felix Kernan, b.1859, a farmer, Drumakill, Castleblayney, Co. Monaghan

When the potato crop failed no other food was available and the people perished by the hundreds of thousands, along the roadside, in the ditches, in the fields from hunger and cold, and what was even worse – the famine fever. The strongest men were reduced to mere skeletons and they could be met daily with the clothes hanging on them like ghosts.

The grandmother of the present writer often told me of her experiences when a girl of seventeen in those awful days. Her people had a little country shop and those customers who called on any particular day seldom or ever returned to the shop. She said it was usual to see corpses lying by the roadside with pieces of grass or leaves in their mouths and their faces stained with the juice of the plants which they were chewing to try and satisfy the hunger.

On one occasion a mother came in with a baby in her arms. The poor little thing was gaunt and thin and kept whining for something to eat. The mother would persist in putting its lips to her breasts which were milkless in order to stop it crying. A drink of milk was given to the baby and its mother and later the same day the mother was seen dead by the roadside with the baby still alive in her arms.

On another occasion a man called at the shop to buy a pound of meal to make porridge for his family of six. This small quantity of meal was boiled in a great deal of water to make more bulk but the thin gruel only hastened the end of the poor starving creatures and the next day four of them were dead in a neighbouring field.[15]

⋇⋇

From old people in 1945, Aughrim, Co. Wicklow

My memory goes back to the early [eighteen] seventies to a farm in Mourne Abbey, near Mallow. The fright of the Famine was still in the people's minds. My mother's people lived in Gleann na gCloch between Donaghmore and Macroom. They were Sullivan (muintir na Cleithe). The house was near the road and a pot of stirabout was kept for any starving person who passed the way. My mother Mary says she was a gearrachaile [young girl] at the time and alone in the house one day when a big fathach [giant] of a fellow staggered in. He wolfed his share of stirabout and made for the door, but there was a tub of chopped cabbage [raw] and porridge for the pigs. He fell on his knees by the tub and devoured the stuff till she was in a fright, then he reeled out to the road and was found dead there a short time after. She said she was never the better of it.[16]

⋇⋇

Thomas O'Flynn, John Melody, Attymass, Ballina, Co. Mayo

Conditions were terrible as few had any money. In one case a man drowned himself rather than suffer the hunger pains any longer. It is related of one family that someone called on them to find the children dead and the parents dead and the parents lying on the floor nibbling grain from a sheaf of oats which lay between them and both unable to rise when the visitor entered.[17]

⋇⋇

*Deóra (Downey), Bean Uí Ghealabháin, b.1858, a farmer's wife,
Druimeanna Mór, Parknasilla, Sneem, Co. Kerry*

I heard my mother saying that a woman and her three children called into her one day. They were after walking from

Cahirsiveen. They belonged to Skibbereen. She came into my mother and asked her permission to boil a few heads of cabbage she had.

My mother gave them bread and tea and she gave her a cake [of bread] and some flour for the road. My brother James was nine years old at the time.

Himself and my father went to Skibbereen some years afterwards. My father had a sloop and he used to trade along the Cork coast. When they landed in Skibbereen, James went up to the town for milk and met a young boy in the street with a churn of milk, himself and his mother. The boy recognised him and drew his mother's attention to him. The mother told him the story then, how they had called to his father's house in the bad times. She had the grass of sixteen cows in Skibbereen. She sent down a keeler of prints of butter the following day to the boat.[18]

⁂

Eibhlín (Ní Chathaláin) Bean Phádraig Uí Shúilleabháin,
Meall an Róistigh, Sneem, Co. Kerry, in 1944

My uncle Mick [Cahalane], he was nearly 95 when he died. He is dead with 27 years. He remembered a family of the Caseys that lived up at the bottom of the mountain, at the top of the farm [Doirín an Mhuirig]. The ruin is still there. There were seven or eight of them there. A neat little family, white heads. My uncle Mick used to cry when he used be telling the story.

The oldest girl went the six days of the week to Sneem for soup [praiseach] and came empty. On the seventh day, five of them died. I remember one of them, she was a withered old little woman. The name of the place where they lived was Cúm an Chárthainn [Doirín an Mhuirig] The olagón they rug [raised] the sixth day, when she came without any food, was something dreadful.

Years after, my father was ditching [fencing] near the ruin and he found the bones. An old man and a child, the arm of the old man was wound around the child.[19]

❧❧

Tadhg Ó Scanaill, a farmer, Cathair Crobh Dearg, Rathmore,
Co. Kerry, in 1942

My mother remembered the Famine of '48. She remembered
finding a mother and daughter on the path, locked in each
other's arms, within a few yards of Rian an Daimh, on the cosán
[path] going across to Claedach, above the Gleann an Phriacháin
Lake. She was sent on a message with another little girl. The
night was snowy, there was a little snow on their clothes, they
were around here the day before.

She remembered one young man dying up here at the City
[Cathair Crobh Dearg] a man named 'Jockon'. He ate the
horseflesh, a horse that got killed or died on them. He died of the
hunger afterwards.

Maire Ní Chriadáin was her name. She was 78 when she
died.[20]

❧❧

Ned Buckley, Knocknagree, Co. Cork, in 1945

Two people, men, died of hunger in Knocknagree but they were
not of Knocknagree. One of those men was of Kingwilliamstown,
now Ballydesmond. He had brought the corpses of his two
children in a bag to be buried in the old churchyard of Nohoval,
an Irish mile and a half from Knocknagree and six miles from his
home. The children had died of want and he brought them all
the way on his back to Nohoval and going back he died of
hunger and exhaustion.

The other man was from some part of Kerry who had travelled
down to Limerick seeking employment which he failed to obtain
and, after some time in that inhospitable place, he was returning
home to Kerry, which he never lived to see as he died in Park a
quarter of a mile eastward of our village and was buried in the
wood there.

Long ago I remember to have heard when I was young, nearly sixty years ago, how a poor woman was found dead in the parish of Kingwilliamstown. She was found on the roadside with a poor miserable child trying to suck at the dead breasts of the mother and the mouth of the poor corpse was smeared with green slime to show that the poor woman was existing on grass and weeds.

Michael Matt Dennehy, [b.1872] Scrahan, Knocknagree, told me this tale a few days ago. It happened in the townland of Lisheen about two miles from our village in the Kerry side of the Blackwater. A man named Dennehy, Old Mick Dennehy, owned a farm at that time and he was one day in the spring ploughing in the field near Lisheen Cross in which there was a fine spring well. It was the will of God that he noticed the travelling woman dragging and pulling a strong little girl of about ten or twelve towards the well. He watched her and the little child was resisting as much as she could. He noticed that when she had the girl near the well she was trying to throw her in and the child was roaring with terror. He ran towards them and found she was trying to put the child into the well.

'Woman what in the name of the Devil are you trying to do with that child?' said old Mick.

'Oh sir,' said the poor woman, 'if the Lord would only call on her I'd be all right. Isn't it better for one to be gone than to have we all gone. She has a wonderful appetite and nothing could give her enough. If she were gone I could get enough for the two more and I must do away with her altogether or she'll starve the rest of us.' She had two smaller children with her and they were all hungry. 'I'm out of my mind,' she said, 'from her and what can I do with her?'

'Stop. Stop,' said old Mick. 'Don't murder your own child. God is good and if you struggle on for a bit more maybe God will send ye all enough. Come on home now with me and ye all can have a bit to eat, and who knows but God would open some gap for you and those children.'

He took them in and told the story to his wife who gave them praties and milk enough and when the woman and her children had eaten and taken a good rest, they followed on their way after

Mrs Dennehy making her promise faithfully that she would never again think of doing away with her eldest little girl.

The poor woman was not of the tramp class, but a poor working man's wife who had to take to the road in search of something to eat for herself and her children. It was said that she was never seen or heard of again in Lisheen or anywhere around, though several enquiries were made concerning her there was no trace or tidings of her or her children ever since.

It was hoped among the neighbours that when she had got over that passion and when God saw fit, in the person of Mick Dennehy, to save her child that day that she never again attempted to do away with it.[21]

❖❖

Séamus Reardon, b.1873, Boulteen, Eniskeane, Co. Cork

The beginning of 1847 saw want and hunger all over the country. The poor were the worst. They had nothing. What made matters very trying and hard in these districts was the number of starving creatures that having left their homes in the Skibbereen and Bantry districts travelled around these parts looking for a bite to eat.

There was an old man dying. All belonging to him were buried, having died with either the hunger or the sickness following it. A neighbour found him in his little cabin and all he asked for was to send the priest to him.

The priest came and he found that the poor fellow had eaten the greater part of an old painting of the Sacred Heart, fearing he was going to die without receiving the Blessed Sacrament.

'There was no need to send for me,' said the priest, 'that poor man was all right.'[22]

❖❖

96

William Doudigan (O'Dowd), b.1863, Redbray, Tullaghan,
Co. Leitrim

The same man told me he remembered seeing a little woman being brought into their house from the dunghill where she had been found searching out and eating juices of potato peel thrown out there and that you couldn't tell was she young or old as her face, which had lost all its natural colour, was wrinkled and puckered and covered with a white downy hair.

Bessy Clarke from the same place and the same age as J. McGrath, told me a similar story about a little stray girl coming into their house in the Bad Times and eating [the] hen's share [of] pounded potatoes and meal. When Bessy's mother offered her bread, she had bother getting her to accept, as she thought the hen's share very good, not having eaten any food for a week.[23]

❖

Peter Sloan, b.1912, a postman, Glenloughan, Mourne Parish,
Co. Down

I heard my grandmother say that up in Tulyframe [Mourne Parish, Co. Down] she knew fine people to be seen lying dead along the roads and in the fields. It seems they fell dead out of their standing and the dogs eating at them.

They mustered up, she said, in bunches like, them that felt getting weak. I heard her say that. And then they went away to some place, away out along like, and one done what they could for the other till they died.[24]

❖

Hugh O'Hagan, b.1900, a farmer, Greencastle Street, Kilkeel,
Co. Down

My granny sayed that the street there, where you see the steps, was cut in the time of the Famine. And she says herself that she often took out a pot of broth out to the door there and the men would run to it and ram their hands into it, and it boiling, looking for the meat.[25]

❖❖❖

Edward McGrane, b.1857, Ballintra, Co. Donegal

A strange death from starvation took place in this district in the winter of 1846. A small farmer, who was the father of several children, was seen by his neighbours to be losing flesh rapidly. They could not understand the cause as he was known to be a thrifty man and was not in dire want, as it was known that there was still a small store of potatoes in the house from which the family used to make a meal once daily. He had a horror of the workhouse and would do anything rather than go there. His condition grew gradually worse and at last he died.

The doctor was puzzled, as he could see nothing which would account for the man's death, and so a post-mortem examination was decided upon. This solved the mystery as it was found that he was full of indigestible potato skins. He had been eating these for a considerable time and gave the inside of the potatoes to his children.[26]

❖❖❖

Mrs Kavenagh, b.1865, Knocknaskeagh, Co. Wicklow

She heard her grandfather tell of a man whose child died of hunger during the Famine years, and when it died he said there was no use in burying it until the other two died. When this happened he took them all wrapped in a sheet to Knockananna graveyard and buried them there.[27]

❖❖❖

Liam Ó Floinn, Cúl an Fhia, Kilworth, Mallow, Co. Cork, in 1935

About three miles from Mitchelstown to the south-west on the road to Araglen there is a townland called Skeheen. There is a small lake in that townland called Loch na gCúigear. Local tradition has it that the reason it got that name is as follows:

Years ago, about the time of the Famine of '47 a woman and her husband were journeying along from Anaglen. They were very poor and food was scarce at the time. The man had some bread, scarcely enough to sustain himself. The woman got hungry and asked him for a bit of the bread. He gave it to her. After a time she asked the same request, and he gave her some more, very reluctantly. She asked him a third time, so he said to himself, 'If this goes on I will starve.' They were near the lake by this time and he threw her in. She was drowned. Almost immediately, remorse seized him and he then committed suicide by drowning himself also.

When the bodies were recovered it was found that the woman was carrying three babies, so that five were drowned altogether. Since then the lake bears the name Loch na gCúigear [the Lake of the Five People].[28]

❖

7

'The Fever, God Bless Us'

❦

The overwhelming majority of deaths during the Famine was due to disease. The link between malnutrition and infection is stronger in some cases than in others, but the general poverty, deprivation and dirt created conditions where a number of deadly diseases were rampant.

'Famine fevers' were mainly of two kinds, typhus fever and relapsing fever. Both were caused by micro-organisms and transmitted by the human body louse, often in the poor housing conditions of the tightly knit and crowded clustered settlements of the cottiers or in the crowded and unhygienic workhouses. Vagrancy, large gatherings at road works and relief centres all added to the spread of fever.

Typhus was acute, infectious and more deadly than relapsing fever. There were no remedies. Symptoms of typhus included high temperatures, mental confusion, skin rash and severe headaches. Where typhus was deadly, death occurred from heart failure after two weeks.

Relapsing fever caused high temperatures, nausea and vomiting, general aches and pains, nose bleeds and jaundice. The fever tended to last about a week with a crisis of sweating and exhaustion. It could recur several times before it ran its course.

Fever tended to start among the poor and spread upwards through the social classes and it appears to have been feared above all other diseases.

Dysentery is a bacterial infection of the intestine and was related to food deprivation, eating unsuitable food or having an inadequate diet, all of which made people more vulnerable to infection. Bacillary dysentery was spread by flies, contact or by water polluted by faeces, causing nausea, shivering, fever and diarrhoea, with the frequent passage of mucus and blood. Mortality rates were high.

A number of other diseases also claimed large numbers of victims during the Famine period. Highly infectious smallpox occurred, although it was independent of nutrition, and it blinded, disfigured and killed many.

A cholera epidemic also spread from Europe to Ireland in 1848.

❖

Barney Gargan, b.1860, Tierworker, Bailieboro, Co. Cavan

There was a lot of fever around here because of the hunger and a good many people died. They were starving so long that when they got oaten meal and made bread and stirabout, they ate too much and it brought the fever on them. It was the same with the beef that they got after they had been starving for a long time. They ate more beef and drank more soup than they were fit for, and it killed some of them, and more of them took the fever. The strong heavy meals heated up the blood and caused the fever.[1]

❖

Conchubhair and Solomon Ó Néill, b.1860s, farmers, Cratloe, Co. Clare

In the same yard as the O'Neill brothers lived a family of Danaghers, in the townland of Cratloe. The household consisted of the widow and four children. All were stricken with fever, the mother having the two younger ones beside her. When she got a 'cool', as Con O'Neill put it, she discovered one of the children dead, evidently for some days. Unable to rise she used to put her hand over to the other child to feel if it were still alive; the second child died also. The other two survived and were later well known to the O'Neills.[2]

❖

Richard Delaney, b.1874, master mariner, Wexford Town

When a person in any house had got fever the people of the house would hide it from the neighbours. If the neighbours suspected there was any fever in a house, they used steal up to the house at night time and put an onion on the window sill. They would split the onion in two. If the onion turned green they would know that there was fever in that particular house and they would avoid it.[3]

❧❧

Eamonn Mac Dhuírnín, b.1878, retired national teacher, Creeslough, Co. Donegal

An outbreak of typhus fever was the most serious menace to life and numbers of people died of this fever. I do not think there were any cases of cholera in this district and the local fever hospital in Dunfanaghy was built by Stewart of Ards in 1845. There are traditions that whole families were wiped out by this fever in 1845 and succeeding years. In other cases half or perhaps three fourths of certain families met the same fate.[4]

❧❧

Mrs Gilmore, b.1867, Moyleroe, Delvin, Co. Westmeath

When the cholera came people were afraid to go near each other's houses. Often when the people would die, they would be thrown into the ditches and often there would be hundreds upon hundreds on top of each other, dead.[5]

❧❧

Seaghan Mac Cártha, b.1893, national teacher, An Bóthar Buí,
Newmarket, Co. Cork

For the first time the doors were locked. A sabh or long stick was drawn as a bolt inside the doors to keep out strangers or people having the sickness. Every cabin was overcrowded at best and the cholera was infectious. There were rows of cabins everywhere. In my district the people seemed nearly all to be closely related to each other. The miracle was that so many lived at all.[6]

⁂

Mrs Lennox, b.1869, a housewife, Hollywood, Co. Down

People became ill with sickness like cholera. Nobody entered the affected house. When death occurred in a house a tar pot was set outside the door. When this appeared a cart came and took the remains away for burial. Holes were dug for graves and numbers buried together.[7]

⁂

Felix Kernan, b.1859, a farmer, Drumakill, Castleblayney,
Co. Monaghan

In the towns things were worse. The number of deaths from the famine fever increased and so numerous were the dead and decaying bodies that the air became putrid with stench and disease germ. Fires were lighted in different quarters to purify the air. Doctors and nurses were kept busy until they themselves fell victims of the dread disease. Priests were worn out by calls night and day. Often when he opened his door a man or woman exhausted with hunger and exposure fell into his hall in a state of collapse and died there.[8]

⁂

Pat Maher, b.1885, Closh, Camros, Co. Laois

The people, when they got a fever, were moved out to the barn and a person put to mind them. The barn door was built up with black turf and whatever was wanted for the sick person was let in the window for him.[9]

❧❧

Mícheál Ó Beirne, national teacher, Cor an tSilín, Bawnboy, Belturbet, Co. Cavan

A woman and son lived at back of Macha's and they got fever. The mother died and was four days there without any neighbour going into the house. Thughey Mhacha's granda (Matthew McGovern) and Mrs Martin's granda (Pat Dolan) took her and made a coffin and left her on the street in the coffin for a day, put her in a handbarrow and brought her to the graveyard with no other help. When these men returned they were not allowed into their own homes, clothes were brought out to them and some water to wash themselves and to put on fresh clothes and to leave the cast-offs on a hedge for days.[10]

❧❧

Máiréad Ní Ailpín, Díseart National School, Dunleer, Drogheda, Co. Louth

The people were too weak to dig proper graves. They dug holes about a yard and a half deep. Very often hungry dogs came and pulled the corpses out of the shallow holes, ate part of them and left the rest exposed. In this way the fever spread.[11]

❧❧

John Phillips, b.1855, New Inn, Co. Tipperary

Before the Famine a man named Guinness of the great Guinness' Brewery had the Knockbrack farm where the present barrack is. He built a big granary for corn and two large malt-kilns under the wrath. They were underground and all solid brickwork. The two malt rooms are still there nearly opposite the barrack garden nearly level with the land.

At the time of the Famine two young men who hadn't any residence of their own got fever. They went into the malt rooms underground and, when the neighbours heard of it, they used bring food, drink and clothing to them and after some time they recovered and walked out quite cured. They went to America and became two great men afterwards.[12]

Thomas O'Flynn, John Melody, Attymass, Ballina, Co. Mayo

The 'black fever' followed. This appeared in black spots which gradually crossed the body, lips became bloodless. Death followed in the home if they were not removed to the Workhouse Hospital and there seems to be no tradition that anyone catching the disease survived. One old person here says cattle also contracted the disease. It was dreaded more than the actual hunger and when persons were found dead in the fields or along the road, their own kith and kin often denied knowing them.[13]

Pádraig Mhichíl Ó Súilleabháin, b.1867, a farmer, Meall an Róistigh, Sneem, Co. Kerry

I heard my grandmother saying that the worst sight she saw was, she saw a woman laid out on the street (in Kenmare) and the baby at her breast. She died of the famine fever. Nobody would take the child, and in the evening the child was eating the mother's breast.

There is an old ruin there across the river where a whole family died. They died of fever. They had to knock the house down on them and the dogs drew away their bodies.

There were several cases back there in Doirín an Mhuirig where whole families were buried in the fields.[14]

❖❖

Ned Buckley, Knocknagree, Co. Cork, in 1945

Jack Conell told me this tale or tales. He is 84 [b.1861] and he heard a lot of the tales of the Famine years from his own father who was a full grown man at that time, a labouring man. I knew him, Old Mick Conell.

When the people were so badly fed on greens and turnips, cabbage and certain kinds of weeds that, as they used to say, 'ran down through them', they were affected with a kind of fever and dysentery that was contagious or 'taking' as they used to say at that time and all the people suffering in this way were put away in a place by themselves. They built huts up against a sheltered ditch, poles were stood on the outside and a roof thrown across them to the ditch and they were thatched with brambles, briars and rushes. Here in those huts or 'scalpts' the afflicted people had to live, their own people or family shunning them. There were few of those scalpts, Jack Conell says, in the field now belonging to Willie Breen bounding the field now owned by Andrew Rahilly, Shanballa. The field or the port near the bounds ditch is a low and sheltered valley and was known as Park na Phooka. The sick poor had to have a vessel of their own and their friends would come now and again a couple of times each day and empty their own gallons containing milk or boiled potatoes or oat meal porridge into them, taking care not to touch them at all as the mere act of touching the vessels used by the sick was suppose to bring on the sickness.

Now poor Ellen Greany, Meentofluck, although about three miles away, often made it her business to bring food and drink to the people living in the Scalpts in Park na Phooka. She too had her own vessel and they were warned not to come near her but to wait until she'd be gone before they'd approach the food she'd bring.

It was supposed that Ellen Greany had a good lot of spuds of her own one of the Famine years and it came about this way. A farmer neighbouring her had such a bad garden in 1846 that he thought the spuds were so small and the crop so bad that it would not pay him to give hire for the digging of them. It held on through the winter and in the spring the small potatoes began to shoot out stalks and the stalks were so plentiful that Ellen one day passing by said to herself it was a pity without giving them a chance, so she began to weed the garden and the stalks grew up and flourished and she kept them clear of all weeds and the farmer left it to her for her trouble. The result was that this garden produced the best crop of potatoes that was in the country that year and Ellen Greany had plenty spuds for her poor sick people all round and for the people in the Scalpts of Park na Phooka, and though a whole lot of them died, a lot more got better and things were on the mend, but before she had used up or dug all her crop poor Ellen, who was always making bolder than anyone else, contracted the sickness and had to go to the Scalpt herself where she died.

Old Mick Conell knew her well and 'twas said by all that she had her soul made and that surely she was a saint in Heaven on account of her good deeds among the starving people of her district in those terrible years of hunger.[15]

❧ ❧

John Mc Carthy, b.1873, Kilcoleman, Eniskeane, Co. Cork

The fever, God bless us and protect everyone, that came with the want, came, she [my mother] used to say, from the people eating bad things. Of course starving people would eat anything, even though it was decaying, and that was what brought on the sickness.

It was so contagious that it was hard to escape it when it got into a district, for the people had so much communication with each other at the time, and there were so many wandering from other places worse off than this place.

It was nearly all over, she said, when herself and her brother contracted it. Her mother knew what she had as soon as she got sick, as good as any doctor could tell it. She knew it was the bad sickness from the colour of the urine. She removed the two of them to an old house in the yard, where another family had lived a short time before, away from the rest of the family, there were seven of them in all.

There was no doctor called in nor was there any doctor's medicine given. The old woman was doctor and nurse herself. They did not get a mouthful to eat but plenty drinks of two milk whey, the lightest and most sustaining drink going at the time.

Although she attended themselves in their sick beds, and done her household work besides, she had some way unknown to them of not contracting it, or taking it to the rest of the family.

She knew again from the colour of the urine when it had cleared away and the first bite they got to eat, when they got well, was a toasted potato, one only, although she said they would eat a dozen.[16]

❖

Sean Crowley, b.1858, Cill Cholmáin, Eniskeane, Co. Cork

Bad, unsuitable diet began to tell, sickness followed and worst of all the fever, God bless us, broke out in places. This was due to using bad food. Fowl that died were taken up and used. Starving people would eat anything but it had dreadful results.

The old and feeble did not stand it long. Death claimed them very soon. The fever then, when no proper treatment was available, began to take away young and old.

There were three or four little houses in that district where the whole family died out altogether and the houses thrown down and what was inside them burned.[17]

֍

J. O'Kane, Dromore National School, Dromore West, Co. Sligo

There was fever and cholera in Sligo town and the neighbourhood. There was no fever hospital here, the nearest was Sligo. The fever must have been bad there because Miss Flynn often heard her father tell of the large open pit into which the corpses were flung with lime thrown over them. He heard too of the bottomless coffin or the endless coffin in which the corpse was carried to the pit.

She tells of a Swiss doctor who came to the fever hospital in Sligo to attend the patients. He laughed at the idea of being afraid of the fever, or at least pretended to. One morning after being little more than a week there, he did not appear on his rounds as usual. After a time somebody went and knocked on the door of his room, and getting no answer, he or she opened the door. He found the doctor lying on the floor, fully dressed, with his feet towards the door and quite dead. He was fully dressed as if ready to go to work.

There was a girl who was nicknamed 'Nurse Biddy' for years after the Famine in Sligo Hospital. She, her four brothers and her father were brought into the fever hospital in Sligo suffering from fever. Her four brothers and her father died but Biddy survived. I suppose because she had no home to return to she remained in the hospital as a sort of attendant. She was for years in Sligo hospital and became a sort of 'character'. She always went by the name of 'Nurse Biddy'. Perhaps, having survived the fever or the cholera, she was immune to further attacks of it and was not afraid to nurse new cases that came into the hospital. Hence the name 'Nurse Biddy', even though she had no nursing qualifications. I was told that at least three doctors, as well as the Swiss doctor, died in Sligo hospital during the Famine.[18]

֍

John Treanor, b.1870, a retired scutcher, Forkhill, Co. Armagh

Then the cholera came out. It started, they say, between the two big toes and worked its way up till it killed you.

My own grandfather was a powerful man. He was alive and well in '46, I heard them say, and he was known to carry great weights. He was afeared of nothing. The cholera was bad at the time, and he used to walk into houses and carry them out and dump them into the carts. I didn't hear then that they buried them anywhere, Urney I suppose [graveyard beside Forkhill]. They had no coffins at all, I mind them to say, but just buried them as they were. And many's a one never knew where they were buried [not in family graves] for they buried them at night, I heard them say. They'd bury them as soon as they heard of [death from the cholera].[19]

❧❧

Mary Nugent, b.1860, a farmer, Dernaroy, Dromintee Parish,
Co. Armagh

I mind Katchy Kerly (of Dernaroy, Dromintee) saying they died with the cholera. And she took it herself, she sayed. So she went down to the field, it to be in the hay-time, and over to a hay-stack, and she got under the hay and the heat and the weight of it was a cure. The heat I think.

They took it first, I mind her to say, between the two big toes, and it turned black and it went up the foot and the leg and into the body, and it turned as black as behind the fire till it killed them on their two feet in no time at all.[20]

❧❧

Hugh O'Hagan, b.1900, a farmer, Greencastle Street, Kilkeel,
Co. Down

We had a driver that time called James Higgins, and a single-horse hearse. It was in Mass Forth all the people were buried (Kilkeel Parish). And my father sayed, and I mind old Higgins myself, but he said he wouldn't have been fit only he was drunk all the time. He sayed himself that the time of the plague he went to houses and there was no one there till give him a hand with the corp and he had to wrestle the best way he could himself. They'd be all down with the fever. Oh, it killed hundreds.[21]

❖❖❖

Michael Gildea, b.1872, Dromore, Ballintra, Co. Donegal

1847 was a worse year here than the previous two. People in general were then weaker from the effects of the two previous years of scarcity, and were less able to resist the attack of any epidemic.

There were more deaths in 1847 than in 1845–46 due more to fever than starvation.

Insanitary conditions had much to do with the spread of the fever. It was a common sight to see dunghills piled close to the door of the dwelling house, of which it and the little byre or stable formed the same range, and stagnant pools were plentiful. These spread foul vapours of a summer sun.[22]

❖❖❖

Mrs G. Kirby, Stradbally, Co. Laois, in 1945

It is said that methods of cooking food were very primitive at that time. Potatoes were easily cooked, but for the making of the stirabout it required long slow cooking and frequent stirring, so it is presumed that the meal was never given sufficient time to soften and swell, and that it was the uncooked meal that caused dysentery from which many of the people suffered, and there was lack of nourishment in the food on that account.

Mr Percival was the medical officer in Stradbally at the time. He used to try to get volunteers to put people in the coffins, who had no friends of their own. He assured them that if they removed their clothes before handling the corpses, and washed themselves afterwards, they need have no fear of infection. I was told by a woman that she heard her grandfather say that he and another neighbour put many corpses in their coffins and never contracted the disease. They used go at midnight, strip themselves naked, put the corpses in the coffins and then leave the coffins outside the doors. They were buried next day the ordinary way in the local cemetery.

I have been told that for many years after the Famine people didn't wish to talk about it, as it was considered a disgrace if it could be said of any family that their people took soup from the soup kitchens, or took the Indian meal or that any member of a family died of hunger; but they were considered martyrs if they died of the fever.[23]

⁙

Paddy Sherlock, b.1865, The Green, Stradbally, Co. Laois

If a poor man went to a farmer's house to look for work he would be refused, as the farmer would say 'I smell the sickness from you, and I can't take you into my house', and that was the reason why so many people lay down and died by the roadside or on the floors of their cabins. No one wished to go near them when they smelled the sickness from them.[24]

⁙

William Naddy, b.1863, Inistioge, Co. Kilkenny

Naddys and Gormans, well-to-do farmers in the townland of Kilmacshane, Inistioge, were very charitable to the poor of the district during these years. Both families often brought a 'jog' of potatoes at night and threw them onto the village square in Inistioge. They often brought milk, cabbage and anything they could spare in the same manner.

They dare not bring these foods in the daytime as the suffering people would flock around them and the consequent danger of infection would be very grave.

Before going to the village on these errands of charity, they disinfected their persons and clothing with some disinfectant and again used the disinfectant on their return. When the cholera broke out in Inistioge they were forced to discontinue their help as it would be impossible to escape infection, more especially as they would have to pass by the cholera house on their way to the village.

Large numbers of people died as a result of the cholera in Inistioge. Those who ate the black potatoes invariably contracted the dread disease and nearly always died as a result. Speaking of this Mrs Lyng told me she remembers her father to say that a person could be well in the morning and dead in the evening should they be unfortunate enough to be stricken by the disease.[25]

❧❦

William Blake, b.1895, a labourer, Rathnagrew, Co. Carlow

Fever patients were not brought to any hospital but a sod shelter was built up around them wherever they might be found on the roadside.

For 20 years after the Famine the Irish Cholera used to break out every year and people wondered what was the cause. It was the dung heaps. Every time they stirred them to plant the crops, it would start again.[26]

❧❦

Jim Lawlor, b.1877, a labourer, Knocknaboley, Co. Wicklow

In Knocknaboley there were people living at Lacey's and one of them saw a dead hare and brought it home and ate it. The hare was infected and they all died one by one and were all dead in a week.[27]

꩜

John Doyle, b.1900, a labourer, Rasheenmore, who was reared
at Craffle, Ballyteigue, Aughrim, Co. Wicklow

They put up a sod house in Aughrim and anyone with fever was
put into it to die. There were no doctors or attendants and no
one was allowed in.

There was also a cave near Aughrim and when the people
used to get fever they were brought into the cave where there
were two doctors to attend them. One day it was full up and
couldn't hold any more. English soldiers were passing by and they
built up the front of it and let all the people die.

A car used go round Aughrim district every day collecting the
fever patients and the driver had to sit amongst them. There was
nearly a new driver every day as each of them got the complaint.

There were so many bodies in the pond at Aughrim that the
government had to get it cleared out. The men who did the job
caught a few big trout and ate them but they immediately got the
typhus from them and died. The cleaning had to be done because
fever was spreading all over the town out of the mill pond. They
had a car there for burying the people who died of fever and they
had a bell on it to ring so that when they would be coming the
people would keep off the road.[28]

꩜

Mary B. Dunphy, Irishtown, New Ross, Co. Wexford

Though the effects of the Famine were not much felt in this area,
there were few, if any, deaths from hunger. The cholera outbreak
which followed, claimed a large death toll. There were three
local hospitals, all overflowing with patients. They were not at
all adequate. Deaths and funerals were multiplying.[29]

꩜

Pilib Ó Conaill, national teacher, Main Street, Kilfinane, Kilmallock, Co. Limerick, b.1878, Wilkinstown, Navan, Co. Meath

The poor in the towns were in an awful state and I've heard that the mortality was greater among them than in the country. In the country the disease swept an uneven swathe, but in the towns the people died like flies.[30]

8

The Paupers and the Poorhouse

❖

In 1838 an Irish Poor Law was introduced with 130 Poor Law Unions being set up by the introduction of a Poor Rate. The number of Unions grew to 163 over the Famine period. From 1843 the £4 valuation scheme was introduced, which made landlords responsible for the rates of all holdings under £4.

From 1840 each Union had to provide a poorhouse and by the outbreak of Famine there was an extensive poorhouse system in Ireland. In 1845 there were 118 poorhouses and each had its own infirmary. After 1845, each Board of Guardians could have a separate building to treat fever victims and in March 1846 a Temporary Fever Act was introduced to allow temporary fever sheds or hospitals to be built beside the poorhouses. By 1846–47 the poorhouses had a capacity for over 100,000 inmates, but those qualifying for entry numbered around half a million.

Harsh regulations and regimes were in operation in the poorhouses. When people entered, they were bathed, classified and clothed in poorhouse uniform and families were broken up and segregated by age and gender. The diet was basic and consisted of bread, stirabout, milk and potatoes, where they were available. There was no privacy, little health care and strict discipline was enforced.

As the crisis got worse, more and more people turned to the poorhouse for food and shelter. In December 1845 there were 38,000 inmates, by March of the following year that figure had risen to 41,000 and by June to 51,000. While the total number of places in poorhouses around the country were still only half-full, in some areas they were totally full and had to turn paupers away. By the following year, in the spring of 1847, the poorhouses were three-quarters full and, by the end of that year, the poorhouse system was in chaos, as ratepayers defaulted, poor law unions became bankrupt and contractors refused to supply food to them.

Diets got worse and were dictated by local conditions and not by the Commissioners. In the winters of 1846–47 and 1847–48 there were two and a half thousand people dying each week in the poorhouses.

In January 1847 the Irish Poor Law Extension Act was introduced by Lord John Russell's government. This meant an end to government funding for relief of any sort and the burden fell on the local ratepayers, the landlords.

By July 1849 over 200,000 people were depending on the poorhouses.

⚜

William Naddy, b.1863, a farmer, Cill Mhic Sheáin, Inistioge,
Co. Kilkenny

There was a fever hospital in Ballyrocksuist and a cholera house in the Mill Road. Patients were removed to the cholera house when there was no hope of their recovery. In some cases the patients were dead on admittance. They were buried in bottomless coffins in a large pit in the corner of the present graveyard. These coffins had hinges attached to the bottoms, a trigger was pulled and the body was let drop into the pit. Some clay was filled in over the body. Lime was then added. The corpse was buried without a habit, a sheet or anything available was wrapped about the body. Oftentimes this sheet or blanket was used again to cover a victim still living. The one coffin was known to have been used in the cholera house for more than twelve months. It was carried by two men like a hand-barrow, having handles front and rear. It is estimated that about three people in every house in the Inistioge district of the parish died either of fever or cholera during these years.[1]

⚜

Thomas O'Flynn, John Melody, Attymass, Ballina, Co. Mayo

It is said that a woman was placed in the dead house in Ballina Workhouse but was found alive after five days there.

In some cases when the relatives were a little better off than the majority, they aimed at burying their dead 'decently' and hired the local cart which was on contract to the auxiliary workhouse to carry the sick there, and they got or hired a coffin with a hinged bottom and used this to carry the corpse to the graveyard. The same coffin served a similar purpose again and again.

Here it may be well to give an account of the contract given by 'the powers that be' in charge of the auxiliary workhouse to a local who had the only horse and cart in the immediate neighbourhood. He was paid at so much per head to convey the sick to the workhouse. The patient was put in a sack, feet first, and the sack was tied closely around the neck and labelled. Up to seven or eight patients were laid out in the body of the cart which then set off on its cogglesome journey to the workhouse. Few ever returned. But the cart did not return empty for the bottomless coffins were ready tenanted, and the driver proceeded to the graveyard at Bonnifinglas and the corpses were deposited in the same grave. The relatives were not even notified of the deaths. The corpse was sewn in a white cloth and a coffin was not used.

The contractor received the name of 'Sack Them Up', from the fact of putting the patients in the sacks.[2]

❧❦❧

Kathleen Hurley, Corlock House, Ballymoe, Co. Galway

The poorhouses also supplied coffins very cheap to any persons throughout the country who were unable to purchase a coffin for their deceased friend. To be buried in a workhouse coffin was regarded as a slur on the friend and on the deceased. Consequently when a death occurred the friends of the deceased went to town for the 'Burial Charge', bought three boards, paint and mounting. Some handyman made the coffin and the coffin was carried to the grave on white linen sheets. This was done up to 40 years ago. A child's coffin was covered with white cloth instead of paint.[3]

❧❧

Pádraig Ó Cruadlaoich, b.1860, a master tailor, Macroom, and Máire Bean Uí Mhurchadh, b.1874, Sráid Ghuirtín Buí, Macroom, Co. Cork

During the time of the Famine a great number of dead were buried in one grave at the Abbey Graveyard, about a mile west of Skibbereen, near the Skibbereen-Sahils road. There is a monument erected over the grave, which I saw myself a few years ago.

When the bodies were being pushed into the huge open grave, the story goes, a little child's body was in the way and one of the grave-diggers pushed it with a spade or shovel. In doing so he broke both knees of the child, with the result that the child woke up. It wasn't really dead. The child who had the marvellous escape from being buried alive was taken to the local workhouse. He grew up strong and hearty but was severely knock-kneed for the remainder of his life.

He was for many years a familiar figure in the West Cork towns, travelling around on foot, a beggarman, from fair to fair. I often saw him here in Macroom. He was known by a nickname I cannot now recollect.[4]

❧❧

Maighréad Ní Dhonnabháin, b.1866, a farmer, Drom Inide, Drimoleague, Co. Cork

But the most remarkable of all Famine victims in this district was Tom Gearins. Tom was a young lad the time of the Famine. With many others he was taken and thrown into the Famine Hole in Skibbereen Abbey. He was not dead and somehow or other he was able to raise his hand. He was eventually rescued but it was found that both his legs were broken and badly deformed from the weight that was on him. However he lived, but his legs were all out of joint. He spent the greater part of his time in the district working with the Protestant Minister.

When the poorhouse was built in Skibbereen, Tom used go in there for the winter and then return to Drimoleague for the summer. Whenever he was getting tired of the work he would say to the Minister, 'Would to God sir, 'tis time for Tom Gearins to go to roost'.

On one occasion the Board of Guardians in Skibbereen were providing poor people with boots. Tom thought that a pair would be a great relief to his bórach [misshapen] legs so he applied. He was told however that he had no hope of the boots unless he composed a verse about himself. Whether he is the author of the following or not, this verse is known to all the older stock in Drimoleague.

I arose from the dead in the year '48,
Though a grave in the Abbey had near been my fate,
And since for subsistence I've done all my best,
Though one leg points east and one leg points west.
And never a tax on the ratepayers I've been,
I've roamed o'er the country enjoying each scene,
I only appeal to you now for a pair
Of boots and I'll vanish again into air.[5]

❧❧

Pádraig Pléimionn, Killarney, Co. Kerry

I heard several accounts of the misery and wretchedness of the people who gathered about the Killarney Workhouse moaning and groaning with the hunger and the cartloads of corpses wending their way to the Paupers' Graveyard in the neighbourhood. There was no visiting of wretched, starving people by the Shoneen well-to-do. 'Bring the carrion as soon as possible' was the order from the local magnate, Irish or Anglo-Saxon, to his hirelings who were brutal enough to cart away dying men and women in the hope that they 'would be dead enough to bury' by the time the graveyard was reached. But why say more? I used to get sick listening to such tales as a youngster.[6]

✣

Dáithí Ó Ceanntabhail, national teacher, Croom, Co. Limerick

In the district about Laffan's Bridge, Co. Tipperary, the cholera was very rife. From the poorhouse in Cashel a sort of covered car used be driven out to carry in the poor sufferer. The driver was callous, by nature or otherwise, and when his patient died on the way to the workhouse his dead body was released through the flooring of the car and left by the wayside.[7]

✣

*Anthony Dwyer, b.1876, a painter and Thomas Magner, b.1860, a
blacksmith, Golden, Cashel, Co. Tipperary*

Anthony O'Dwyer's father told him that he saw people dead, dying and staggering about at a rest house at Knockroe, a short distance on the Cashel side of Golden. These people had been on their way to Castlelake, near Cashel, where there was then a workhouse. The people who died along the road were so numerous that they were thrown inside the ditches near where they lay, and buried there without the sacred rites of scripture.[8]

✣

*Seán Breathnach, b.1891, a labourer and shepherd, Coill Mór,
Cloughane, Co. Kerry*

The people died on the roadside, fields and ditches. They very
often stayed at home until they were very weak and then started
to try and journey to some other place and died on the way. They
were buried without coffins and they were taken to the
churchyards on ladders. They were buried in the family graves,
but those from the poorhouses were buried in a special corner in
the graveyards called the 'Paupers' Corner'.[9]

~~~

Peter O'Brien, b.1860, Clonmore, Tinahely, Co. Wicklow

The cholera was very bad in this district and the affected person
was brought to the poor house in Shillelagh in an ass cart by a
man named Dunne who received the sum of 1/6 for each person
he brought in. On one occasion he brought two; he left one of
them in the dyke outside town until he delivered up the first one
and got paid 1/6, and then he went back and brought in the
other and got paid also.[10]

~~~

*Pádraig Ó Cruadlaoich, b.1860, a master tailor, Macroom,
and Máire Bean Uí Mhurchadh, b.1874, Sráid Ghuirtín Buí,
Macroom, Co. Cork*

During the 'fever' warrants were issued against escapees from the
workhouse, and it was said that begging was officially prevented
or 'frowned upon' on account of the danger of spreading the
fever.[11]

~~~

Tomás Ó Cearbhall, b.1875, a shopkeeper, Kildorrery, Mallow, Co. Cork

A few fever hospitals of which the sufferers had a horror were established. The victims preferred to die at home, and the Poor Law Unions were also hated, even the destitute refusing to avail of their open doors.[12]

❦

Mícheál Ó Beirne, national teacher, Cor an tSilín, Baunboy, Belturbet, Co. Cavan

Patrick Reilly, Culleagh, tells of people found along the roads weak with hunger, grass on their mouths and who were brought to the poorhouse and given brandy, as the authorities found that brandy caused death quickly.

Fever or Black Fever, also called Cholera, came.[13]

❦

Kate Flood, b.1882, Cranally, Granard, Co. Longford

Auld Mrs Corcoran, the wife of Peter Corcoran, went into Granard Workhouse and took out three children out of it. These three children were belonging to Ballinuty and their father and mother died of the faver, and the childer were brought away to Granard Workhouse.

Inside the green wall of the Workhouse in Granard, where the houses are now, a row of beds was inside the wall, and some thatch or something covering them, and all the people in them beds had the faver. And Mrs Corcoran, she went into Granard with a neighbour to the workhouse and it was believed that if you threw green fruit into each bed, you'd escape the faver. She went and she had the neighbour with her and she had a bag of green apples, and she went along the row of beds, one bed to other and she looking for the childer, and she threw a green apple into each bed she passed, to keep her from bringing home the disase with her.

She got the childer and brought them home with her, the three of them. She had no child of her own. But after a while some friends [relatives] of the childer came and took them away from her and sent them to the United States to friends out there.

And I often seen that auld woman crying and she telling that story and how the childer were taken from her and sent to America, after she taking them from Granard Workhouse.[14]

❧❧

Mrs Mary Kettle, Cohaw, Cootehill, Co. Cavan

There was a lot of deaths from cholera round them years, and Cootehill workhouse was crowded with sick people and old people and people that were driven to it through want and destitution.[15]

❧❧

Patrick Redmond, b.1872, a farmer, Forrestalstown,
Poulpeesty Parish, Co. Wexford

When the Poor Houses were built they put the poor people from the doors and the curse of God came on the country as a result. The Poor Houses were built in 1841. That was the reason for the Famine.[16]

❧❧

Michael Morris, Carnanrancy, Co. Tyrone

They used to give out what they called 'Poor Meal' in Gortin. That was Indian meal. That was the first time it was ever seen in the country. But it was counted a great disgrace to take it. It was given out in the workhouse.

124

The porridge made from it was called Indian Buck. It was a disgrace long after, like I mind this well, to be seen or heard of eating 'Indian Buck'.[17]

⁂

Mrs James Clarke, b.1873, Dromore, Bailieboro, Co. Cavan

So many died in the workhouse that the contractors for burying them were kept busy carrying the remains to the old graveyard on the hill near the old Protestant Church. There was a big trench dug in the graveyard, the corpses were carried in a coffin with a detachable bottom, they opened it in the same way you'd open the bottom of bawrthogs [barrdóg, a pannier with collapsible bottom] when putting out dung. The same coffin was used again and again.[18]

⁂

Terence Clarke, b.1872, Bailieboro, Co. Cavan

In the years before the Famine there were between 200 and 300 inmates in Bailieboro Workhouse. In the year 1852 there were 1,350 treated in the workhouse, the hospital and the auxiliaries. There were three auxiliaries set up in 1852 to deal with the fever cases. There was no general sickness until the fifties.[19]

⁂

Charles Clarke, b.1873, Tullynaskeagh, Bailieboro, Co. Cavan

A lot of people had to go to Bailieboro Workhouse, and a good number of them died in it. The contractor for the supply of milk to the Workhouse delivered chalk-water instead of milk. This was discovered, and there was a sworn enquiry into it, and he lost the contract. It was put up for contract again, and his tender was again accepted. I think he supplied proper milk the second time.[20]

❦

Hugh Clarke, b.1873, Bailieboro, Co. Cavan

Old James Stafford, of Bailieboro, told me that he was a youth during the Famine, and that he remembered seeing a crowd of men walking down to the workhouse every day for dinner. Free dinners were given in the Workhouse at that time. I think it was oaten porridge they got. I think the Indian meal only came in after that. They went twice a day to the workhouse to get food. Bailieboro Workhouse was only built to accommodate 699 people, but at times during the Famine there would be over 1,000 people in it, between the fever hospital and the body of the house.

There were contractors for burying the people that died in the workhouse and fever hospital, and an old man told me that the contractors would be working with lanterns till twelve o'clock at night, burying the people that died in both places.[21]

❦

William Keane, b.1891, a farmer, Ballingrenia, Moate,
Co. Westmeath

The poorhouses were dreadful. People hated to have to go in; and the outdoor relief and free meal were hated too. In cases where a homeless person was forced to go to the poorhouse, even in 1847-52, it is taxed to their relations up to the present day. 'The paupers' as the poor were called, were badly treated in the Workhouse. The food was poor and stingy. Those over them had no feeling for them.[22]

❦

Liam Ó Danachair, Sunvale, Athea, Co. Limerick

One morning in the very height of the trouble a man named Fitzgerald was passing by the workhouse (at Newcastle West). He noticed a little girl lying on a bundle of hay or straw beside the gate. He got off his car and going in asked with much indignation the meaning of leaving the child thus abandoned. The attendant told him that there was no room for more inmates. Fitzgerald went out and raising the child in his arms took her in and insisted on finding a place for her.

Next day Fitzgerald himself fell sick and died. He was buried among the graves of the famine and fever-stricken people and on the day of his funeral the whole body of the workhouse inmates insisted on accompanying the remains to its last resting place.[23]

❧❧

Pádraig Ó Seaghdha, Fearann tSeáin, Castlegregory, Co. Kerry

There were deaths in the parish of course, chiefly among the landless population. There was also a floating population of people who drifted in from poorer areas. Many of these became ill and had to be removed to the workhouse hospital, Dingle.

At that time a gentleman named Edward Hussey, descendant of Gregory Hoare, Lord of Castlegregory, had a fine house and demesne at Liscarney, Cloughane, Castlegregory. In his pity for the plight of his poor neighbours he vacated his mansion and handed it over to the authorities to be used as an auxiliary workhouse. Many of those admitted died and were buried in the lawn in front of the mansion. When conditions became normal again the house was surrendered to Hussey but as it was then, and still is, called the Poorhouse he took a dislike to the place and sold it out.[24]

❧❧

Tomás Aichir, b.1859, a farmer, Coill a Tonna, Kilmaley, Ennis, Co. Clare

By 1852 however, matters had much improved and the Poor Law Commissioners could report that the rate of mortality in the Co.

Clare was less than the average rate for Ireland and the workhouse accommodation in the county exceeded the actual number of inmates by 2,000.[25]

❖❖

Kathleen Hurley noted this from a man born in 1853

My father worked as baker in the Workhouse [in Castlerea] during the years of famine. I frequently heard him say he, assisted by five more bakers, baked into bread half-a-ton of flour on the same day.

They kneaded the flour with the ordinary spade used by farmers in tilling land, divided the kneaded dough into large lumps and baked same. The bread was called 'Gandough'.

So great were the crowds of starving people who called at the workhouse during each day that the authorities were obliged to attach iron bars onto the outside of the windows of the bakery to guard against attack for bread, and my father told us that before he or any one of his five assistants appeared in public, they made sure to wash their hands and remove any whiteness of flour dust from their clothes or they stood in danger of being eaten alive by starving people.

There were three deep pits sunk outside the workhouse, one on the women's side, beside the piggery; one on the west side of the workhouse, and the third pit close to the mortuary or dead house.

The workhouse was overcrowded, packed like herrings in a barrel with victims of cholera. When a victim died the remains were lowered on a sliding door from the window into one of the pits and covered with quicklime. The pits became filled with corpses.

The walls and woodwork of the windows, from which those sliding doors were attached, were thickly covered on the outside with a thick coating of black tar. The black tarred walls are still to be seen (1938) in the ruins of the workhouse, also the site of the gruel boiler and the three pits.[26]

❖

Kathleen Hurley, Corlock House, Ballymoe, Co. Galway

Johnny Callaghan lived to be 90 years, died a few years ago.

'My father who was also named Johnny Callaghan was a baker during the Famine years and for years after the Famine in the workhouse, Castlerea, Co. Roscommon. And I as a young lad assisted my father at the baking trade. I distinctly remember the Famine and every time I think of it I shiver all over. In the bakehouse in the workhouse my father and I were engaged all day baking. My father was always nervous to appear in public with flour dust on his clothes, so ravenous were some people he feared they would attack him and kill him.

There was one large pot resting on stones in the workhouse yard and in this huge pot was made gruel to be distributed to a constant stream of starving people. The people came by every road to the workhouse for their measure of gruel. Another large pot was erected on stones at the back of the present National Bank. This pot was fed with water running in the demesne outside the town. There was a third pot erected and in the three pots gruel was boiled for the starving people. Seeing people die of hunger was awful but it could not equal seeing them die of the cholera that set in. On the road leading from Ballymoe to the workhouse a son was wheeling his dying father (dying of cholera) on a wheel barrow. On reaching the workhouse the father was dead and the son collapsed and died in a few hours time.

The workhouse was full with sick people. When a person was near death, he or she was removed from other parts of the workhouse to a large room at the other gable-end of the workhouse (the gable nearest the town of Castlerea). This room was called 'The Black Room' and the gable the 'Black Gable' for in this room the sick person was allowed to die. Sometimes there were up to seven persons in this room. From the window in this room there were a few boards slanting down to the earth and beneath was a huge grave or pit. When a death occurred the corpse was allowed to slide down the boards into the pit beneath and lime was put over the corpse, along the boards and along the wall of the gable. This caused the wall to go black and gave the name to the 'Black Gable'. This black gable was to be seen up to a few years ago and had retained its black colour.

The people who died of cholera in the workhouse at this time were buried immediately after death without a coffin and wearing their own clothes in which they died. There was also another large grave or pit at the back of the workhouse into which more corpses were put, mostly those who died of hunger. He told me more people came into the workhouse dying of cholera from the Ballinlough side of Castlerea and from the villages between Ballymoe, Ballintober and Castlerea than other parts'.[27]

⁂

Séamus Reardon, b.1873, Boulteen, Eniskeane, Co. Cork

The poorhouse in Bandon was soon full of sick and starving people. Deaths were reported by the score. Still they were coming in such numbers that those in authority decided to take over the cotton mills as an auxiliary poorhouse, for the time being at least.

He was a very old man that told me it was nothing strange to see people by the fences at the roadsides in a dying condition. They had left their homes and were looking for a bite to eat from anyone that could give it to them. Some of them were strangers to the locality. They were not left on the roadside. Someone with a horse or donkey took the poor creatures to the poorhouse where they did not live long. One poor man took his mother in in a donkey and cart. On his way home he found two poor creatures by the roadside, he turned and took them in also. Three journeys he made on that day and, the last time he went, the place was so overcrowded that they were lying near the laneway to it.

A meal given to some quite often caused their stomachs were so weak from long fasting that solid food was only poison to them.[28]

❧❧

J. O'Kane, Dromore National School, Dromore West, Co. Sligo

Later when the poorhouses were built, the poor tried to get as far as one of these before night. They slept in one poorhouse tonight and tried to get as far as the next poorhouse before the next night. But even after the poorhouses began to function, many of the wanderers, except the real hardened cases, preferred to shelter in the cottages of the small farmers.

After a time the young, when grown up, got work, made as much as brought them to England, but the older drifted at last to the workhouse where they ended their miserable existence.[29]

❧❧

9

Boilers, Stirabout and 'Yellow Male'

✥

The main relief food used in Ireland during the Famine was Indian meal. It had been used during previous food shortages of 1800–1802 and in 1827, when other crops failed.

Indian meal was made from the whole maize grain. It was very hard and had to be chopped in steel mills before being ground. In Ireland people were unaccustomed to it as a food and initially did not know that it required pre-soaking and long boiling to make it properly digestible. In fact, they often didn't have the fuel necessary to cook it properly or were so hungry that they ate it raw and suffered the consequences. The hard grains in raw or under-cooked Indian meal could, at worst, pierce the wall of the intestine or, at best, cause intestinal discomfort.

It was brought into the country in the period of the Great Famine by the Prime Minister Peel in the autumn of 1845 and stored until March 1846. Some of these early imports were of old, dry and inferior corn which made it even harder to mill.

In August 1847 the government changed its policy of confining food relief to the workhouses and followed the example of many charitable organisations by providing outdoor relief. In February 1847 the 'Temporary Relief Act' or 'Soup-Kitchen Act' was introduced and soup-kitchens replaced public works as the main source of relief. At the height of their operations, the soup-kitchens were distributing an incredible three million meals a day.

Relief was free for the destitute and landless, while wage-earners could buy rations. An estimated 800,000 people were getting this outdoor relief in July 1848 and 1849. While the soup-kitchens were short lived, they were a success in administrative and humanitarian terms.

The Society of Friends, who had been very active in Famine relief between 1846 and 1849, decided that charity was ultimately useless and of no permanent benefit and urged changes on the whole land question. Many other charitable organisations, and the contributors to them, became weary at the unrelenting nature of the Famine and they gradually withdrew their extensive and worthwhile relief schemes.

As the government had spent eight million pounds on Famine relief between 1845 and 1849, cost was a major factor in its decision to stop funding relief schemes.

❧❧

Michael Corduff, The Lodge, Rossport, Ballina, Co. Mayo

During the Famine years around 1847, there was a scheme of relief of distress and hunger operated by the Society of Friends, commonly known as the Quakers, instituted in north-west Erris. The scheme was administered by the local landlords and part of the procedure was the installation of large iron vats for the cooking of Indian meal porridge which was rationed out to the peasantry every day. Those huge vats or pots were known in each locality as 'the boiler', and a couple of paid men were always in attendance to minister to the cooking, distribution and supervision of the work of maintenance. One of these boilers was situated at Rossport and another at Rinroe. I cannot say definitely if there was one at Pollathomas, but the meal was distributed there by the landlords O'Donnell, and probably the boiler was in operation there too. Landlord Bournes was in charge of the boiler at Rossport and Landlord Knox at Rinroe. Of course, the work, especially the distribution, was in the hands of trusted servants of the 'big house'. The meal was imported by a ship which came regularly from Westport.[1]

❧❧

Pádraig Ó Briain, 83, Corbally, Kilrush, Co. Clare

Long ago during the Famine there was a family in Dunbeg and

they wern't as badly off as they let on. Anyway the old mother went into Kilkee one day to see the man who was giving out the help, as she wanted him to put in a spake for her with the workhouse in Kilrush where they used give out the fish, meal and potatoes to the starving.

'Will you write me a letter to Mr J. M.,' says she to this man in Kilkee. 'I have nine childer at home and they're all starving.'

Now the man to whom she went knew that she wasn't as badly off as she pretended and he wrote a letter for her alright, but this was what he put in it:

Here comes an old hag
Scarce able to wag,
She's feeble, crippled and lame,
And my dear honest Jack,
As you're in charge of the sack,
Will you poultice her gizard with male [meal].[2]

❦

Seosamh Ó Dochartaigh, b.1894, a farmer, Ballagh, Cnoc Glas, Malin, Inishowen, Co. Donegal

I hear tell of a ship called the River Erne leaving Dublin and going round the coast with a cargo of Indian meal and boilers for cooking it. The ship came on round as far as Aranmore Island and the last of the cargo was spent there. Every port that they put in at they left some oaten meal and a boiler.[3]

❦

Michael Corduff, The Lodge, Rossport, Ballina, Co. Mayo

It was during the Famine years, around 1847, the landlord of the Dooncarton Estate which includes Glengad where O'Donnell the poet lived at the time, was distributing relief meal to his tenants. Co-incidentally the name of the landlord was also

O'Donnell, but that did not mean they were better friends on that account. In fact the poet was by no means a favourite of the landlord who was only too well aware of the other man's views on landlordism.

The landlord had a storekeeper named Shaun Doherty who had a rather bent back, and it was he who doled out their rations of yellow meal according to the number of each family to the tenants. He had a measure of capacity, a wooden measure like a small pail, which he filled up with the meal and then over the mouth of the vessel he passed a curved board like a barrel-stave so as to make the contents even on top. Those recipients who were in the landlord's or storekeeper's favour got their measures completed by Shaun the storekeeper passing the board over the meal with the concave side beneath, which left a heaped measure and a well satisfied and grateful recipient. For those people who were not favourites such as Daniel, the reverse or 'humpy' or convex side of the board was pressed over the meal, which left a hollow in the centre and therefore that person got much less meal than the favoured individual.

Daniel, who perceived this practice of favouritism, and on examining the contents of his little bag, and being dissatisfied naturally with the inequality of his dole showed his resentment as he shouldered his little 'mongeen' of meal, by breaking into a rhyme as he was about to move away while the hunchback storekeeper and perhaps the landlord also listened, as well as the others present:

Tá cruit ar Seáinín
Is tá cruit ar an gcláirín
Agus tá an diabhal ar an máilín.
[There's a hump on Shauneen
And there's a hump on the boardeen
And the devil is on the bageen.][4]

⚜

Laurence Mc Intyre, b.1865, Kilcrossduff, Shercock, Co. Cavan

A relief committee was formed in Shercock, and they raised funds for the poor to keep them alive. They gave out Indian meal stirabout. It was cooked in a boiler in Nelson's yard, where the Sloane family are now. A pint of thin stirabout was given out for each member of a family that was entitled to receive it. They would come with gallons for it every day, and when they'd be on their way home it would get thick. Some of them would wait for the 'screb' [scríob: scraping], the crust of burnt stirabout that would be at the bottom of the boiler, and they'd eat out of their hands the same as if it were bread. They got that in addition to the pint of stirabout. They employed Nelson as a paid official, to cook the stirabout and distribute it. They bought turf at five shillings a load to keep the boiler going. My father drew turf to it.[5]

❦

Charles Moran, b.1862, Bailieboro, Co. Cavan

Relief schemes were set up. Local Relief Committees were responsible for these schemes, and they continued until the Poor Law Relief schemes were put to work. Shercock Relief Committee had a committee room in the village and met regularly. Mr Charley Adams, who was one of the landlords of the district, was President of the Committee, and devoted a lot of time to the raising of funds and the giving out of meal to the poor. He succeeded in getting a good subscription from the Relief Commissioners.[6]

❦

Terence Clarke, b.1872, Bailieboro, Co. Cavan

Indian meal was imported into the country, and a number of agents were appointed to distribute it, and it was said that some of them mixed lime through it in order to make a profit, and the people took dysentery after eating the stirabout that was made from it.[7]

❖❖

Mrs Peter Stafford, b.1895, Delvin, Co. Westmeath

For some of the time they were able, through the good offices of Brien Geoghegan of Archerstown, a kind, enlightened and patriotic farmer, to get rice. This they boiled with oatenmeal and made into a porridge.

There was a relief depot opened at Archerstown. It was then owned by a man named Doyle. There was a large boiler erected at Doyle's premises, and Fr Dowling, then the Parish Priest, put Brien Geoghegan in charge of the depot. This good man, Geoghegan, went every day to Doyle's to see that the Indian meal was cooked clean and right and he himself distributed it to the poor who came for it from as far away as Fore.[8]

❖❖

Tuosist, Kenmare, Co. Kerry from Seán Ó Súilleabháin,
Irish Folklore Commission

The following is a fragment of a song made, Johnny Bat said, by Thady Tim of Derrynambrack, about the famine relief scheme.

1
Attention my ditty to straighten,
A chlanna cheart Éire gan treo,
Our gentlemen wanted to treat us
Gan bheatha, gan adach, gan ghnó.
The rations were stopped from the neighbours
They had not a potato to sow,
They wanted to follow the legins
That were promised last season in woe

2
...Our Committee, the wicked thieving schemers
Kept it to feed their own parents at home.[9]

❧❧

*Pádraig Ó Cruadlaoich, b.1860, a master tailor, and
Máire Bean Uí Mhurchadh, b.1874, Sráid Ghuirtín Buí,
Macroom, Co. Cork*

Re Coolea soup-kitchen [at Athleacach]. Pádraig Ó
Cruadhlaoich relates that the man in charge was a stoop-
shouldered man named Domhnall Bán Ó Loingsigh. A poet
named Ó Buachalla had a son of Domhnall's working for him
some time afterwards, who was also a minor poet. He composed a
verse for Buckley which rattled Buckley and Buckley's verse in
reply was:

An cuimhin leatsa tigheas in Athleacaidh
Aimsir na praisce is na 'rations'
Nuair tháinig an drainn [hump] úd ar t-athair
Ó bheith ag scríobadh is ag measca an bhiléira [boiler]
'Tally ho, hi hó, is tally hí hó the grinder.'[10]

❧❧

*Tomás Ó Ceallaigh, b.1860, a farmer, Caherea, Ennis,
Co. Clare*

There were no local food-centres, the nearest being in Patreen,
part of the adjoining parish of Meelick, within a short distance of
the power-house at Ardnacrusha.

A soup-kitchen was set up by the Delmedges who lived near
the Longpavement Station. On a certain Friday the locals were
invited to 'dinner' while the worthy host had his own group of
interested spectators. The people were ranged round boilers
waiting for the order to come along, when one Matt McNamara

of Cratloe (Gallows Hill townland) came up to the first 'cooker' and, taking a heavy hammer from beneath his cloak, 'made smithereens of the pot and sent the soup all over Meelick'.

To the surprise of all he was not apprehended, but the crowd was dispersed (I know his son personally, also Matt). This however was not looked on as an attempt at proselytism – just misapplied charity.[11]

❖❖

Tomás Aichir, b.1859, a farmer, Coill a Tonna, Kilmaley, Ennis, Co. Clare

The enormous amount of work in relieving the distress that ensued proved altogether beyond the scope of the Board of Guardians. Relief works were started and charitable organisations came to the relief of the dying people but finally the Government had to give the Guardians authority to assist people outside the workhouses and outdoor relief was given in 1848 for the first time.[12]

❖❖

Francis Mac Polin, Ballymaghery School, Hilltown, Co. Down

Indian meal and Indian meal porridge 'Downshire's Porridge' was in those years distributed to the poor at some centre in Hilltown. Local tradition recalls the poor running along the Briansford Road to Hilltown with their 'wee tin cans' for their rations. I think the Marquis of Downshire was anxious to do all he could to relieve the poor on his estates.[13]

❖❖

Stiofán Mac Philib, Edenmore National School, Emyvale,
Co. Monaghan

There was a food kitchen in the townland of Brackagh. Both broth and porridge were distributed. The meal was brought from Newry in carts and this took three days to go and three days to come back. It was usually a Protestant farmer's house was chosen for the distribution of porridge. A ladleful was given for every member of the family and it was distributed every day except Sunday, when two ladlefuls were given out on the previous Saturday. The people used to line up with their noggins for their share of the food.

There is no account of either souperism or proselytism in this district.[14]

❧ ❧

Felix Kernan, b.1859, a farmer, Drumakill, Castleblayney,
Co. Monaghan

The government set up food centres and local soup-kitchens to try and alleviate the suffering somewhat. The soup-kitchens were situated a distance of about two miles apart. There were three of these kitchens set up in the town of Castleblaney for the benefit of the people there. There was one set up at Oram and the nearest one to us was one in the townland of Tullynaghan. It was in the hands of a family called Murtagh. From this centre food was distributed to the people of the district. A huge boiler or cauldron was used to cook the soup. It was made from small quantities of meat but chiefly vegetables, nettles and other herbs were largely used in its make up. A quantity of the steaming liquid was given to each person daily. Many bad accidents occurred at the soup kitchens for hungry creatures, often unable to wait until they were served, plunged their hands into the boiling cauldrons and died most painful deaths as a result of the burns.[15]

Seán Ó Beirne, Malin, Inishowen, Co. Donegal

There was a soup house at the place here in Malin known as Willie Starret's at the upper end of the village. The giving of the soup was under the direction of a Rev. Canning of the Church of Ireland. Then the Youngs (landlords at Culdaff) distributed soup or broth to their tenants. Some members of the family went up to the house at Young's and received a ration dependent on the number in the family. I think they went each day.[16]

Seán Mac Cuinneagáin, Scoil Mhín an Aodhaire, Carrick, Co. Donegal

There were soup or broth boilers set up in places. As far as I can find out these were managed by servants of Protestant ministers. Souperism or proselytism never had been tried to any extent at all.

In Glencolumkille district meal was supplied to the Protestant Minister for distribution to the poor. The distribution was most unsatisfactory. Men and women fasting walked a distance of nine or ten miles and were refused and told to return next day. When the crowds queued up there was a man who was supposed to keep order. He was most cruel and often beat unmercifully those waiting with a heavy cudgel or a stick.

The then minister, who condoned such conduct on the part of his servant, died of diabetes. It used to be said that his food had to be barrowed to him and that while the food was still being barrowed to him he died of hunger. It was also said of him that he would not distribute to the Catholics their meal until it was infested with maggots.[17]

Michael Kilemade, Ferefad, Longford

During the years of the Famine a soup-kitchen was set up in a large house owned by Lord Longford. The soup was given to everyone who had a ticket, which was got from one of the landlord's officials. There was no discrimination against Catholics.[18]

꧁꧂

John Burke, b.1849, a farmer, Dunblaney, Dunmore, Co. Galway

The original meal-centre was in his house [he pointed out the store room to me]. It lasted thus for a year and since, apparently, they were too generous with it, it was transferred to Blake's of Claddagh whose plan to stop the people coming was to give them the meal in the form of 'brocán buí' [yellow porridge], using a big pot to boil it. The people came for a can for a while but those who came a distance thought it not worth their while and stayed away. There was no proselytism in the district.[19]

꧁꧂

Thomas O'Flynn, John Melody, Attymass, Ballina, Co. Mayo

The only relief committee in the district was in Ballina. Indian meal was used for the first time in 1847 as human food and was made available to the committee from government sources. A Mr Fenton was chairman and he was assisted by a committee composed of members of the ascendancy.

Fr O'Flynn struck such an appealing note that he secured a generous weekly allowance of Indian meal for the parish. This was put up in three hundredweight sacks and conveyed weekly by the contractor Melody ('Sack Them Up') in his cart to Fr O'Flynn's home in Carrick.

Here the parishioners gathered on the appointed day for the distribution of the meal and took with them bags or vessels for

142

their weekly allowance. Very often all the members of the same household arrived, each to claim his or her own share, for one would not trust the other, as great was the temptation to steal even the brother's or sister's share or even the child's. Fr O'Flynn assisted at the distribution while other members of his household served porridge from a large pot, always kept boiling to feed the multitude awaiting their allowance of meal. An outhouse in the farmyard of Mr Thomas O'Flynn (nephew of Fr O'Flynn) still carries the chimney erected in '47 by waiting stone-masons for the purpose of providing the fire to prepare the porridge.[20]

✥✥

Pádraig Mhichíl Uí Shúilleabháin, b.1867, a farmer, Meall an Róistigh, Sneem, Co. Kerry

The soup house was where Mrs [David] Fitzgerald is now. They had a big boiler and they used to put about a sack of meal into it, and two strong old men stirring that with two sticks. Sometimes that [porridge] wouldn't be half boiled, and it would give them colics and kill them. They used to take it away in wooden cans on their heads, very thin. Those that were in charge of it would take home whatever remained.[21]

✥✥

John O'Reilly, a farmer, Glenville, Co. Cork

Patrick Forde of Raheen gave out tickets to the poor to obtain Indian meal. Den Dunlea of Ballyvourisheen, Carrignavar was the distributor of the meal. When the poor went to him for meal he had none for them. He kept it to fatten pigs, and sold more of it dearly. It was said that the priest cursed him and that there would not be one of the name in the place, and now the name has disappeared in the district.

A soup-kitchen was provided in connection with the local hospital. To make this soup meat of an inferior quality was used, with turnips and cabbage to thicken it. It was from Hudson's house that the supplies came from. It is not stated who dished out the food at the hospital, probably it was people appointed by the 'ladies' of the House.

Many people visited the Great House to get food and the 'ladies' were very kind and good. Whatever was left after the household was given to the poor. Susan Buckley aged 80, of Glenville told me this.[22]

❧❦

Ned Buckley, Knocknagree, Co. Cork

I heard my mother and several other older people talk about the public boilers established in several villages. The meal was given by the Government and a local person of influence was put over the making of gruel or stirabout in the boilers. Many were the cases of fraud done by those people where the meal was given to their own friends to fatten pigs with and left the hungry people without.

Often I heard of a glaring case of this kind. A priest, Fr Naughton by name, was in charge of the Indian meal boiler at Boherbue (my mother who died in 1934, aged 90, is my author for this. I often heard her mention it in my youth). Instead of dividing the meal and the stirabout honestly to the worthy and poor, he gave large quantities of it to relations of his called Gormans, who used it for fattening pigs and grew rich on account of it, so that they bought the land of Moule near Boherbue and grew rich and important on the spoils of Fr Naughton's misbehaviour. My mother and people of her age used have no respect for people who grew fat by robbing the poor but I understand there are Gormans in Moule to this day, so that all people who do wrong and profit by it don't disappear from the earth in a generation or two.[23]

❧❦

William (Bill) Powell, b.1869, Eniskeane, Co. Cork

It was the Indian meal sent here from America, and sent free on sea and every other way, there wasn't to be one penny of cost no matter what part of the country it was sent. It was that was given out as food. Even that would in some way save the people if it was distributed in any kind of a just way. But no, the biggest and worst of the Protestants were given the doling out of this meal and allowed to act on their own discretion.

Through the country they selected places as centres to which the starving people should come to get an allowance daily. These centres the people called soup houses. In some of these places the meal was boiled into thin stirabout and given out, but here in this village it was not boiled but a certain allowance of the meal was given out, still the place was called the soup house.

These couple of lines from a poor old wit of the time, that people often quote, will tell you how things were working:

Shorten and Daunt and Scofield from Phale
They did cut me short in my three pounds of male.

So you see, as little as the allowance was for a poor man with a family, he did not get his right, no, for we have it on good authority, these men fed it to their cattle. In this village of 300 inhabitants at the time, it is something to say that seven bullocks died from being overfed with relief meal. It wasn't here alone that occurred, it was done all over the country. It was being fed to the cattle.

To the east of us here the big Protestants of Manch had a soup house but they kept men of their own boiling meal. They used a copper boiler and this boiler, when heated, gave off a poison that mixed in the stirabout. This caused any amount of deaths and there were more deaths in the locality than anywhere around.

One day the big fellows came to the man boiling and sharing out the stirabout.

'Well,' he says, 'how are things going on?'

'Ah good,' says the fellow in charge, 'there is so-many deaths reported again this morning.'

145

'That's right, that's right,' says the first fellow. 'Keep the copper boiler going.'

About the Indian meal when it first came into this district, I was told it caused the deaths of several. The people did not know how to cook it, I was told, and it caused diarrhoea, punctured the bowels and the people bled to death. They cooked Indian meal as they always cooked other meal and the hard grains of the Indian meal did the damage, especially when eaten by people who had not anything like a substantial meal for months.

Pamphlets were distributed among the people by government orders giving instructions as to how the Indian meal should be cooked. I was told that most of these instructions were wrong or most misleading. Anyhow, the new meal at first caused widespread sickness and many deaths, I was told. Many people were afraid to use it except very sparingly until they found a method of boiling it to the proper degree.[24]

***

Miss Anderson, b.1865, living in Brooks, Forkhill, South Armagh

I don't know if I can be of much use, but it is a fact that my grandfather, who was Brooks of course, was the first to bring Indian meal into this part of the country. He brought in a full boatload and had it carted up to keep the people from starving.

You'll see a huge boiler outside here in the shed which was used in the Famine years for cooking porridge. It was set in the board-room of the church then of course. It was built in, of course, and they made porridge in the morning, and soup in the evening. I'm afraid I can't say what kind of soup. The porridge was of Indian meal, of course.

It was definitely an individual thing. A charity I suppose. That's definite. It had no connection with any government scheme to relieve hunger or want. My own grandmother superintended it all.[25]

***

Susan Murphy, a farmer, b.1848, Dromintee, Co. Armagh

They had this big trough or boiler or whatever it was, oh it was way out [about two yards in diameter from her gesture] and he [Willie Jordan] always had a lot of meal, oaten meal, and they paid him for it too [to make the porridge at McGuill's, Dromintee]. And I mind me going up to a rock above our house [Jordan's, Tifferum] where the roses grew and taking them down and cleaning the roots and all for them and cutting up the leaves, and that went into it [the boiler]. And many a time they'd just go into a field of oats and pull the pressaugh and put that in. There was nothing at all.

And at McGuill's they'd come with their wee tin in their turn and get some, and Willie Jordan was over it. And it wasn't every day they'd make it, but maybe every other day, and it would be in the evening.

That was the time the priddies went bad. Some died with the hunger, but not many.[26]

❖❖❖

Mr Gwynn, b.1846, a Protestant gentleman, Ballymoney, Rostrevor, Co. Down

I mind my father and my grandfather collecting off the gentry to provide for the poor people. Only for that the people would have starved. They had no money. There was plenty of other food, although the potatoes all went rotten in the fields, but the people had no money to buy it. They had to sell their cattle to get money, and at that time you could only get about 14 shillings for a fat sheep. A fat bullock would bring you six or seven pounds, or seven pounds ten.

The food was bought with this collection and was distributed at the old barracks in Rostrevor. Apart from that, the ladies had a fund of their own to provide for the poor.

In those days the poor had nothing to provide for them. There was no poorhouse and one had to be set up. With the money collected they bought turf. My father and my grandfather attended the meetings, many times indeed. The turf wasn't given out at once, you see. The poor were careless and wouldn't look after it and, if it was all given out at once, they'd have none when the time of year came [winter].[27]

⁂

Jimmy Quinn, b.1869, a shoemaker, Newry Street, Kilkeel,
Co. Down

Soup was give out at the old church (Newcastle Street, Kilkeel) and porridge as well, Indian porridge it was. I heard my mother say that them that went for it be to bring something for to get it in, and they couldn't wait till they got home, but they'd run with it down to the river and hold it in till it'd cool so as they could ate some, they were that far gone with the hunger.[28]

⁂

Thomas Brophy, b.1858, a labourer, Inistioge, Co. Kilkenny

Soup-kitchens or porridge kitchens were established in Inistioge village, in Ballygallon, Inistioge, in Ballygub, Inistioge, in Rower village and in Raheen, Graignamanagh parish. The food was distributed in Inistioge from the courthouse. Yellow meal porridge was cooked in this place in a huge metal pot with a tap attached. Each one entitled to porridge came with a container and received his or her ration of porridge or stirabout. A committee met regularly and decided how much each applicant was entitled to receive. A portion of this house was used as a hospital where the sick and aged were treated and fed with whatever food was available. Soup was sometimes given to the needy. The soup was made from bones. The porridge and soup that was distributed was a government scheme, while the hospital attached was financed by the landlord, Mr Tighe.[29]

⁂

Richard Power, b.1875, a farmer, Shanbo, Co. Kilkenny

The meal that was sent here to relieve the Famine went under the general name 'Galatz', after the Black Sea port from which it came.

Old sailing vessels, some of them rotting from age and letting in water, were pressed into service. Carried in the holds of such vessels the meal became saturated with sea-water and, by the time it arrived here, the stench was unbearable. This was the stuff that was doled out to the poor starving people.[30]

❧

Tomás Aichir, b.1858, a farmer, Coill a Tonna, Kilmaley, Ennis, Co. Clare

The Famine abated in most parts of Ireland after the first two years, but it is interesting to note that in 1851 in certain districts in Co. Clare, especially in the Kilrush area and as far as Loop Head, Ennistymon, parts of Kilmaley and Inagh and Scariff, the effects of the Famine still continued to be felt to an extent to which there is no parallel to be found in any other part of Ireland. In 1850 the number in receipt of outdoor relief was given as high as 30,000.[31]

❧

J. O'Kane, Dromore National School, Dromore West, Co. Sligo

The British government gave a belated help in the form of Indian meal. The Indian meal may have come perhaps in 1849, the people here could not say exactly, but they are positive it did not come during the three years of the failure of the potato crop. As far as I can judge from what I heard there was no distribution of Indian meal free of charge, but it was given in lieu of work on relief works in the years immediately succeeding the Famine, '48, '49 and '50.[32]

❧

10

New Lines and 'Male Roads'

⁘

The Irish Board of Works was set up in 1831 to supervise and advise on proposals for a range of public works including road, harbour and bridge building, bog clearance and drainage. These were supposed to provide manual labour at the lowest rates possible.

Central government in London funded relief works set up locally by the Board of Works or the Grand Juries who were in charge of schemes at a local level. The government advanced monies for the schemes set up by the Grand Juries, which was supposed to be repaid, as was half the cost of the Board of Works' relief schemes. While spending on these works did not begin until March or April 1846, by that summer there were 100,000 people employed by the Board of Works and another 30,000 by the Grand Juries, mostly on road works. By the spring of the next year, 1847, there were 750,000 people engaged in the Famine relief works. That three-quarters of a million people accounted for one in every three males between the ages of 15 and 65. The speed of the uptake of the schemes may partly explain why there was no strategic planning of them for long-term benefits. In the summer of that year, 1846, Lord John Russell's government decided that each local area should bear the full cost of relief works, but the government did continue to pay for them in the short-term. From October 1846 landlords were allowed to sponsor improvements to their own property. The decision to close the relief works was taken in January 1847 by Russell's government, who decided they were a waste of money, and they began to close in March. It has been estimated that ninety percent of the money spent on these works went in badly needed wages, in cash or in kind.

The Grand Juries were unelected bodies and were largely composed of property owners. They were often corrupt, as members favoured their own areas and tenants, who were then in a better position to pay their rents. As a result, other areas and other tenants suffered discrimination and neglect.

The local relief committees which administered the Board of Works relief schemes were also dominated by the men of property. Those areas lucky enough to have active landlords, landlord's agents or clergy, who could lobby and organise on their behalf, tended to fare much better from the system than less-fortunate places with less active or absentee landlords. These were often the poorest areas and those which most needed relief.

❖❖

Mick Kelly, b.1878, Gartley, Castletown-Geoghan, Streamstown, Co. Westmeath

My father worked on the Relief Scheme splitting the Hill of Dromore (near Garthy, Castletown-Geoghan). The pay was 8d., 6d. or 4d. a day, hardly anyone got as much as 10d. a day. It was all task work. The gangers treated the labouring man something cruel. They never gave them time to draw their breath.

The people round here had to go to Clara for Indian meal. I heard my father saying he bought half a stone of meal. It used to be wet before the people got it so they couldn't sell it. The poor got the meal for nothing, and got a certain amount according to the size of their family.

There was only a track across Dromore before the relief scheme. The hill was split then and the road made.

The Railway was laid during the Famine. They began to clear the track in '49 and were working on it for three years. My father worked on the line for the three years. He walked to Ballinderry and back every day when the line got as far as that. The men had to be at their work from 6 a.m. to 6 p.m. in all weathers.

The work was very hard at times. He often told me they were six weeks in Bunnanaugh Bog, between Streamstown Station and Jamestown Bridge. They were working night and day staunching. At first all the ground that they'd clear in the day would be flooded with water next morning. The men worked in water up to their waists at times. They couldn't staunch it until they began to work by night, then the men worked on it in shifts. There was an army of men employed clearing the track. The work was a godsend to the people.[1]

❖❖

Luke Smyth, a farmer, b.1875 at Coolatore, living in Ballinbeg, Mullingar, Co. Westmeath

The only relief works I can recall are the lowering of the road in Ballintubber Hill and lowering the hill of Horseleap.

Darb Casey worked on both of those. At one time Darb was without a taste of food for three whole days hand-running when he first got employment in this relief work. His mother used to come up to a bush near where they were working at dinner-time and he'd go down to her as if to his meal like any man, but for those three days she hadn't a morsel of food.[2]

❖❖

Brigid Keane, Ennel View Terrace, Mullingar, Co. Westmeath

All these works were of permanent value.

The people were very glad to get employment on these Public Works and accepted it rather than take the 'free meal'.

The gangs were so big that work could not be found for all and a man would be employed for three days and be idle for three days every week. The pay was 10d. a day for the common labouring man. The overseer or ganger got 2d. a day more, that was the highest pay.

The men worked in gangs digging out the hills, removing stones and filling in the hollows. There would be six or eight men loosening the earth, four filling barrows with the stuff and four wheeling. Two men worked at each barrow and they took it in turns to shovel and wheel. They had to make a double run of

24 to 30 yards and back. It was knacky work and a man had to be very careful. He had to run down along a nine-inch plank with his full barrow to the tip-head, tip out the stuff and turn back. If he was not careful and knacky he might topple his barrow over and maybe fall after it himself. The tip-head was the worst part.

The 'whip-up', as they called the ganger, watched them all the time while he walked around cracking his whip. If a man showed any slackness or weakness at all he was knocked off at once. There was always plenty of men waiting around to get work. There might be a hundred men sitting on the boundary to see if any man would drop out. If the labourer was not able to do a certain amount of work every day, he was knocked out of employment. Some men had to walk four or five miles daily to their work, or even farther.

The only rest during the day was the dinner hour, before and after that it was back-breaking heavy labour all the time.

Tom Keenan, Darb Casey, Matt Kinahan and other old men that worked on those schemes often talked about the terrible hardship they endured, and of the cruelty of the gangers. Only the strongest and ablest men earned 10d. a day, most of them only got 5d. or 6d. or even 4d.

The overseer visited the works on horseback twice a day.

Only the destitute was entitled to employment on those public works. Anyone with as much as a rood of ground was not regarded as in need of employment on those Relief Schemes. There was a Relief Committee in every town which met on certain days and made out lists of men looking for employment under the relief schemes. The Parish Priest, the Protestant Minister and the gentry were on this committee. A Poor Law Inspector used attend those meetings and arrange for the men to get employment at the different places. This man was in touch with the engineer in charge of the various works and knew how many labourers he required at any particular spot. Work on the railway line began here in '49. The first train ran on the 15th of August 1852. During all those years there was great employment given by the Railway Company.[3]

❧❧

John Hanrahan, Inistioge, Co. Kilkenny, in 1945

Many relief schemes were started locally during and soon after the Famine. Hugh Green, landlord of Fiddaun, Cappa and Raheen carried out many relief schemes. He reclaimed all the land on his estate, clearing away existing fences, 'squaring' the fields, re-erecting much more modern fences thereby enclosing greater areas than previously, and draining the land.

A large number of people were employed in this scheme. Men came long distances to find employment, some coming even from Waterford. A man and his wife who lived in Garan, Tullagher parish, about seven miles from Inistioge, came to work on the draining of the land in Cappa every morning, returning home every night. Two other women from Inistioge, Mam Long and Nellie Whyte, worked for Green with shovels at this time also. They made drains just like the men. They were paid four pence per perch at the drain making. Out of this miserable wage they had to buy yellow meal, the only food they had to exist on. Not alone were they badly paid, but for quite a time they were wronged by a Scotch overseer who gave incorrect measurements when overseeing the work they had done. The balance due to them he kept for himself. When at last the landlord heard of the dishonesty, he had the Scotch man dismissed and appointed one of his own tenants, named Keefe from Cappa, as overseer.

The privations of the workers were very acute. When dinner-hour came each one washed his shovel, put some raw yellow meal on it and wet it from the water that fell into the drain and ate it. This was all they had for dinner.

Those who came a long distance from home to work stayed in one of Keefe's lofts in Cappa, and lived a sort of community life. The ration of meal that was left after the dinner was collected, each man giving his share. This was cooked for them by Keefe. They ate it on the loft where they slept.[4]

❧❧

William Blake, b.1895, a labourer, Rathnagrew, Co. Carlow

The New Line at Kilcarney was made as a relief work during the Famine, while the mill owned by a man named Law at Ballinglen, three miles away, was the centre from which the Indian meal or Yellow Buck was distributed.

The meal was imported in coarse lumps and was ground in the mill. At first it was distributed in the coarse condition and people say that when it was boiled it spat steam and boiling water all over the kitchen. The children had to be put into the room while it was being boiled.

People working at the public works got a small weekly ration but others had to pay for it at a rate of £2 per 16 stone bag. They got 4d. a day for working on the road.

One man died working on the New Line and he had to be thrown into a ditch till after the day's work was finished before they could bury him.[5]

❖❖❖

John Doyle, b.1900, a labourer, Rasheenmore, born at Craffle, Ballyteigue, Aughrim, Co. Wicklow

His grandfather worked for 4d. per day building the ditch at the straight mile near Aughrim. He was also employed as a gravedigger and on one occasion was engaged by the landlord to open a shore with 21 other men. Three or four of them died every day and were buried beside the shore under the sods thrown up from it. Only himself and four others survived. They were paid 2d. a day and a turnip.[6]

❖❖❖

Edward McGrane, b.1857, Ballintra, Co. Donegal

In 1846 a road-making scheme was launched which came in for much criticism, especially from the landlords who were most concerned about the order of their making.

South-west Donegal had by then almost emerged from the feudal system of rundale in the allotment of land, and from primary 'striping', lands were 'squared' and laid out in fields.

When officials came along to lay out roads under the Famine Relief Scheme, landowners were much annoyed by the lack of any set plan. No account at all was taken of the newly squared fields and the roads in many cases cut through them diagonally, spoiling the fields in the process and also farms.

If anybody objected, no heed was taken, the roads went on until the money ran out and they sometimes wound up in the middle of fields and have remained so ever since without any attempt being made to connect them with any highway.

Several new roads, however, were completed in the district which to the present day are referred to as the 'New Lines', and those already in existence were distinguished by calling them the 'ould road' whenever it became necessary to mention one of them.[7]

❖❖

William Torrens, b.1872, Lisminton, Ballintra, Co. Donegal

Relief was slow in coming owing to the slow methods of transport and the long distance from Dublin from which relief methods were directed and money sent to pay the men on relief works, which largely consisted of road-making.[8]

❖❖

Sarah O'Hare [Sarah the Racker], Balnamatha, Dromintee Parish, Co. Armagh

There was relief works. That ditch up Slieve Gullion was done then for fourpence a day, and the women be to take up the men's dinner of Indian porridge to them every day.[9]

❦

Michael Gorman, b.1868, Doontrusk, Carrowbeg, Westport,
Co. Mayo

Subscriptions were made up all over England and Scotland and in other countries and it was estimated that the amount collected would give £5 to every family in Ireland. Many families got none of it. Relief works were started but no one was allowed to work except those who had cards saying they were entitled to do so, and officials, gangers, timekeepers etc., got most of the money.[10]

❦

John O'Reilly, a farmer, Glenville, Co. Cork,
who heard it from his father, 1826–1906

There was a government soup-kitchen at the Mallow crossroads, about three miles west of Glenville. This soup house was in connection with the relief schemes in that district. Old horses, cows or any eatable animal was used in the manufacture of the food and drink supplied there. Salted water and not soup was doled out to the workmen mostly. This soup house was under the care of the Board of Works.

The government grant for the relief scheme '46–47 was, we are told, £100,000. This was to relieve suffering humanity but the greater part was used up by clerks and commissioners.

It was mainly the opening up of new roads through waste places and never used afterwards. I have estimated the amount of roadway as twelve and a half miles but it was more, as in travelling near where these roads were made, I find that branches from here and there lead to nowhere.

When the poor starving men heard the 'good' news of a big sum of money being spent on works, they left the farmers in the lurch and applied for jobs. The result was that the farmer was not able to till his lands as heretofore, and the result was that the farmers became poor themselves, so much so that the poorer threw up their lands or were evicted to join the labour gang. Money was very scarce then and many labourers were merely working with farmers for their keep and certain prerequisites which was of small value.

Now these labourers had to find food to bring with them. Very many of them had no meat at all going to work but depended on the soup-kitchen for to sustain their strength. The pay was from 2d. to 4d. a day, while the overseers had the lion's share. It is said that many poor starving men were unable after a day's work to reach their home in the evening and were found dead in a dyke or trench the following morning.

The landlord [Hudson] too had his relief scheme. Those who had given up their farms had emigrated and now started the destruction of those lands into large ranches of from 50 to 70 acres.[11]

⚜

Thomas O'Flynn, John Melody, Attymass, Ballina, Co. Mayo

New roads were begun. The principle one was to connect Foxford with Bonniconlon, running at the foot of the Ox Mountains. Several hundred men were employed here in gruelling labour as the ground was covered with huge boulders. They received from 2d. to 4d. per day or a quart of Indian meal. The usually took the latter as food was not available in any large quantity for cash. It is related that from about mid-day the pot was hung on the fire and kept replenished with water, awaiting the return of the workman and his parcel of meal. This was put in the pot and a thin porridge was made to fed the starving family. Some was left for the breakfast of the workman. He also rolled up some of it in a handkerchief as his food for the day. Many died on the job and on the journey to and from the work. The gangers were spoken of for their harsh methods only. The road was started about mid-way and was never finished or never used for the purpose it was intended, if indeed it was meant to serve any purpose but that of a wild scheme to provide casual relief to the starving population. Sand and stone were carried in baskets and there were no carts at work. Another road was commenced along Ballymore Lake and would have proved a useful one if completed. It remains to be seen to this day but was never used These roads came to be called the 'male [meal] roads'.

Killala was the metropolis of these parts in Famine times and still bears witness to its great trade as a port. Huge derelict stores still stand there gaunt and gaping as proof of Killala's great past. But a relief scheme was begun in 1845 to clear the sand-bar which lay across the mouth of the Moy between Bartragh Island and the mainland on the far side from Killala. The sand was cleared at the rate of 6d. per day per man and ships have sailed to Ballina Quay since then, to about one mile of Ballina town. Ballina sprang into fame as one of the principle seaports of the west. Killala's day of glory passed away.[12]

⊰⊱

Martin Manning, b.1875, Carrowholly, Kilmeena, Westport,
Co. Mayo

Father Tom Hardiman P.P. Kilmeena got all the relief schemes in the parish in working order, the making of roads, the cutting of hills on the roads. There were a good many hills cut around Carrowholly those years which proved to be a benefit to the people ever since. The workman got 4d. a day and the ganger 8d. There was meal stored at Ayer's which was sold at 2/6 per stone. My father was ganger on these works, just because there were few men could write or keep men's time in those days.[13]

⊰⊱

Tomás Ó Méalóid, b.1865, a farmer, Corra Bán, Cnoc Breac,
Móta Gráinne Oige, Co. Galway

Máire Ward, who lived at Tom Melody's house and who related her recollections of the Famine to him, worked for 4d. a day drawing stones and sand from a sand-pit beside the village to improve the road, now the main road from Ballinasloe to Athenry and Galway. She worked with a box-barrow. The hills which were cut away and the raised hollows can still be seen in that portion of the road between New Inn and Ballyfa. Many poor people used pass the way to whom she often gave half her dinner.[14]

❖❖❖

Felix Kernan, b.1859, a farmer, Drumakill, Castleblayney,
Co. Monaghan

Several local relief schemes were organised during the Famine. New roads were made and fields and bogs drained. Churches and bridges were also built. Two churches in these parts bear the date 1847 and locals say they were erected in the time of the public works. They are very high and spacious but are built with very narrow walls. Folks say that men were too weak to carry large heavy stones up ladders for the building. These buildings are very easily heated in winter and very cool in summer. Mr Swansee, a local landlord, had all his land drained or intersected by 'shores' at that time. The men worked for him without any pay. They received plenty to eat and considered that was ample reward for their work.[15]

❖❖❖

Stiofán Mac Philib, Edenmore National School, Emyvale,
Co. Monaghan

This district was well provided with relief schemes, due largely to one of the local landlords, Leslie of Glaslough. The Broad Road from Monaghan to Clougher was made at this time. Some of the hills or roads were cut and made less steep. New roads were made. According to the County Surveyor this is the most roaded part of Co. Monaghan, which for its size has the largest mileage

160

of roads in Ireland or, perhaps, in Europe.

A considerable amount of drainage was also carried out under the supervision of the landlord.

A number of mills were built, notably a large flour mill at Em, Emyvale and a linen factory in Mullan, Emyvale. To provide power for these mills a 'race' or water-course was constructed between Emy Lough and the Ulster Blackwater.

Wages on these schemes were very small, 4d. per day for an eleven- or twelve-hour day. Penalties were imposed on men for want of punctuality, scheming at work etc. It is said that for each fault a man lost a quarter of his day's pay. It used to be a standing joke in this district about a man named Callaghan of Drumturk, Emyvale, who complained about being quartered five times in one day.

Other works carried out includes the building of a high boundary wall round Leslie's Demesne. The wall is about four miles long. Masons were paid 6d. and labourers 4d. per day. Men from Carrickroe area walked more than seven miles to and from their work each day. At these works the strong men tried to see who was the strongest and the weak men died of the hard work.[16]

⚜

James Donnelly, b.1848, a farmer and fisherman,
Roskeen, Coalisland, Co. Tyrone

Locally the Verners of Verner's Bridge [landlords who built up a reputation for eviction on religious grounds] had charge of a scheme of drainage in the townland of Derrylee. This was a bog. The scheme aimed at helping the tenants of the Verner Estate and was not of great value. The drain made is still to be seen and is locally referred to as 'Stirabout Drain' because its main object was to afford a means of providing stirabout [porridge] for the workers. Any person working on the scheme received in return one pound of yellow meal per day.[17]

⚜

Tomás Ó Ceallaigh, b.1860, a farmer, Caherea, Ennis,
Co. Clare

Under the heading of local relief schemes comes the case of one of the landlords, Lord George Quinn, owner of the townland of Ballymorris.

At the government's request he employed a staff of from between 15 to 20 men. They were employed in different ways, some being engaged in the erection of three large two-storied houses in different parts of the parish, all in prominent positions. For example, one was built on high ground in Ballymorris overlooking the Shannon; another facing the railway and the third almost right on the summit of Cratloe Hills, the idea being to show what was being done to relieve the conditions of some of the tenants at least.

Other parts of the property were drained and fenced, in one case a farm of considerable size in those days had no less than 27 gates here and there through it. It was not all charity however as four percent was added to the rent. The wood used in the construction of the houses was of the best pitch-pine. One cannot fail to notice the difference between them and the other dwellings in the locality, from the point of view of size and architectural design. The names of the families who lived there are Griott, Cherry and Donoghues and, at the present time, although the Cherrys and Griotts continue to live there, in a short time these families will become extinct, while the other has long since died out.

Two locals were engaged as stewards, Mick Shanahan being over the drainage and John Flannery over the housing scheme. No trace of the Shanahans is now left. We still have the Flannerys.

The workers were chosen from those who could produce a note or letter from the Parish Priest stating that they were in need of employment. And as the work was hard and hours long (from 7 to 7) none but the best need apply. As regards the stewards these were selected by the landlord's agent and as they were looked upon as his 'pets' you may be sure they were not very popular with the workers, and with good reason too. The wages were ten shillings per week of six days and was considered good, while the works carried out under the relief scheme proved beneficial to the surrounding little farms especially the drainage. These works continued for many years afterwards, up to 1890 or so.[18]

❖❖

John D. O'Leary, Lynedaowne, Rathmore, Kerry

Choice of workers was left to the farmers on whose land the work was done, the landlord reaped the benefit as he used the improvements as an excuse to raising the rent. Attitude of the people – anything that meant food was a godsend. The farmers were glad to improve their farms. I don't know how the local schemes were financed but there is a local tradition that the landlords helped. The stewards were usually the landlord's demesne steward.[19]

❖❖

Pádraig Ó Seaghdha, Fearann tSeáin, Castlegregory, Co. Kerry

The principle local relief scheme was the building of boundary walls on the mountains. The men employed were the able-bodied poor of the parish and the pay was fourpence a day, the men to find their own food. As I write I can see nine or ten miles of dry stone wall on the face of Binn Ós Gaoith. These run up to a height of 2,000 feet on the mountain side and enclose land which is not worth 4d. an acre.[20]

❖❖

*Seán Ó Domhnaill, b.1873, Scairt na nGleobhrán, Ballylooby,
Cahir, Co. Tipperary*

Local relief schemes were numerous. Two new roads were laid
down in my district, the main-line from Cahir to Mitchelstown
and the line from Cahir to Clogheen via Ballylooby. Many steep
hills were cut through in these works. The mountain road from
Clogheen via the 'V' to Melleray was laid down about 1848.

The pay for the labourers employed on these works was 4d. a
day. These men often were obliged to walk a distance varying
from 10 to 15 miles. Yellow meal was the only food available.

A local inhabitant, by name James O'Brien, was a ganger on
one of these schemes. These schemes were financed from state
grants. Drainage work was carried out on a landlord's estate, a
portion of which was very marshy. Long deep drains were dug
which can still be seen. Workers suffered much from the fact that
they were obliged to stand all day in water-logged areas. They
were allowed one meal of stirabout per day.

As far as my parish was concerned the relief schemes were of
advantage to the people generally. The roads opened up easy
ways of getting to the nearest towns, hence greater increase in
trade and business. And the drainage increased the amount of
arable land.[21]

❧❧

Liam Ó Brien collected this in Co. Fermanagh

About 1907 I heard James McGrath, Kilcoo, Garrison, Co.
Fermanagh, then about 70, say he worked at the making of a road
in that place called still 'The New Line'. He said they used to get
two feeds of stirabout (India buck) in the day, one in the
morning before starting and another in the evening after
quitting, and they used to bring a quota of oatbread in their
pocket going off then to work in the morning and that was all
their support.[22]

❧❧

William Doudigan (O'Dowd), b.1863, Redbray, Tullaghan,
Co. Leitrim

Women as well as men used to work on the road, the women barrowing clay and stones. The women one and a half pence a day and the men 2d. He often saw the women falling in the barrows, weak with hunger.

He also said that every day, and sometimes several times a day, funerals used to pass. A couple of old people and children carrying naked remains covered with a bit of sacking on an old handbarrow. The gaffer used to allow the squad of workers to carry the remains to the next squad, and so on as far as the workers went, but the old people had to finish the journey on their own. Having reached Garrison graveyard, a square Famine pit 30 feet or so square and having a pair of great doors, that shut down were opened and the remains being dumped in, were closed again. The stretcher was carried back again for future use.[23]

❧❧

Pádraig Mhichíl Ó Súilleabháin, b.1867, a farmer, Meall an Róistigh,
Sneem, Co. Kerry

A poor man, Seán Chrócháin [Ó Biorainn, a poet who lived at the old quay of Sneem] worked with him when they were making the Board of Works road up here to Sliabh na Seasca. It was a frosty hard black morning in the month of January. Fourpence was the daily wage then, and 'tis often they would have to walk 12 or 14 miles to the work. They had no boots, Seán and this other man. The daughter came to him (to this other man) in the morning with the breakfast, yellow meal wet with cold water. He drank it, swelled up and died.[24]

❧❧

11

'Soupers', 'Jumpers' and 'Cat Breacs'

❧❧

As a result of the 'second Reformation' in the 1820s, evangelical Protestants established a number of 'colonies' in Ireland, notably in counties Mayo, Galway, Kerry and Cork. These colonies were to serve a number of purposes. They functioned as refuges for persecuted converts from Catholicism who were attacked or suffered from 'exclusive dealing'. Converts also received substantial material benefits as the colonies were designed to be model economically self-sufficient communities, able to provide education and employment.

Most controversially, during the sectarian tensions of the period in general and during the Famine years in particular, the evangelical groups were accused of providing relief to the distressed in exchange for their conversion from Catholicism. While attempts at proselytising had also been made before the Famine, a new and more intense campaign was funded from Britain, especially between the years 1848 and 1850.

The evangelical preachers, teachers and clergy had no shortage of people to attend their services and proselytising schools. Indeed, their offers of material comforts in exchange for conversion had a high degree of short-term success in some of the most deprived areas of the west. The offering of food in exchange for conversion gained them the nickname of 'soupers', while those who converted were sometimes known as 'jumpers'. 'Cat breacs' (speckled cats) is understood to have referred to covers of books they used in their preaching and educational works. In the areas where their missionary work was most concentrated, converts would have numbered several hundred, and in Dingle and Achill, for example, the colonies continued their missions on into the 1850s and 1860s.

❧❧

The Donegans, Ballintoy, Co. Antrim, in 1956

There was a soup-kitchen run by people named McKinnan in the townland of Cloughcur. They called them the 'Brockan-men'. It was porridge they would give if you would change your religion.

At the time there was a lot of youngsters and these big people, the gentry, would take them to some place and give them food. The children would bless themselves before they would ate; and these one would have their hands tied behind their backs so's they couldn't bless themselves. That happened round here as far as I heard.

And another thing I hear them tell, they would offer to give you brogues and a top coat if you would ate bacon on a Friday.[1]

❧❧

Patrick O'Donnell, b.1863, Cam, Mostrim Parish, Co. Longford

The parson gave the grass of a cow to a man if he'd go to church for three Sundays. So the man agreed to the bargain and went to church for three Sundays, but he was going to mass as well and the parson found out about it. So the next time they met the parson says,

'I hear you're going to mass.'

'Why wouldn't I,' says the man, 'I go to you for the grass of me cow, but I go to mass for the good of me sowl.'[2]

❧❧

Walter Furlong, b.1871, a farmer, Carrigeen, Grange, Rathnure, Co. Wexford

There was a soup-kitchen set up between the present church of Rathnure and Tomenine Bridge. Somewhere on the stretch of road the soup-kitchen was. There was a public works scheme working on the road leading down to the Bridge of Tomenine. The men working on it got fourpence a day and their soup. The soup-kitchen was set up by a Protestant Society. They used to give tracts to the men to take home to their families. People took the soup at that time because they had nothing else and made a laughing stock of the soupers.

I asked Morgan Dunne what used to be in the tracts. 'I'll tell you what was in one of the tracts I got from my father, when he came home from the Public Works,' says he.

Come all ye blind, dead papishes, wherever that ye live,
Never depend on papish priests, for they will you deceive,
Never bow down to wooden gods, or images adore,
But join our Orange heroes and we'll sing 'Dolly's Brae' once more.

The Public Works and soupers worked in conjunction with each other. Yellow meal was given free and each got a tommy-can [a tin holding about a quart of liquid] full for his dinner.

The head ganger over the Public Works was also in charge of the soup-kitchen and gave out the tickets for the soup. I never heard of the soup being given except for renouncing the faith.

People would renounce their faith for the time being, in the hope of going back to the old faith as soon as times got better.[3]

❧❧

Cáit Ní Bholguibhir, Rathnure, Enniscorthy, Co. Wexford

In the district of Carna, near Fermoy, Co. Cork, where my mother came from, the people suffered a great deal. They died by thousands by starvation and disease and the workhouses in Cork were full. She often told about the soup-house in Bandon. Over the gate to the entrance was written: 'Jew, Turk and Atheist are welcome here, but not a Papist'. A poor destitute scholar, left homeless, was passing by it and saw it. Under this he wrote: 'Whoever wrote it, wrote it well, for the same is written o'er the Gates of Hell.'[4]

☙☙

Charles Clarke, b.1873, Tullynaskeagh, Bailieboro, Co. Cavan

There was a soup-kitchen at Ervey, near Kingscourt. A minister called Peadar a Willan [an Mhuilinn, of the mill] was teaching an Irish class at Ervey, and the classes were held on Wednesdays and Fridays [both fast days] during Lent. It was only on those two days of the week that those classes were held, and the people attending the classes were offered soup and feeds of beef and bacon. People came from far and near to get the feeds, but the majority attending the classes refused to eat the beef or bacon, and they wouldn't drink the soup.

One of the Sullivans of Breakey, they called him Peadar Bany, was attending this class, and the priest of Tierworker objected to it. This was during mass, and Sullivan said he would put the priest off the altar. The priest told members of the congregation to shove him out of the chapel, but not to abuse or strike him. They shoved and elbowed him when they were putting him out. He was dead before that day week and was buried in Moybologue graveyard. But some of the neighbours came that night and lifted the body out of the grave and threw it in Clugga Lake.[5]

☙☙

James Argue, b.1865, Galbolia, Bailieboro, Co. Cavan

Relief Committees were set up at Bailieboro and Shercock and the Indian meal came as the first relief. The landlords had boilers for boiling soup and Indian porridge. Lord Farnham, of Cavan, had soup-kitchens, and any Catholic who went to him and turned Protestant, or ate bacon or beef on Fridays, got as much soup and meat as they wanted to take. But anyone who refused to eat beef or bacon on Fridays got nothing at all. The majority refused but a number of Catholics did eat the meat. In my young days it was cast up to people that 'they ate Lord Farnham's bacon'. I heard of people who turned Protestant and, when the worst of the Famine was over, they turned Catholic again.[6]

꧁꧂

Seán Ó Domhnaill, b.1873, Scairt na nGleobhrán, Ballylooby, Cahir, Co. Tipperary

Souperism was practised in the south-east of our parish so the tradition has it; and in the Ballybacon parish which is adjacent. To speak of a person as a 'souper' in our district was tantamount to the greatest taunt and insult.

These soupers wore black hats and could be easily identified at the local fairs. This idea of souperism has died out during my time.

A condition of reception of soup was to forswear allegiance to the Blessed Virgin and to disregard the Catholic law of abstinence with the denial of mass. Proselytism was widely practised by local Protestants.[7]

꧁꧂

Dáithí Ó Ceanntabhail, national teacher, Croom, Co. Limerick

Souperism on a wide scale was inaugurated and carried on with a certain amount of success in the Ballingarry, Co. Limerick area, in the poor district of Knockfierna the poverty and misery of the people provided for the proselytisers a ready lever to effect their nefarious work. The result of their activities was but very temporary but it was marked enough to win from the neighbouring people the nickname of 'soupers' or the 'Ballingarry soupers' for the people of that district.[8]

꧁꧂

Pádraig Ó Seaghdha, Fearann tSeáin, Castlegregory, Co. Kerry

The Dingle and Ventry areas were of course notorious areas of souperism. I met a Dingle man one day and the conversation turned to matters of religion. 'Are there many Protestant families in Dingle now Jim?' arsa mise. 'Oh only two or three Protestant families,' he replied, 'but there are a couple of soupers too.'[9]

❧❧

Tomás Ó Cearbhall, b.1875, a shopkeeper, Kildorrery, Mallow, Co. Cork

Another story I heard was of a poor Catholic family on the brink of starvation, being fed by another family who were of a different faith – the snag being that they were to attend church service, instead of going to mass. On the following Sunday the poor old woman and two sons attended the church at Rockmills near here. She entered and put out her hand for the holy water stoop, then she trailed up to the foremost portion of the church, knelt down on the floor and said her rosary continuously while the minister officiated. She was rather an incubus to this divine, as when the service was over he told her that she was not bound to return again to his church.[10]

❧❧

Seaghan Mac Cártha, b.1893, national teacher, An Bóthar Buí, Newmarket, Co. Cork

In Famine days some of the Protestant ladies tried to buy the babies in the district with gifts of food and blankets, but were refused.

Lady, here are your blankets clean.
Take back your meat and gold
I could not part with my heart's blood
I could not see them sold.

But souperism fared better in Newmarket district. Here Lady

171

Mary Allworth, a famous proselytiser, tempted many starving victims with the soup-kitchens. There was no proselytism in my home district as there were no Protestants. They never settled down in a poor district.[11]

❧❧

Máire Bean Uí Mhurchadh, b.1879, Sráid Ghuirtín Buí, Macroom, Co. Cork

There was a soup-kitchen attached to the rectory of Clondroichid, three miles west of Macroom and in charge of Rev. Mr Kyle. There was no doubt whatever about proselytising having been carried out here.

It seems that a neighbouring farmer's wife, Mrs O'Donoghue (grandmother, I believe, to Dr O'Donoghue retired M.O.H, Macroom) started a rival kitchen on her own, to combat the hunger and the proselytism. She gave of her beet, potatoes, sour milk and oatmeal to her less fortunate neighbours.[12]

❧❧

P.J. McNamara, b.1895, national teacher, Boys' National School, Newmarket on Fergus, Co. Clare

Souperism appeared in a very mild form even in this backward district. It existed under the form of a type of night school known as the 'Cat Breac', so called from the picture of a speckled cat on the front page. Its object was the spread of reading ostensibly but really to make the people English Protestant, and the Irish language was used as the medium and fostered for that purpose. It was financed by some government agency such as the Kildare Place Society. There was a local family named Healy who were traditional schoolmasters. One of them became an untrained assistant in Coolmeen School and resigned from here on pension in 1914. The Healys whom I have mentioned were often called in derision the 'Cat Breacs'. This title would be hurled at them in a drunken squabble perhaps, and was fiercely resented.[13]

❖❖❖

Mrs Lennox, b.1869, a housewife, Hollywood, Co. Down

Church Missionary Societies opened soup-kitchens and distributed soup. Great care was taken that the soup was made from meat and vegetables and distributed on Fridays so that Catholic population could not partake. The Catholics in these parts died on the roads sooner than partake of the soup. These soup-kitchens were run by the aristocracy. The Indian meal which was sent from England was unfit for pigs and the people could not eat it.[14]

❖❖❖

Patrick McGinley, b.1871, a tailor, Malinbeg, Glencolumkille,
Co. Donegal

Minister Carr in Cashel, Glencolumkille, assisted by Philip McNelis (a Catholic), and Minister Hume, assisted by O'Reilly (a Catholic) were the individuals responsible for distribution of Indian meal (a half stone per family) and soup. Large cauldrons about four or five foot in height, was the receptacle used. None but the very poor received food supplies for which work, such as the conveyance of sea-wrack to fields, had to be done in lieu. People in good circumstance secretly obtained the meal by payment. Recipients of soup and meal were on the whole grateful.

Proselytism and souperism occurred in Cashel, Glencolumkille. Cashel was, and still is, the district where the Protestant Minister resides. Three Mac Neilis families and one O'Reilly family are known who turned Protestant. Land was the inducement held out. These families, still Protestant, reside in the district.[15]

❖❖❖

Lughaidh Ó Maollumhlaigh, Ard Achaidh, Edgeworthstown,
Co. Longford

Soup was given out by Protestant families who tried to get the
people who took it to turn Protestant. Some did so. An old
couplet said of them:

They sold their souls for penny rolls,
For soup and hairy bacon.[16]

❧❧

Kathleen Hurley, Corlock House, Ballymoe, Co. Galway

In the town of Ballinlough there lived during the Famine years,
and for some years after, a Protestant clergyman of the name
'Parson Blunder'. This parson gave soup and aid to the stricken
people around Ballinlough and succeeded in proselytising a
number of families, so much so that there are a number of
Protestant families up to the present day around Ballinlough. A
Protestant church, a Protestant school were also built in the
town and those who gave up their religion and attended
Protestant worship got contracts for coffins, contracts for roads,
contracts for selling manure, were given good farms of land so
that the newly turned Protestants in and around Ballinlough
became rich while the Catholics remained poor.[17]

❧❧

Austin Concannon, b.1882, Cloonthoo, Tuam, Co. Galway

The Christian Brothers had a house and school in Tullinadaly
Road and they were evicted by Mary Plunkett, sister of Bishop
Plunkett, Protestant Bishop of Tuam. The students set fire to the
desks in the school before leaving and the house was burnt. Mary
Plunkett rebuilt it and used it as a soup-house in conjunction
with Dean Seymours. She had to cross over from the back of the

palace to it as she was afraid to go through town. They sent agents dressed up as ministers and called 'Bible Readers' out the country who threw tracts on the road and tried to draw people to the soup-house. It was badly supported. They did everything to annoy the priests, including getting the people to spit on the Blessed Sacrament in the Corpus Christi Procession.[18]

❖❖

Bean Uí Sheoighe, b.1873, a farmer's wife, Dawrosmore, Letter, Letterfrack, Co. Galway

Brocán was the food eaten by the people. It was made of oaten meal. This was bought in a certain house in Tully. Any Catholic who became a Protestant got plenty of food to eat and soup to drink. They were also educated in the Protestant schools. This was carried out in Renvyle but not in Letter. A Protestant school was erected in Letter but the roof was not put on it, as the people would not allow their children to attend it.[19]

❖❖

Martin Manning, b.1875, Carrowholly, Kilmeena, Westport, Co. Mayo

A fair contingent went to the Colony in Achill. Others held out by getting food in Ayer's kitchen and a little meal in return for this attendance at church or by sending their children to the Protestant School [Ayer's Kitchen has reference to Rev. Mr Giles Ayers who was Protestant rector in charge of Kilmeena Parish at the time].[20]

❖❖

Seán Ó Duinnshleibhe, Glenville, Fermoy, Co. Cork

The Protestant clergyman at the time (name unknown now) in the Protestant Church at Glenville had the giving out of alms to the poor, the Catholics, on condition that the recipients would attend their church on Sundays. Several people availed of this charity which consisted of food and clothing, but as there was no response, that is attending church, the supplies ceased. Only a few Catholic families, the heads of which went to church. They were Forde and Sullivan. It was not to become Protestants that these men attended the Protestant Church, but to get relief for their families. Forde and Sullivan lived at the foot of the Nagles Mountains and had large families, and rather than see their families die, they did as I have stated. Of course, they did not turn their backs on the Catholic Church, but went to the Catholic church and to mass, and to meet their demands they went to the Protestant church later in the day (Sunday) at twelve o' clock. I was told they only presented themselves at the service, but did not pray or take any active part in the ceremonies. When the Protestant Church Board saw that only the heads of the two families were present at service, an order was made to bring in the children. It was hard on these people to do so, but want compelled them to bring in their young families to divine service at the Protestant church. This is how the Board succeeded by having the children and bringing them up as Protestants. These people were then called 'soupers'. The Forde family followed up as Protestants and three of that generation married and settled in farms near their birth place, one in his father's house. This Forde (the souper) died about 40 years ago and was buried in the Protestant graveyard adjoining the church.[20]

✤❧✤

Séamus Reardon, b.1873, Boulteen, Eniskeane, Co. Cork

During that time a poor woman and her son were very badly off.

The boy was almost dying. A lady knocked at the door and offered them food, food in plenty, if they would renounce their faith. She came daily but her offer was not accepted. Things were so hard on the poor creatures that one day the mother asked her son was it better take the food or die. In Irish he spoke 'Is fearr an bás, a mathair,' he answered. 'Tis better die, mother.'[22]

⁘

John Mc Carthy, b.1873, Kilcoleman, Eniskeane, Co. Cork

The parish of Desert during the famine years, and the lean years that followed, was a nest of soupers or bible readers. Their names were all recorded in an old song afterwards:

Near Maulnarougha schoolhouse I saw a great number
Of big-bellied preachers assembled together,
Wren, Sealys, Harris, the Daunts and the Lambes,
Buttimer, Baldin and grey-whiskered Farr,
Shine, Hosford, Attly, Moore, Green and Bateman
Longfields and Gallach, the Joyces and Teagans.
May the devil transport that band to New Zealand.

They were offering bribes, food and money to the starving people to renounce their faith and turn Protestants. The head of this band of 'bible-readers' was a man named Buttimer. He was known as 'Big-bellied Buttimer'. He was also called in Irish the 'Rughra Rahar' [rugaire reatha – interloper, raider].

He could translate his ould bible from English to Irish
To give us a taste of his polluted Irish.

As much poverty, hunger and disease was raging at the time, their families is all that turned with the 'soupers'.

I forgot to relate Seán Bán O'Spillane and Henry McCabe
Who altered their jackets for a mere little trifle.

I forgot Dickeen Barry that smuggling old monkey
Who goes every Sunday to get his fat shilling,
And he says to his Joney 'tis far better than scripture.
Owanamso Joney, this man will do more
He says he will give us buck porridge galore
And besides our Johnny will be a fine scholar
But if he said as much more he's the 'Rughra Rahar'.

It was during the Famine and the years that followed that the Irish language was lost. Old people advised their children to learn English in order that they may not read, or in any way become interested, in tracts printed and circulated by the bible readers. These tracts, extracts from the corrupt or polluted bible, were thrown into the cabins by the roadside, handed to children to take home, or thrown about in public places. It was all the work of the soupers and their agents to induce the people to forsake their religion.

The old people made the sign of the cross on themselves when they heard of the couple of families that had turned over.

The biggest soup-kitchen in this parish was in Dery Castle. It was a government soup kitchen run by Lady Bandon, whom the people called Lady Porridge. It was relief 'by the way' for the poor. It was not soup, Indian meal boiled into thin porridge. Any person likely 'to turn' got the best of it.[23]

❖❖❖

Sarah (Wiley) Grant, b.1860, Faughil, Jonesboro, Co. Armagh

Yes, I mind hearing of that. I'll tell you where they gave it out. They did then give it out in Jonesboro. There's people you see don't want it mentioned. Some scorned, and some went and took it. It was given out in a house called Carpentiers. It was given by Benson. Haven't you heard of Benson's Gravey? My uncle, Tom McGinnity, made a song about a man that took Benson's Gravey.

Benson was over there in Chambree's and was trying to corrupt the people that time. They dropped tracts along the road as well and would stand to see who would pick them up.

And cabbage too, to kitchen Benson's Gravey.

If you'd take Benson's Gravey they'd have a claim on you and you'd have to sent the children to the Protestant school in Adavoyle.

It wasn't for saying his prayers, you know, that Cahmree lost the eye.[24]

❧

Owen Rafferty [known as The Bar], b.1885, a farmer, Carrifamean, Carrickbroad, Dromintee Parish, Co. Armagh

It was big Protestants give that out, and it was of a Friday you got it, and you be to go and eat a feed of beef and soup and meat, and they gave you a whole lot to take away. It was only turncoats took that.

Where they gave it out I can't say, but it was in all the big Protestants' houses up by Ravensdale, Plunkett's and Heuston's and Talford McNeill's.[25]

❧

Mrs G. Kirby, Stradbally, Co. Laois, in 1945

There was only one soup-kitchen here during the Famine. There was an old ballad composed by some local bard denouncing the landlords and, judging by the information contained in two of the verses, I have come to the conclusion that the food must have been supplied by the Protestant gentry locally.

In '47 they contrived a plan
To pervert poor Catholics with their soup can.
Their chums from London all came there
With hairy bacon soups to prepare.

But their soup and meal did not entice
Poor hungry victims to their low vice.
They died of want in fields and dell
But their faith to them they would not sell.[26]

❧

William Blake, b.1895, a labourer, Rathnagrew, Co. Carlow

There was a soup-kitchen in Kiltegan and anyone who was prepared to turn Protestant would get a feed there. They made a song above which contained the lines: 'Goodbye God Almighty till the praties grow.'[27]

❧

*Thomas Kelly, Rockfleet, Carrowbeg, Westport, Co. Mayo,
b.1855 in Rosturk*

There were soup schools in Mulranny and Murrevaugh (just east of Mulranny). Some of the people turned with the soupers and remained with them till they died. A few of these went to Inisbiggle in Ballycroy when driven from home by shame, fear or otherwise.

One man, not a native of this parish, turned. He was passing by the priest's house one day in his native place and raised his hat.

'Ah', says the priest, 'you cannot please God and the devil.'

'Ah father,' said he, 'It's only till the praties grow.' He turned back later. His son was also a Protestant, but only for a time during the Famine.[28]

❧

*Mary Daly, b.1874, a farmer, Faughart, Co. Louth, and a native of
Creggan Parish, Crossmaglen, Co. Armagh*

'Aw, bad luck to you, oul bottle the soup.' Sure I heard that cast up to people at home myself. You'd get so much soup yourself, and so much to take home to your own ones in a bottle.

At that time the courthouse in Cross was where the old barracks was. They had beef and soup and were giving it out. And Minister Ashe, I think it was from Philipstown he was, he was trying to convert the Catholics [to Protestantism].

And fever was awful prevalent, but in them times all men was bled for that. Someone would take so much blood from them. That was common. But when Minister Ashe come he was able to give the people more than the priest.

It was Minister Ashe tried to convert them all. The fever was raging at the time and this man and his family were all bad. This was out at Cross. He hadn't the land or anything tilled. So Minister Ashe come to him and said he'd till it.

'I'll till it,' says he, 'if you come to the church.'

So he said he would and I think some of them died. It's long since I heard them at it. But he got the crop in anyway. And so he was to go to Minister Ashe's church this Sunday, to get the communion I think. So when he didn't come Minister Ashe come to him, but he wouldn't go into the house for fear of the fever. He had him converted up to that to get the communion. So he says 'I thought you were to come to my house for the communion?' 'Aw,' says he, 'sure I'm not fit.' So he got a shovel and he put it into him on a shovel. 'I'm not able to lift it,' says he to Minister Ashe. 'Well own up to it and that'll do,' says Minister Ashe.

So anyway he got over the fever and when he was able to go about he went to the chapel and Minister Ashe come to him again.

'You were at your own chapel today,' says he, 'and you were to come to my church. You and your whole family was it. And,' says he, 'I put in your crop and I want the price of it.'

'Aw,' says the man back, 'own up to it and that'll do.'[29]

⚜

12

The Bottomless Coffin and the Famine Pit

❖

Over one million deaths in Ireland during the Great Famine were due to hunger and disease. Over two-thirds of these deaths happened in Munster and Connaght with Connaght, for example, having a Famine death-rate twice as high as Leinster. Most of those who died were children and old people. It is estimated that three out of every five who died were under 10 years of age or over 60.

The problem of finding materials for coffins, of transporting the corpses and digging graves for over a million dead, was made worse by the dire poverty and the physical exhaustion caused by hunger and disease.

❖

John Doyle, a labourer, Rasheenmore, b.1900 at Craffle, Ballyteigue, Aughrim, Co. Wicklow

There were so many deaths that they opened big trenches through the graveyards and when they were full of dead they filled them in. His father worked at the opening of these trenches and he was paid by the government.

In some places they had trap doors in the floors of the houses with a trench underneath and when anyone died they dropped them into the trench and shut down the door.

His father told him that his father saw 40 funerals going into one graveyard in one day and he was covering all the graves. No one was allowed into the graveyards except the men hired to cover the graves. Two guards were always on to keep the people out and there were many rows with people trying to get in. They dug graves 12 foot deep and put seven or eight bodies into each grave. They never put coffins on them at all. Some of the bodies used to swell up and when they would be dropped into the grave they would burst and the gravediggers would have to run until the smell would ease. Often they would get the disease.[1]

◦§§◦

Jim Lawlor, b.1877, a labourer, Knocknaboley, Co. Wicklow

In Knocknabooley there was a fever and people who would get it got as black as tar and used swell up. There were special coffins for putting them into with a trap door in the bottom for letting them into the grave. No one would be allowed to the funeral except people who were let out of gaol to bury the dead. No one else would be allowed to go near the corpse. Wheels were fitted to this kind of coffin.[2]

◦§§◦

Michael Gorman, b.1868, Doontrusk, Carrowbeg, Westport, Co. Mayo. He heard this from his father, 1819–1911

A man in Lettermaghera was sick of the fever. He died. There was no one in the house with him except his wife. It seems the neighbours avoided the house through fear of the fever. The wife dug a grave by the bedside and rolled her husband's dead body out of the bed into the grave. Then she covered it in.[3]

◦§§◦

Seán Mac Cuinneagáin, Scoil Mhín an Aodhaire, Carrick, Co. Donegal

A woman from the Teelin district, Una Gaughan (maiden name), Una McDermot in marriage, on the death of her little son, not having the wherewithal to get a coffin, put the child in the cradle, strapped the cradle on her back and carried it five miles to the nearest graveyard and buried it.

183

Coffins of fever victims were always tarred on the inside as a precaution against any ooze and as a sort of disinfectant.[4]

⋰⋱

Dáithí Ó Ceanntabhail, national teacher, Croom, Co. Limerick

Those who died from cholera might not be brought to burial through a village or town for fear of spreading the contagion. Yet a whole family who died almost together, 'because they were too proud to admit their hunger, to beg', in the townland of Cluais Meirgín – now and long since Ploughlands – were coffined and brought by the neighbours through the village of Croom and interred by night in Manester Abbey.[5]

⋰⋱

Mrs Peter Reynolds, b.1871, Ballykilcline, Kilglass, Co. Roscommon

My father was only a little fellow during the Famine but I often heard him tell that he saw a whole cart full of corpses and the bodies all swollen, and they brought the cart of corpses to the graveyard and made a big hole and put the corpses in the hole as they were. They put a big mat over the corpses and then filled in the clay over the mat, and that's how they were buried.[6]

⋰⋱

Joe McConaghy, b.1892, a farmer, Mullarts, Ramoan Parish,
Ballycastle, Co. Antrim

She [mother] talked of people being in a coma. They would be waking them and they wouldn't be dead at all. She talked of some man from Carry that was burying his wife that time and the man noticed some movement in the coffin, and took the lid off and his wife was there wondering where she was. She said he had nothing but his overcoat to put round her and take her home and

184

she lived for long after that. It was true enough that, and there were others like it.[7]

⚜

Mrs M. Twolig, Battery Road, Longford

When she saw the people coming they shut the door and they were afraid to let any stranger into the house. When a person died they got a plank and tied the feet of the corpse to one end of it and the head to the other end, and the hands together, then two men took hold of it at each end and carried it to the bog nearby, she pointed out the place, where there was deep water and threw it in. The people had neither the material nor the strength to make coffins nor dig graves. She said she was telling the truth for she saw it happening herself.[8]

⚜

Charles Clarke, b.1873, Tullynaskeagh, Bailieboro, Co. Cavan

A great many died in the hospital and workhouse, and the funerals to Moybologue were numerous. My father told me that he saw a man carrying his brother's corpse in a coffin on his back for Bailieboro to Moybologue graveyard. He had no one to help him and he had to dig the grave and bury the corpse himself. There were so many funerals at the time and people didn't like to attend the funeral because the man died of fever, and they were afraid they might take it. He died in the hospital. My father said it was the saddest sight he had ever seen.[9]

⚜

Mrs Gilmore, b.1867, Moyleroe, Delvin, Co. Westmeath

It is said that during the sickness there was a man for burying the dead. He would have maybe 16 or 20 corpses thrown on a cart.

185

The people had no coffins. They were buried just as they were. This man would get a pound for each corpse. He used to get this money from some rich people who were away. No one round was rich at that time, except the man from burying the bodies.[10]

❧❧

Seán Ó Domhnaill, b.1873, Scairt na nGleobhrán, Ballylooby, Cahir, Co. Tipperary

The local authorities (Guardians) looked after the burials They paid labouring men to bury the dead at so much a body. My informant saw one of these fellas who earned their money in this detestable manner. He knew him by the nick-name of 'Paddy the Puncher'. He earned this title from the manner in which he used to dispatch to eternity those poor people who were on death's doors. He received a shilling or so per body, and consequently his whole interest lay in the number of his burials. In later years when Paddy returned to the district he was set upon by an old woman who recognised him and cursed him away from the house.

Graves were made anyplace. As far as possible relatives did their best to bury their dead friends in their native churchyard. Graves were made outside of graveyards where deaths were numerous and entailed too much trouble to transfer to other places.

In a homestead ravaged by the famine disease only two brothers remained alive. Finally the elder brother passed away, and the onus of his burial rested with the younger brother who was himself weakened out also. He began journeying by night, to the local graveyard, with the dead body upon his back, but was not able to reach his destination. A relation of my own uncle helped the corpse-bearer to bury his brother in the churchyard (Whitechurch).[11]

❧❧

Dáithí Ó Ceanntabhail, national teacher, Croom, Co. Limerick

They were buried where they were found by opening the fence and shifting the poor corpse into the gap so formed. The ditch was then built over the body and some stones set into the bocastwork of the fence to mark the grave. The memory in later years of a Famine burial having been made at a certain point produced a superstitious fear in the minds of the people, a fear which had its origin, I think, in the horrible dread of contagion which filled the survivors in an area where death mowed a wide swath.[12]

⚜

Tuosist, Kenmare, Co. Kerry, from Seán Ó Súilleabháin,
Irish Folklore Commission

One day Stephen Regan met a dog dragging a child's head along. He took the head from the dog and buried it and set a tree over it. The family to whom the child belonged were getting relief for the child and for that reason did not report its death.[13]

⚜

Pádraig Pléimionn, Killarney, Co. Kerry

I heard many harrowing details of how people died by the roadside when travelling to Killarney to the workhouse, and how the bodies used to be buried coffinless in old forts and at disused cemeteries.

There was a general rush to the workhouse and many died going there.[14]

⚜

Gerald Fitzmaurice, improvements and drainage inspector,
Knockrour, Scartaglen, Co. Kerry

The dead were put into a kind of coffin, a few boards nailed together, and those who died around here were mostly buried in Kilsarcon Church. There was a corpse once left inside a gap in the townland of Knockrour. It was left there by some poor people farther east who could not carry it any further. It was brought by night. The following morning when the young men of Knockrour stopped work, they took it on their shoulders to Kilsarcon Church (five miles away) and buried it. They didn't know if it was a man or woman they were carrying. This frequently happened. One party brought the corpse as far as they could and left it there, then others would carry it another bit and leave it, when a third party would sometimes finish the job. The shoulders of the young men around here used be sore from carrying corpses.[15]

❧❧

Mrs O'Brien, b.1874, Kilworth, Co. Cork

My grandfather was at work cutting wheat in Tobar na hOla and my grandmother was with him taking out and binding. My mother was a young girl at the time and she was with them in the field. They saw the man coming along the road – Scanlan was his name – and a load on his back. My grandmother asked him what he had there and he said it was his wife that was dead and he was taking her to Leitrim graveyard to bury her. He had her sitting on a súgán fastened over his shoulders, and she was dressed in her cloak and hood just as she'd been when she was alive. His little son was with him. My grandmother went into the house and brought them food and milk. Scanlan wouldn't take anything; he said it would overcome him and he wanted to have his wife buried before the dark. The little boy drank the milk.

Every time my mother would talk about that, she'd cry.[16]

❖❖❖

Maighréad Ní Dhonnabháin, b.1866, a farmer, Drom Inide, Drimoleague, Co. Cork

There lived in Dromore to the west of Drimoleague one Joan Hayes. Her husband was one of the early victims of the Famine. Towards the end of the Famine the children got sick and as each one died she took it in a 'kitch' to the graveyard in Caheragh and buried it beside the husband. The distance she would have walked was about eight miles.[17]

❖❖❖

Pádraig Ó Cruadlaoich, b.1860, a master tailor, Macroom, Co. Cork

Pádraig Ó Cruadlaoich told me of a somewhat similar story. He heard of a lone man taking the coffin containing the body of his dead wife all the way from Cork through Ballyvourney to Kerry. The old man was giving out a caoineadh [lament], of which he remembers one verse:

Is fada síos do rugas tú
Agus is fada aníos do thugas tú
Agus thiar i gCiarraí a chuirfí tú
Ologón – mo bhean.

Children were buried near the county bounds on the Cork-Kerry road in Ballyvourney parish, and the local Protestant clergyman regretted he had not heard of the burial in time, otherwise he could have them buried in Ballyvourney (St Gobnait's) graveyard.[18]

❖❖❖

Stiofán Mac Philib, Edenmore National School, Emyvale,
Co. Monaghan

It is said that some of those buried were not quite dead and curses
are spoken of where the 'dead' shouted in his coffin on the way
to the graveyard. It was noted that a person with a clear drop at
the point of his nose would be dead the next day.[19]

⚜

John Fallon, Cloonadra, Ballymoe, Co. Galway

In 1847 Edward Fallon lived with his parents in Cloonee, on the
holding now occupied by Michael Butler. He was one of a large
family and when the cholera swept the district young Edward was
the only survivor. He was then about nine years of age and found
himself alone in the world to fend for himself the best he could.
His native village of Cloonee and the neighbouring villages of
Corliskea, Cloonadra and Bookla suffered severely. With very few
exceptions the entire population was prostrate at the same time
and deaths occurred every day.

At that time there was only a donkey and cart in the district
and that was the property of Michael Green of Bookla. The few
who were lucky enough to escape the cholera gradually availed of
this one means of taking the coffins to Kilcroan graveyard, some
two miles away. Young Fallon was delighted when he was given
the task of driver and day after day he worked from dawn to dark,
always sitting on the coffin and making an average of six
journeys daily. He was accompanied to each house by two men
who put in the coffin over the half-door. The corpse was placed
in it and the coffin was pushed out on the street. It was then
placed on the cart and taken to the graveyard.

Whenever the opportunity afforded, young Fallon went into
the house of the victims and gave them hot drinks, yet he never
contracted the cholera.

Afterwards he was taken to Glenamaddy Workhouse and
reared there and the ownership of his father's holding was lost.

Some years later he returned to this parish where he was given a tiny patch of bog on the Roscommon-Galway border. Here he built a hut and reared a family and on this same patch of ground his son John lives today.[20]

⁘❧⁘

A man born in 1869, Co. Roscommon

I heard my father say it was the custom that people who died from cholera and starvation during the famine years were buried near the spot where their remains were found, by the person who found the remains and that the remains were interred without a coffin. That being the custom it will explain the following incident.

Early one October morning two priests celebrated the Station Mass in a country thatched house in the village of — Co. Roscommon. They travelled to and from the Station Mass on a sidecar. While driving along the public road in the direction of their home they saw an old man lying on the side of the road under the shelter of a hawthorn bush. The priests were seen to draw up their horse, they came off the car and examined the corpse, for the old man was dead of cholera and the remains were emaciated. He was a stranger in the locality, likely a beggar, who took ill and lay down to die by the roadside. The priests were seen to kneel in prayer beside the remains and afterwards get to their feet, mount the sidecar and drive home to their presbytery, leaving the corpse on the side of the road. Now it happened that this was witnessed by the man whose house was situated nearest the spot where lay the remains. He was much annoyed by the conduct of the two priests for he considered it to be their duty to see and have the corpse interred. The priests were the first to find it. After the two priests had disappeared out of sight, the man came forward, examined the remains, found it to be the remains of a stranger in the locality. He got a wheel barrow, placed the corpse on it and wheeled it to the presbytery, the house of the two priests and left the much wasted corpse on the step outside their hall door, that seeing it there might remind them of their duty to the dead.[21]

❖❖❖

Thomas O'Flynn, John Melody, Attymass, Ballina, Co. Mayo

Most of the dead were buried in fields or along the roads. The difficulty was to get men to carry the corpse to a graveyard but many men were buried in the local graveyards situated about twelve miles apart.

Tradition says that every few yards of the way contains a grave, for the corpses were buried along the way when the bearers became too weak to travel farther. There is a gap on the way leading from the main road called 'Bearna na gCorp' from the fact that the bearer or bearers rested there with their burdens before taking the near-way which was rugged and forbidding.

One man, Martán Fada, whom I knew well and who died about 20 years ago, having reached about his hundredth year, was reputed to carry a corpse from his own townland, alone, to Kilgarvan, about seven miles away. Martán could not find anyone to help him.

The corpse was frequently wrapped with straw ropes and buried in this way without a coffin. Corpses were sometimes carried to the graveyard on donkeys' backs.

Tombstones were not erected as it was difficult to find men with the strength to make the graves. Sometimes a large stone or flag was placed at the head or foot of the grave to mark it out. This practice still continues in the absence of a tombstone.

Bodies actually lay unburied by hedges for rats soon devoured the flesh and only the skeleton remained. There is an instance of a family being found dead with their skeletons only remaining and the neighbours' efforts failed to frighten away the rats which were feeding on the flesh.[22]

❖❖❖

Conchubhair Ó Súilleabháin [Connie Cornelius], b.1866, a farmer, Drom Tathuile, Sneem, Co. Kerry

They was four men here, I remember one of them Paddy Cahalane, I knew him, he lived in Srón. He was very old.

They [the four men] used have an old bogdeal chest with two sticks under each end of it. That was the affair they used have drawing them [the corpses].

There was a house there at the quarry, above the road, to the eastern end of the quarry, and a cooper lived there named Paddy Doyle. I knew him. And they were coming up from Ros Deóchan, along by Glaise na Cómhrann, tis below Glaise na Craoú. Anyhow this old Paddy Doyle was in the last agonies, dying, and they went in and they examined him and of course he had life, and old Paddy Cahalane said (to the others) to carry him, not to be coming again for him.

Well, all right, he had presence of mind enough. He understood what he said, and he gave them to understand, with the little life that was in him, that he wouldn't go in the chest.

He lived for years after. He never spoke to Paddy Cahalane after that. He got some aid and lived a long time afterwards.[23]

※

Seán Ó Duinnshléibhe, Glenville, Fermoy, Co. Cork

Part of the Protestant graveyard was used for the burial of Catholics of the district and hospital. A common coffin was left in the graveyard for all, and when a corpse was to be brought to the grave, the corpse was buried and the coffin left for the next. It was not told whether it was a bottomless i.e. sliding bottom or not. This coffin was constantly in use, and probably the grave was a large open trench. This Catholic part of the graveyard is a northern wing. No Protestant is buried in this quarter. There are no tombstones where Catholics are buried in the Protestant graveyard at Glenville.[24]

❖

Thomas Kelly, Rockfleet, Carrowbeg, Westport,
b.1855 in Rosturk

A woman carrying a child in her arms came into the house of his
uncle Paddy Kelly, at Rosturk, and asked for a night's lodging.
They kept her and gave her part of whatever food was going. The
child died during the night, and the mother took the baby with
her in the morning without telling the people of the house what
happened. She brought him up the rise behind the house, laid
the corpse beside a sod fence and knocked part of the fence to
cover it. When the fence was noticed, and they went to make it
up, the body was found and buried there.[25]

❖

J. O'Kane, Dromore National School, Dromore West, Co. Sligo

There is a story of Grace Wallace who lived in Croagh. Her
mother died and she, Grace, carried the corpse on her back in a
creel across the fields (there were no roads then as now) to the
graveyard in Kilmacshalgan. She rested at every fence and stile.
At last she arrived at Somerville's, a Protestant's house about a
quarter of a mile from the graveyard. Old Somerville, great-great
grandfather of the present Bob Somerville, saw her and brought
her a bowl of oatmeal porridge and milk. She ate it and went on
and buried her mother. Old Somerville was very anxious for days
lest the porridge would kill Grace Walker in her weakness from
having eaten little or nothing for days. However she survived.

It was a common sight I was told to see corpses being carried
in Creels, or cross-wise on the backs of people to this
Kilmacshalgan graveyard, mornings and evenings, and more
often at night.

There was little communication between neighbours as far as
I could learn. If somebody died in a house, the corpse was left
unburied unless there was somebody in the house able to carry, in

one way or other, the corpse to the graveyard and do the burial.

Miss Flynn tells the following. She had a grand-uncle, John Flynn, who lived beside Leharrow chapel. One day he saw a man named Philibín passing with an asscart with his two dead children in it, bringing them to Kilmacshalgan graveyard to bury them. Flynn saw that the man Philibín looked weak and tottering. He thought this man will never be able to dig a grave. He took up a spade and shovel and crossed over the fields to the graveyard. Near the graveyard he met another man, Miss Flynn could not remember his name, but Flynn asked him to come and help him make the grave. He refused, and said to Flynn if he began that work, grave-digging, he would be at it every day and would be able to do nothing else. That evening this man's arms became paralysed, and Miss Flynn could not say if he ever recovered the power of his arms again.

As for coffins they were few. Corpses were buried wrapped in sheets. People could not pay for coffins. I was told that people broke up dressers and tables to make coffins, some sort of rude home-made coffins, but the majority were buried coffinless.[26]

❖❖

Brigid Keane, Ennel View Terrace, Mullingar, Co. Westmeath

Old Tom Keenan of Laragh (born 1830 or 1829) often told me that on one particular evening in the Famine times he attended nine funerals below in Cargrove. At that time there were 47 little houses along the bog road there. The seven corpses were carried to the graveyard in Horseleap and were all in coffins. The bearers would carry one coffin a certain distance, then stand while another set of men bore the coffin along on their shoulders. When the second coffin came as far as Tom, he and his fellow bearers took that on their shoulders for a further stretch of the road, then stopped and waited for the third and so on, until they had carried each of the seven corpses in turn. After that they stepped on to the first coffin and continued so. All those corpses were coffined at all events. These seven persons had died of the 'sickness'. The corpses turned black.[27]

❖❖

Jim Lawlor, b.1877, a labourer, Knocknaboley, Co. Wicklow

People who died at Crossbridge were thrown in the river. They had the river dammed and when there would be a lot of bodies collected they let off the water and it would carry the bodies away.[28]

❖❖

13

Landlords, Grain and Government

꧁꧂

Before the Famine, Irish landlords were the main holders of both the economic and political power of the country. They lived most on the rents they got from their tenants and, to a much smaller extent, on the export trade and on industrial production. After the Napoleonic wars in the earlier part of the century, there followed an economic depression as there was a drop in demand, and profits, from Irish grain, beef and butter.

As well as external pressures such as this, some of the landlords had been gradually dissipating their inherited family wealth and their estates had accumulated huge levels of debt. Other landlords remained wealthy.

The landlord class provided the men who were elected as Members of Parliament and many of them funded their political careers in the British parliament from their Irish rents.

The British establishment often let it be known that it felt that Irish landlords had failed in their responsibilities and were largely responsible for the state of Ireland and Irish poverty.

Nevertheless, following the blight of 1845 the money voluntarily contributed for relief by the landlords was unprecedented.

A disproportionate amount of taxation to pay for the cost of relief schemes in Ireland fell on the landlords and large farmers, especially those with greatly sub-divided estates. The charging of the cost of relief schemes to local taxes, and the steadily growing arrears among badly hit small farmers and middlemen, gave landlords a double burden to carry. For many landlords, the loss of rents during the Famine and the burden of taxation imposed on them by central government was their final ruin and saw many of them lose their traditional wealth, power and lands.

꧁꧂

Michael Howard, b.1883, a farmer, Gladree, Belmullet, Co. Mayo

When the Famine of Black Forty-Seven was nearly over, and the most of the people of West Connaght were dead of cold and hunger, a man left Belmullet with his boat and went to England for a cargo of meal to try and save some of the lives of the poor people. This man was known as John Lally, who had owned a boat of his own, and was living in a small house in Belmullet. When this man came from England with his boatload of Indian meal to the pier at Belmullet, the landlords that were in Connaght at that time took all the meal that was on the ship and fed the pigs with it.[1]

❖❖

Frank Craig, b.1891, a farmer, Ballykeel Middle, Brockley,
Rathlin Island, Co. Antrim

He [my father] minded the Erin's Hope coming in to the Island, the Irish sent it from America. She had yellow meal. Gage [the landlord of Rathlin] got that. Now, listen to this, Gage was the landlord, the Irish paid for that yellow meal to be given free, but Gage made people pay for it. That's true for I heard it told here. My father's father, my grandfather, was a blacksmith, and he went for his share of the meal off Gage. What did Gage do? Says he, 'You're well fit to pay for it, you have money. Get the money and you'll get your share of meal.'

My grandfather had a forge in Fallyyack and there were other friends, from above where Sandy Maguire lives now. They went for their share of the meal and Gage says 'Yous have money. Pay for your share.' They told him they had no money. 'Well, yous have friends that have money. Get it off your friends and pay for it.'

He made money out of that and it given free.[2]

❖❖

Liam Ó Danachair, Sunvale, Athea, Co. Limerick

During the worst period of the Famine the local landlord was Wyndham Goold. Like other landlords of his time he exacted excessive rents from his tenants but was otherwise considered a kind landlord. Where cases of want among his tenancy were reported to him he constantly sent food to the afflicted.

For example, when Mrs Carrol of Gortnagross was ill and in want of food he personally brought her soup, food and remedies, inquiring on the way of the Parish Priest whether she might be allowed to use meats on a Friday owing to illness.[3]

Conchubhair and Solomon Ó Néill, b.1860s, farmers, Cratloe, Co. Clare

One landlord (Lord George Quin) cleared out several families in the townland of Ballymorris, for non-payment of rent.

Against this, Mr Maunsell (afterwards Lord Emly) gave seven pounds to each householder who left (1852 and for years after). If they remained he did not press them in any way, or leave a process at any man's door. Neither did he ask a vote from any of his tenants in O'Connell's time. He was elected MP for Limerick and also became a Catholic.

The general attitude of the local landlords was cold and merciless, but with the exception of the O'Briens, who are still with us, they all lived across the water. Merchants and shopkeepers did not count for much as there was very little intercourse between them and the people since the staple food was the potato. The priests on the other hand did all in their power to help their afflicted parishioners.[4]

Séamus Reardon, b.1873, Boulteen, Eniskeane, Co. Cork

Anyone who had anything to give, gave it with a good heart, always regretting that they had not more to give. The gentry and the landlord class were an exception to this. They gave only on condition that those who received would turn away from their faith and join the Protestant Church.

Our local landlord always turned those seeking aid or food from his door with a 'Get away to hell you strumpet.' When the poorhouse was established he used to remark 'Get away to the poorhouse you strumpet.'

'The poorhouse [must] have been a great saving on souls,' one poor old woman remarked as she turned empty handed from his door. 'Before, it was go to hell. Now, it is go to the poorhouse.'

Another landlord that lived locally had men working under him. He offered them food in plenty if they would renounce their faith. Not one of them took it.

One poor old woman that lived under him he threw out on the roadside where she was starving, yet she would not take what he offered. She was taken to the poorhouse and died there.

She had asked a neighbour, before she died, that she be buried in Desert with her own if at all possible. A coffin was procured but only seven men could be got to bear the remains to Desert, seven miles distant. The people were afraid of the landlord to attend her funeral, he was so mad as she didn't turn Protestant. Nevertheless the seven men brought her to Desert taking every short cut they could. There wasn't much worry about funeral roads or funeral routes during those yeas. Corpses were taken across the fields.[5]

⚜

William Torrens, b.1872, Lisminton, Ballintra, Co. Donegal.
He heard it from his father, William Torrens, 1828–1912,
in the townland of Rath

The well-to-do class caught the fever as well in trying to bring aid to the stricken. Mr Alexander Hamilton of Coxtown near Ballintra, a local landlord and land agent for many big estates in south-west Donegal, caught the fever in May 1847 and nearly died from it.

This man rose from very commonplace people and in his early years lived in a common thatched country house, but he got on rapidly and well after securing the agency of a small estate. He had a record of stern harshness to poor tenants who could not pay their rent promptly and many evictions took place on his land.

At the time of the Famine many people were evicted from farms surrounding his own homestead and he eventually found himself in possession of between 200 and 300 acres of good land.

This man also attained notoriety by his severity as a local magistrate. There is still a story current in the district regarding a priest from Pettigo who was brought up at a court in Ballintra on some charge of which he was entirely innocent. The attitude of Alexander Hamilton on the bench was so entirely hostile to the priest that it drew comment from many Protestants. The priest eventually was acquitted, and arising out of it, he is said to have made a remark that there would never be an heir for Coxtown which ran in the male line.

Shortly afterwards Hamilton's wife was brought to her confinement and gave birth to something with a head on it like a dog which vanished under the bed.

It is know for a fact that there has never been an heir for Coxtown in the direct family ever since.[6]

❖❖

Martin Donoghue, Ryleen, New Ross, Co. Wexford, a native of Ballinasloe, Co. Galway

Another day he [Martin Donoghue's grandfather] was driving home from town in company with his landlord. They met on the way a member of the Board of Guardians, and delayed to talk.

'Well,' said the landlord, 'are they dying fast?'

'Oh,' said the Guardian, 'they are dying so fast we can scarcely bury them.'

'That's good. That's good,' said the landlord.[7]

❖❖

J. O'Kane, Dromore National School, Dromore West, Co. Sligo

I was told how Jones of Woodhill prosecuted three women for gathering up the tops and ends of the turnips left in the turnip field after the turnips were pulled, before being put into pits or brought into the yard. I was told it was common to see women and even men in the turnip fields gathering and taking home the tops and bottoms of the turnips cut off when the turnips were pulled and cleaned.

Ormsby gave orders to his men, it seems, that they were not to be 'too careful' about the cuttings of the tops and bottoms of the turnips, so that a share of turnips might be left attached to stem and leaves, and to the root, for the hungry who came to gather them.

Jones on the other hand gave orders that nothing was to be left. I was told that a man found stealing a turnip or turnips on Jones's land was shot dead by him or some of his employees.

Ormbsy owned a great portion of the land of this district. If the bread winner of a family died, I was told that he never asked for rent from the widow until a son or somebody else was able to take the place of the bread winner. If a tenant owed him £20 in rent, he often accepted £5 as a total payment. He had very few evictions. The result was that he and his tenants were always on good terms. But with the rent the tenants were obliged to do 'duty-work', to give so many days in each month gratis.

There was another landlord here, an absentee for part of the year, a Colonel Howley. He periodically, I was told, visited the houses of his tenants to inspect them. When he found them dirty or required white-washing, he paid for lime to have the work done.[8]

❧❧

Edward McGrane, b.1857, Ballintra, Co. Donegal

Some resident landlords did much to help the sufferers not only among their own tenantry but also those of adjoining estates, the landlords of which were mostly absentees, with no interest in those occupying the land beyond that of collecting the rents.

One landlord of the resident class who did much good at the time of the Famine, as well as in the years before and afterwards, was Mr John Hamilton of Brownhall and St Eunans, who at that time was an active man 45 years of age. He died in 1854 and is buried in the crypt of the Protestant Church in Ballintra.

John Hamilton often spoke of his experiences of the Great Famine in the district where he lived.

Speaking of 1845 he has often said that up to the summer of that year things were looking bright with cheering signs of success apparent on all sides, but in the autumn appeared the harbinger of the black Famine years 1846, 1847 and 1848. According to his observations, the potato crop, though not wholly destroyed in 1845, was in greater part but a decayed mass.

He saw that the advent of famine meant the vanishing of rent paying and that the evil threatened to be of much greater magnitude and longer duration than that of 1831, seven years before the establishment of the Union Workhouses.

He was of the opinion that for the people to enter these places, or to live solely upon alms meant demoralisation, in that it destroyed feelings of self-respect, independence and industry.

When the soup-kitchens and other temporary measures of relief appeared in the district John Hamilton had thought out a scheme to employ people at works on the land, by the improvement of which they could earn wages of immediate benefit to themselves and of permanent benefit to the district.

In the winter of 1846–47 he began relief works with money advanced through the Board of Public Works. This not only gave employment to the poor on his own estate but to those of neighbouring ones as well.

An absentee landlord had an estate adjoining on which there was a population of nearly 10,000 who did nothing at all in the way of trying to relieve their wants and threw the entire burden upon the public authorities or those, like Mr Hamilton, who chose to exert themselves.

Drainage works were started by him in the winter of 1846–47 and he calculated to have them finished by the autumn of 1850 but, as the government failed to pay the instalments of advance on the times agreed on, he was involved in a series of difficulties and then the government availing itself of an ex-post facto Act of Parliament demanded repayment from April 1848.

This upset all his plans. He had to raise money on short notice in a time of panic and had to dispose of produce and cattle by forced sales to meet the engagements which he had entered into on the faith of the government.

One Saturday in the winter of 1846, with snow lying deep on the ground, a gang of poor hungry roadworkers turned up in the town of Donegal expecting payment, but the government official, who was a young artillery officer, told them he had received no money for them. His job was to take the accounts from the various gangers and send them on to Dublin before payments would be sanctioned, and in this case the workers would have to wait another week before the money came along.

The crowd were in despair when this was made known to them. They had been working in starvation all the week, hoping to obtain some relief with the money which they expected would turn up at the end of it, but the officer could do nothing to help them.

Mr John Hamilton of St Eunan's, who then came on the scene, put forward the suggestion that he would advance the money to pay the men, and when their wages came along from Dublin in the course of the following week the money could be handed to him. The official was agreeable to this and very much relieved that an awkward situation was got over so easily.

Mr Hamilton then borrowed some £40 from shopkeepers in the town and the roadworkers were paid, but when this arrangement was made known to the head officials in Dublin they sent a sharp reprimand to their local man in charge for the irregularity of the proceedings. He was ordered to pay the men, and their good Samaritan never received a penny of a refund from official quarters.

The men, however, agreed to pay him themselves, and one of their number was appointed to collect a certain amount every week until the money would be paid up. All but a small sum was forthcoming in the end, as some of the men died soon after before the debt was discharged.[9]

⁂

Michael Corduff, The Lodge, Rossport, Ballina, Co. Mayo

There was yet another very important fact which came to the aid of the local people. Up to 1844 or 1845, the landlord of Rossport, Samuel Bournes lived near Kilalla some 35 miles distant. Samuel Bournes decided to come and live in Rossport where presumably he considered he would be in a better position to look after his estate. The dominant factor in Mr Bournes' preference for the site selected was the depth of water of the estuary at this particular spot suitable for landing of ships.

During the progress of the erection of the 'Big House' as it was locally called, and is so even to the present day, the reclamation of the land in its immediate vicinity, the construction of landing facilities for shipping, and the numerous other works incidental to such a large scale operation, all the able-bodied tenants were employed. In the first place they were compelled to give their twelve 'laethantaí dulgais' 'duty days' free. This was an additional labour levy to the rent and was enforced by all resident landlords. Apart from the 'twelve days' the tenants received a wage of eight pence a day, which labour was accepted in lieu of rent according to circumstances.

The settling of the Bournes in Rossport took place about the year 1846. It was about the beginning of the 'Bad Times' and though it seems somewhat unorthodox to record written encomiums on Irish landlords as a rule, yet it has been conceded on all sides that Samuel Bournes was a generous and a charitable man. Whatever his motives, he was indeed a philanthropist. He preserved the people of a large area, not merely his own tenants but those of adjoining estates also, from the rigours and starvation caused by the Famine in other parts of the country.

In addition to the development works instituted by Mr Bournes at Rossport, he was also instrumental in procuring food – Indian meal and loaf bread – for the people. It is said that this relief was obtained from a Quaker Society. Hookers plied between Rossport and Westport, Sligo and even England and Scotland, if the story is true, carrying cargoes of meal (Indian), 'min bhuí', and other food stuffs for the stricken population.

In 1847 (approximately) there was instituted at the Big House at Rossport a huge iron cauldron which people used to call the boiler. On this boiler a number of men were in constant attendance, cooking stirabout and doling out the cooked article to all destitute people who called for food and so people came regularly every day to partake of an allowance of the 'broohan'. People came from far and near to have their hunger allayed, but the landlord's tenantry who were working for him had first preference on the relief meal and stirabout, and so the fame of Rossport as a food centre spread throughout a large part of Mayo. Consequently there were incursions of numerous individuals and families into Rossport which became the Mecca for the food-seeking pilgrims from places as far apart as Castlebar and Ballina.

In Rossport there is an old Irish expression born of the relief food doled out and distributed to be carried home by emissaries. The saying is applied to a person who is impatient for something, usually for food, for instance, by a hungry child home from school. 'Bíodh foighid agat agus tiocfaidh do chuid ón Teach Mór chugat'. 'Have patience and your share of food will come from the Big House to you'.[10]

❧

Séamus Reardon, b.1873, Boulteen, Eniskeane, Co. Cork

I must say they [the landlords] were not all alike. My grandfather, God rest his soul, went to pay part of his rent to his landlord, he was a Bantry man.

'Feed your family first, then give me what you can afford when times get better,' he told him.

So when times improved there was two years rent due on the majority of the small farms and very little hope of paying it later. This was a serious matter for the poor landlords. The rich landlords could afford to lose a little.[11]

⁜⁜

Ned Buckley, Knocknagree, Co. Cork

The fact that our people escaped so well was owed to the landlord of the time, Mr Cronin Coltsman. He earned the everlasting gratitude of the people. When he saw the awful plight of the people, his tenants, he caused a mill to be built half a mile below our village, and the place of the mill was also used as a courthouse and was 'the courthouse' until about twenty years ago. The little river called Awnnaleinga Bawna still washes its old walls. The water of this stream was dammed up a mile eastward towards Knockeenagullane and the millstream was dug and prepared to bring water to turn the mill and ever since there is very little trace of the millstream's course. The fields of different farmers through which the millstream ran are called the milleens. When the mill was ready the landlord, Cronin Coltsman, bought the Indian meal in Cork City and got his tenants to go with their horses and bring the meal free of charge to the mill where, when it was ground, everyone who needed it got a measure or scoop of meal for each one of their family.

There was a caretaker or steward over the distribution of the meal. He was John B. Cronin, commonly known as Johnny Batt, who died about fifty years ago at the age of 99. I knew him well.

He was also Clerk of the Petty Sessions Court which was held in a room adjoining the mill.

This man had great influence at that time and a good word from him often meant an extra scoop of meal to some happy family. His youngest daughters, about 80 years of age, live in the courthouse still.[12]

❧❧

Kilmaine (Kilcummon), Co. Mayo, from P.J. Walshe,
national teacher, Cloghans Hill National School, Tuam, Co. Galway

There was one landlord, or rather, lady, Baroness De Clifford, daughter I think of the Duke of Bedford, on whose property no eviction ever took place. People who were evicted by Irish landlords came into her estate and were allowed to build in the bog and wastelands. The De Cliffords were English. They purchased property from the Kerwins and were model landlords, kind, charitable and good to their tenants. Their mansion, now derelict, was for a time the Columban's College.[13]

❧❧

Conchubhar Mac Suibhne, Aughrim, Co. Wicklow

The local landowners were wealthy and ruled as benevolent despots. Evictions were almost unknown under the Fitzwilliam of Meath estates. There were some small landowners who, trying to keep up with the earls, were poor and or harsh with their tenants: Revel, Ram, Whaley and one or two more.[14]

❧❧

John D. O'Leary, Lynedaowne, Rathmore, Kerry

The local landlords, I believe, helped the poor in the towns and the farmers certainly helped their poor neighbours. Priests helped everyone. In fact, owing to low rents and a good supply of corn, this area was one of the most fortunate. A landlord named Freeman Dave of Castle Cor, Kanturk is believed to have given all he had to feed the poor. His property was sold after the Famine.[15]

William Keane, b.1891, a farmer, Ballingrenia, Moate,
Co. Westmeath

When Sir Richard Nagle died, Rosemount House and 450 acres fell to his nephew John Nugent of Jamestown Court. Sir Richard had nothing at his death in 1852. Every acre he had was heavily mortgaged. The Nagles had a People's Bank. All that money was lost when Sir Richard was defeated in the last election. Jack Reilly has a receipt for money deposited by his grandfather.[16]

Pilib Ó Conaill, national teacher, Main Street, Kilfinane, Kilmallock,
Co. Limerick, b.1878, Wilkinstown, Navan, Co. Meath

You can imagine the wealth of corn produced on these big fields all over Meath, but just as the land did not belong to the people, neither could they control the crops or corn which grew upon it. It is a matter of common knowledge that famine conditions spread among the workers of England and that food prices ran to exhorbitant heights. Corn prices began to go up and up. Corn was sold for high prices and was sent to England where the money was to pay for it. Black-marketeers, in the shape of big farmers, landlords, shopkeepers and gombeen men started to store and hold up corn in hopes of a still further rise. People like our family and others at the time that grew some corn could get it ground at the local mills, and in this were independent of the ruling price.[17]

Richard Delaney, b.1874, master mariner, Wexford Town

Although people died there was plenty of food in the country. Corn was stored in Wexford Town at the time and in Briens of Coolmaine. The corn at Coolmaine was for Power's Distillery, and the corn was drawn out to Dublin though there was famine.[18]

Martin Manning, b.1875, Carrowholly, Kilmeena, Westport, Co. Mayo

In the year 1847 fourteen schooners of about 200 tons each left Westport Quay laden with wheat and oats for to feed the English people while the Irish were starving. This happened one morning on one tide and was repeated several times during the Famine. The corn had to be sold to satisfy the landlords whose rents were very high then.[19]

Tomás Aichir, b.1859, a farmer, Coill a Tonna, Kilmaley, Ennis, Co. Clare

The foods during the Famine were Indian corn and Indian meal but sad to say, a shipload of American corn coming would pass a shipload of Irish corn going out of Ireland to England – corn which they had to sell to pay the landlord's rent and escape losing their homes and their all.[20]

Séamus Reardon, b.1873, Boulteen, Eniskeane, Co. Cork

The Young Ireland movement at the time, of which there were many staunch supporters in these districts but no active body, advocated the breaking up of the roads to prevent the carting of wheat to the quaysides. This was not done, for as I said, the people were not united at the time.

The landlords on the other hand, knowing that if the harvest was not exported they could not get their rents, so they saw to it that with the exception of seed for the following year, the wheat was sent away. If the people starved, all the better.[21]

❧❧

William (Bill) Powell, b.1869, Eniskeane, Co. Cork

Yes, the Famine was man-made. It was our rulers that saw to it that our food was shipped away to England from us, and left the people here starving.

There was no one to 'talk'. The men in power were all Protestants, men that could get enough for themselves and their families no matter what came. They were in league with England and it was their delight to see the population decreasing by the thousands dying with hunger and what followed.[22]

❧❧

Mrs Peter Stafford, b.1895, Delvin, Co. Westmeath

I often heard it said by the old people that a lot of the flour that came as relief from America, was stored in Athlone and that it was not given out at all and had to be thrown into the Shannon afterwards, as it went bad from being kept so long.[23]

❧❧

*F. Corbett, b.1874, whose father was from Cork
and his mother from Tipperary*

Victoria sent £50 to relieve the Irish, at the same time, 1847, The Grand National Race Course was being laid down outside Liverpool and the same Victoria gave £5,000 towards the project.[24]

❧❧

Peter Clarke, b.1872, Usker, Bailieboro, Co. Cavan

I heard my father saying that the government didn't allow the Indian meal to come in until it was too late. I heard my father saying that how 'generous' Queen Victoria was that what relief she allowed would come to about quarter of what was needed by the starving people.[25]

❧❧

14

Agents, Grabbers and Gombeen Men

❖❖

Many absentee Irish landlords rented their estates or parts of them to wealthy farmers and to resident middlemen. These middlemen often sub-let their land in small holdings to farmers at higher rents. At the bottom were the landless labourers who provided labour to the farmers in exchange for a patch of ground to build a house and grow potatoes.

When the blight struck it was these very poor who were worst hit by the loss of their crop. But the effect of the loss of food and labour had an effect up the line as well and this increased financial difficulties for the middlemen who often failed to collect their rents and were therefore unable to pay their own rents to the landlords. If they were evicted their tenants were also casualties, as the landlords had no contract with them.

Among those who took advantage of the Famine and the cheap price of land were members of the old landed and professional elites who had the money to speculate. Many others who benefited were strong farmers who managed to get their neighbours' lands cheap when they died, emigrated or were forced to sell their small holdings for badly needed cash. This caused lasting resentment as these 'grabbers' were seen as having taken advantage of their neighbours' misfortune to increase their own holdings.

Some gombeen men were also greatly resented for gaining land from those less fortunate when they demanded people's land as payment for failure to repay debts incurred during the Famine.

❖❖

Ned Buckley, Knocknagree, Co. Cork

Between Knocknagree and Cullen in Meenagloherane townland

there are so many ruined 'botháns' [hovels] and 'fothrachs' [ruins] as to give people the impression that the place must have been alive with people a century ago, old ditches, old trees, old haggards and half-dead trees, that a whole community must have dwelt there in pre-Famine days.

All the townland was only one farm about the Famine days and I've often heard tell of a man named Denis O'Sullivan, nicknamed Donagh an Coopla, who grabbed the whole townland in the bad times and it was said of him that he evicted 16 poor people and quenched 16 fires and tumbled down 16 houses with his own hands on a certain day in the Famine times. It was cruel heartless work but it was usual in those days.

There's neither trace nor tiding of those poor people or of any of those who came after them today. There's no great luck following the kin of Denis O'Sullivan too, as the people say. No invader could be more heartless than some of the peoples' own neighbours whose only ambition was to come by land and to drive the people from their homes to starve or to die.

Denis O'Sullivan's great grandchildren live there today but hold only a third part of the farm he came by, and his son, Eugene O'Sullivan, died insane in Cork Mental Hospital about 50 years ago.

I often heard that the old man was cursed by each and all of his victims whom he left homeless and houseless.[1]

✥✥

Mick Kelly, b.1878, Streamstown, Co. Westmeath, living at Gartley, Castletown-Geoghan, a shopkeeper and postmaster in Streamstown P.O. He heard this account from his father, b.1830

There were 70 families evicted in the Woods of Carn in the Bad Times, in 1847 I'm sure. The Sheerins were hasping the doors before the people were well outside the door. They were paid for that. That is how the Sheerins are all big farmers now around there, with three big slated houses that you see near the Railway Line as you go on to Jamestown.[2]

❧❧

*P.J. McNamara, b.1895, national teacher, Boys' National School,
Newmarket on Fergus, Co. Clare*

Many people who are today strong farmers in the district acquired
their holdings at the time or perhaps later. Many of them were
acquired because they acted as 'touts' or sycophants to the local
landlord or his agent.[3]

❧❧

Thomas O'Flynn, John Melody, Attymass, Ballina, Co. Mayo

There were thirteen estates in the parish but eleven were
administered by agents who did not even reside in the parish but
their absence did not benefit the tenants. On the contrary their
subagents, bailiffs etc. were cruel, though Catholic and of the
people themselves. One bailiff took the roof off his brother's
house, although the latter, his wife and family were inside and
refused to quit.

There were no merchants in the parish, but in the town of
Ballina many were forced to close their premises due to loss of
trade. They became very poor and resorted to begging in the
country. Others took to robbery as a means of living and added
greater hardship to the poverty-stricken country folk.[4]

❧❧

Liam P. Mac Coiligh, Moate, Co. Westmeath

In Rahin (Co. Offaly) neighbourhood, near Tullamore, an
eviction occurred shortly after the Famine. A Protestant family of
three brothers and a hunchback sister took over the farm which
was of considerable size and use, and set to work it under police
protection, for those people's action was unpopular locally.
Nothing occurred for a time and the police withdrew but the

brothers continued to take every precaution for their safety. They had their windows steel-shuttered, slept with pistols under their heads, had a man-trap (a hole into which an intruder would fall) inside front and back door etc. Time passed and one day as one brother and the sister were working in the house a 'beggar woman' came to the door asking alms. When 'she' got her chance she shot the brother dead. At the same time the other brothers were out ploughing some distance from the house, when another 'beggar woman' came into the field and asked leave to pick up the potatoes turned up by the plough. This permission she got and when the brothers passed up the field 'she' shot both dead, although they had a pistol stuck in the handle of the plough.

As for the sister, she was sent to some friends near Moate and her son is still living, a well-to-do-farmer in Moate neighbourhood. (Names would serve no useful purpose here.)[5]

⋅⁂⋅

Thomas O'Flynn, John Melody, Attymass, Ballina, Co. Mayo

Some local families were unaffected by the Famine or at least they managed to live. These mostly composed the agents of the landlords – bailiffs, bog-rangers, wood-rangers, game-keepers, hands etc. Not only did they manage to live but they got large tracts of land adjoining their own, when holdings were forsaken by those who emigrated.

A local landlord has a farm of about 200 acres and practically half of this was in the possession of seasonal tenants before the Famine. A good deal of this is small fields, some not bigger than the usual 'cabbage garden'.

Millers were supposed to be the best off in the period. They held a quarter of the grain they received for distribution to beggars. There were five grinding mills in the parish, four in one townland which has yet the reputation of being best off in '46, '47. The upper class had one ambition in those days, to marry the miller's daughter, as she had a good fortune.[6]

❖❖❖

*Fred Bell, a farmer, b.1902, Ballingrenia, Rosemound, Moate,
Co. Westmeath*

The Bannons, landlords near Ballymahon, were a bad lot. The Malones of Shingles beyond Ballymore were very good landlords, never evicted anyone. Russell that bought Lisanode, Fred Russell's father, was only an agent. He offered the landlord a higher rent than the tenants were paying him and got that estate in his own name. The first thing he did when he got possession was to evict all the old tenants. This took place back in those days, in the '50s or so.[7]

❖❖❖

Ned Buckley, Knocknagree, Co. Cork

In my young day I used to hear old people discuss the awful cruelty practised by farmers who were fairly well-off against the poorer and less comfortable neighbours. The people who were old when I was young, I'm 66, were never tired of discussing how some of those, taking advantage of the poverty of their neighbours, used to offer the rent of their farms to the landlord, the rent which the owners could not pay, and grab their farms adding some to their own farms.

I used to hear how back in Bawnard on the Kerry side of the Blackwater, how old Johnny Mahony paid the rent and grabbed the farm of old Owen Casey, without poor Casey knowing a bit about it. Mahony just paid the year's rent, got a receipt for same and came home, with his own hands doing the bailiff and evicted himself, turned out poor Casey and his wife from their house and home. Poor Casey had the spring work done, the oats and potatoes sat, but had to leave them all. The garden grew and the time came when the spuds were fit to dig and the woman who helped to get them, Mrs Casey, came one morning to dig her breakfast of the praties she herself and her husband had sown, but old Mahony came at her and beat her and broke her spade and broke her hand and sent her off without anything for the breakfast. The old people use tell how no luck ever attended the Mahony family after and now there's no one belonging to them in the place, and they pointed out a lot more of people who came by farms in this way whose families melted away and of whom there is no trace to this day. Several people would be glad if the Famine times were altogether forgotten so that the cruel doings of their forebears would not be again renewed and talked about by neighbours.[8]

❧❧

William Doudigan (O'Dowd), b.1863, Redbray, Tullaghan,
Co. Leitrim

The landlords were not counted a bad lot in these parts though, as a rule, were fairly exact and had to be paid the rent in money or kind. But the agents were the mischief makers and always out to make the most of every situation to feather their own nests.[9]

❧❧

Gerald Fitzmaurice, improvements and drainage inspector,
Knockrour, Scartaglen, Co. Kerry

The homeless were numerous, so numerous that some people kept dangerous dogs. Evictions were rare as nothing was gained by evicting people. The local landlords were only like the tenants themselves. They had a few townlands under a head rent and when the tenants failed, they failed. The people wouldn't be too bad but for the middlemen. They had to get a pig every year. 'Nonger Pork' was the name given to the middleman's pig.[10]

❧❧

Mairtín Breathnach, Inistioge, Co. Kilkenny

Hugh Green, landlord of Fiddaun, Kilkieran, Brittas and Cappa took advantage of the poverty of the people. He evicted families wholesale. His one aim seemed to have been to clear the peasants out of his property, at least out of the fertile portions of it.

The landlords were not always to be blamed when evictions took place. Middle-men and well-to-do farmers [were] very often responsible. 'Grabbing' was quite common in the district. Farmers who had any money to spare were only too ready to approach the landlord or his agent and offer to pay back the rent on a neighbouring farm on condition they would be given possession. Sometimes landlords were asked to dispossess tenants from holdings, the rents of which were fully paid up.[11]

❧❧

Thomas Ashe, b.1862, a water bailiff, Cill Chrois, Inistioge, Co. Kilkenny

Merchants were by no means charitably disposed towards the poor or those who were unable to pay cash for purchases. If a man were unable to pay for his goods, he should secure two solvent friends as sureties. If the account were not settled by an arranged time, the sum of a shilling would be added to the bill every month that would elapse until the bill would be paid. Should the debtor be unable to pay, his sureties would be responsible. If sureties could not be procured, oftentimes the owner had to mortgage his farm. Many small farmers lost their homes and lands in this way. A merchant named Cody, Inistioge, secured a number of small farms in this manner. The Cody family is now dissolved.[12]

❧❧

William Torrens, b.1872, Lisminton, Ballintra, Co. Donegal.
He heard it from his father, William Torrens, 1828–1912

Protestants in general over the parish at large were in better circumstances in the 'hungry forties' than their Catholic neighbours and pulled through the difficult times of a century ago comparatively lightly.

Numbers of them were not slow to take advantage of the difficulties which the stress of the times brought on those of the other faith and were out to buy anything of value for a trifling sum, ranging from land to personal effects.[13]

❧❧

Micheál Mac Carthaigh, b.1891, a farmer, Cnocán an Mhuilinn,
Sneem, Co. Kerry

There is an old ruin to the north of the house here and there is another old ruin in Myles' Matthew's [Ó Súilleabháin] place, a man named 'Blanket' Mac Amhlaoibh lived there.

Myles Matthew told me that he heard old people saying that he (Blanket) went to Cork and bought a blanket, [and as he was on his way home] a snowstorm came and he put on the blanket. That's why he was called Blanket Mac Amhlaoibh.

Blaud owned the cnocán [little hill] that time and he had an agent. Darby Connell, a sort of an agent.

Blaud had turnips and a son of Blanket's used to go down this way and down by the sea, a half-naked creature and the rest of them starving at home. He used to pull the turnips and eat them, and come up this way again and bring some of them home to the rest.

One evening the Darby [Connell] happened to be passing this way, and there was a man of the Connors with him from the village here. They saw this poor half-naked fellow coming up by the river. Darby asked Connor who he was. He told him. 'Oh, by gor, he's the man that's stealing the master's turnips.'

He called him over and he pulled a root of furze and started beating him on the naked limbs until Connor had to tell him to stop.

He went home and took the bed and died, and Connell died too soon afterwards and got a bad death too, he fell off a stairs in a public house in Sneem.

The agency was gone. His wife and children had to go begging and he had three daughters imbeciles. 'Blanket' moved down to the Oyster Bed and he built a little shack there, and the times were improving. Connell's wife and family came begging to him. He wanted to give them a bad send off but his wife said 'return good for evil' ['maith in aghaidh an oilc']. She gave them a dish of potatoes and sent them off. The ruins of 'Blanket's' house is still there and there is another old ruin near it.[14]

⁘⅋⅋⁘

Mrs Concannon, b.1852, Carnagur, Dunmore, Co. Galway

Roddy Kieley of Carrowkeel was a most severe agent for Blakes of Carraroe. He once summoned a hungry man for pulling a turnip. Local people killed and tarred cattle on Roddy from time to time in revenge. Apparently they blackened their faces to avoid recognition. A servant girl who worked for Roddy Kieley was joking a servant boy of same and blackened his face with polish. He is said to have no connection with cattle stealing. He was arrested shortly after leaving Kieley's and later convicted and hanged.

Kieley was called as a witness for the defence and he said that the only 'character' he could give him was that his mother once stole a turkey from him. Some people say she stole it from hunger, others say she didn't steal it at all. All however blamed Roddy for his death as he was in a position to clear him and they say that as a punishment for this his tyrannical career was ended by a fall from his carriage outside my great-grandfather's house in Carrantrola.[15]

⁘⅋⅋⁘

Tomás Aichir, b.1859, a farmer, Coill a Tonna, Kilmaley, Ennis,
Co. Clare

Old Marcus Keane who was an agent for the landlord carried out a lot of evictions in Kilmaley (agent for Westby and Connyngham estates). Westby gave a present of Knockstona and Rathcoona to Old Marcus Keane. Old Marcus Keane married Westby's daughter. Denis Lynch and Thomas Kinane were evicted out of Kilcolumb by Marcus Keane. There were several curses from widows. A lot of people evicted in Kilmaley went to Sydney and America. Old Marcus Keane was buried in a vault in Kilmaley. His coffin and that of Miss Barnes were taken by night and thrown outside the wall. They were reinterred afterwards at the back of Beechpark near Ennis where his son, another Marcus Keane, lived. Old Gurbary Keane was thrown into a bog-hole in Drimanure by Michael Connors of Drimatehy for being doing bog-ranging for Old Marcus Keane. Soup-kitchens were being run for Old Marcus Keane in west Clare and perhaps in Kilmaley too, on condition that you renounced your faith.[16]

❖❖

Mrs Fitzsimons, b.1875, Sheepstown, Delvin, Co. Westmeath

There was a man called Manning lived in Turin, about four miles from Delvin, he used to charge very high rents during the Famine and the tenants were not able to pay as they were very poor. A man named Heffernan lay in ambush for him one day and shot him. The tenants cut him up in pieces and threw him in a hole.[17]

❖❖

Seán Ó Domhnaill, b.1873, Scairt na nGleobhrán, Ballylooby,
Cahir, Co. Tipperary

Lord Waterpark had a storehouse built beside our village in which he stored corn and other farm produce that he confiscated from his tenants as payment for their rents. Waterpark's agent, O'Brien, looked after the sale of the confiscated goods. This agent is still remembered in our parish for his infamous treatment of the absentee landlord's tenants.

A Quaker settler, Jackson by name, was kinder to his neighbours. He does not appear to be a landlord. He spoke Irish fluently and helped the Famine victims by giving them plots of potatoes and free milk.

A further incident which happened about 1852 illustrated the harshness of the masters of the people in those days. My great grandfather and great-grandmother were employed by an estate agent Jellico to gather weeds in cishes [ciseáin: baskets] as a method of cleaning up his land. Jellico stood by watching the operations. In the evening they had collected a few small potatoes [criocháin] for themselves. He, having seen this, harshly ordered them to forfeit these seemingly useless potatoes. They received 4d. each per day.

On another occasion he granted them, with other workmen, a half-day to go to Cahir town to see the execution of two men who had been convicted of stealing some timber from a local wood. 'Twill teach ye to obey the law', he remarked.[18]

⁂

Michael Corduff, The Lodge, Westport, Ballina, Co. Mayo

During the time of the Great Famine, a century ago, there lived in the townland of Kilgalligan a landlord's bailiff who was known by the name of Jack Mór a Raighailligh. Like his neighbours, he was a small farmer and used to have some tillage. Like most of the bailiffs of his kind he was an oppressor and with sternness he dominated and exercised his despotism over the community amongst who he lived. People speak in scathing terms of landlords in the past and not without much justification in may cases, but my opinion is they were not half as bad as the native hirelings in their employment and Jack Mór it appears was one of the worst of his ilk.

There was a widow in the village whose husband had only died recently and she had two little orphan boys. The father had died indirectly of starvation, for in these days the primitive and scanty nature of the people's food was unable to sustain life in numerous cases for long. The two children were one day discovered by the bailiff on his land searching for stray potatoes in the soil called 'prátaí romhair' [digging potatoes]. These were potatoes which having escaped the digger the previous season, grew up again, but they were invariably of very inferior quality and were only fed to animals. Of course, in the time of the Famine people would eat almost anything and these two children were out to procure the makings of a 'cast' to roast in the ashes for themselves, but the merciless bailiff soon put an end to their operations. He seized the two children and brought them to his house, and secured them to the cow's stake at the end of the kitchen, he then returned to his work in the field, having told his wife not to release the children until he would come back to his midday meal. She was making stirabout and it is said she gave some of it to eat to the two children in the absence of the husband. The plight of the two children owing to their cruel captivity and fear was extremely sad. Their mother came to the house of their confinement and begged their release, but the woman of the house who was kind and charitable, and the direct opposite of her haughty and wicked husband, was afraid to incur her husband's displeasure by letting the children go. The mother then went to the field where the bailiff was working and begged for the children's release. Instead of showing any sympathy or mercy for the poor woman in her woe, he merely threatened to do the same to herself and that there was further punishment awaiting the two boys on his return to the house.

She told him to do his wickedest and perhaps he would repent of his cruelty sooner than he expected. On reaching home she went through all of the prescribed formalities of the widow's curse and on her knees she exercised her incantations for evil on her enemy, the bailiff.

Before the appointed time for returning for his dinner Jack Mór was seized with a severe pain in his side, so he had to return to the house and lie on his bed writhing in agony.

In the consternation which followed in the household consequent on the suffering of the man of the house, no attention was paid to the chained boys and one of them managed to release himself and his brother. When leaving the house one of them said to the other 'Now, thank God, we are free, but neither God, man nor devil will ever release you'.

The suffering man sent for the woman whom he had injured and begged her forgiveness, but she merely said she would leave him to God to deal with him, as he was only reaping the fruits of his bad deeds. He died in a few hours.

Many misdeeds could be quoted against him. He even used to intercept the fishermen and compel them hand over to him any quantity of fish which he demanded.[19]

⁂

Mrs Fitzsimons, b.1875, Sheepstown, Delvin, Co. Westmeath

There was a man called Morgan living in Killallon during the Famine. He used to sell the meal to the poor at a cheap rate, and often gave it to them for nothing. The meal mongers did their best to get him to sell it to them but he said he would not, that he wanted it for the poor of Killallon. They asked him nine or ten times to sell it to them but he would not. They watched him one day and shot him. He is buried in Killua graveyard.

There was a man named Connell living at Robinstown, Kilskyre, about seven miles from Delvin. He used to sell meal very cheap to the poor people during that time. The meal mongers used to be very vexed with him because he would not sell the meal to them. They gathered together one Sunday and watched Connell going home from Kilskyre mass with his sister, and pulled him off the cart and beat him to death with blackthorn sticks, and one of them put his fist through Connell's stomach.

Meal mongers were men who used to buy meal and corn from the farmers during the Famine. They would then sell it out in stones and half-stones to the poor people and charge very high prices for it.[20]

✤

*Mrs Kate O'Carroll, b.1877, native of Mullingar, Co. Westmeath,
living in Bailieboro, Co. Cavan*

My grandmother showed me a house outside Mullingar, from
which a poor widow was evicted at the time of the Famine. She
wasn't able to pay her rent, and one day she was cooking the
children's dinner in a pot that was hanging from a pot hook over
the fire. The old bailiff came in and took the pot off the fire.

'Oh,' says she, 'let me boil the children's dinner.'

'No,' says he, and he flung the pot out of the door, and he put
the widow and children out as well. My grandmother told me
that, after his death, he was seen going about that road with the
pot-hooks hanging around his neck.[21]

✤

*From a manuscript by Donnchadh (an Céama) Ó Loinsigh,
a schoolmaster, Cúil Iarthach, Ballyvourney, Co. Cork*

Charles Colthurst (in Ballyvourney) agent who doubled rents in
1840, were never paid. He became insane. Joe, his brother, built
public house and bakery attached. Grinding mill for tenants and
a tucking mill besides by landlord. Joe and family left. A Scotch
family was imported, another premises given them. Consisted of
three brothers, named Peter, Robert and John, with two sisters,
Mrs Hauge with daughter, and Anne.

Peter and Anne received public house and grinding-mill with
shop. They were Presbyterians but attended Protestant service.

Chisolms gave credit all round and kept many from starving.
None died of hunger. Landlord borrowed money from Board of
Works and gave employment in building farmyard, making farm
roads, erecting fences between townlands on the 'give and take'
system, straightened boundaries, hillsides adjacent to roads were
planted with trees. All the work done at 4d. per day, after
increased to 8d.

Coachroad to Killarney and road to Kenmare made by Grand Jury. Superintended by O'Duffy. Two public restaurants.

In the meantime the farmer and cottier were evicted for non-payment of rent, or else were flying to different places. Emigration was in full swing, old families scattered. The gombeen man, the conacre man, the well-to-do neighbour watching the opportunity to add to his farm. Small cottiers were done away with and became the labourers of another day. All this was effected under the aegis of Harry Grod, the rent-warner who took care to see himself rewarded by presents in various ways.[22]

⁕⁕

Thomas Flynn, b.1860, a farmer, Carntulla, Ballinaglera,
Carrick-on-Shannon, Co. Leitrim

There were a few 'gombeen men' who charged the poor pound for pound but this priest, Fr Keaney P.P. brought it down to 2/6 'under pain of absolution'.

The method by which the usurer got his interest was as follows: the person in need of a pound in spring or summer went around to these gombeen men and found out which would give the highest price at November following for a firkin of butter. The gombeen man agreed to allow a certain amount for the butter in lieu of the pound lent. But it often happened that a firkin was worth £6 at November so that the lender had a very high interest indeed on his money. The priest stopped this abuse.[23]

⁕⁕

Thomas Whyte, b.1880, a farmer, Cappa, Inistioge, Co. Kilkenny

An Inistioge boatman named Billy Sinnott owed a shopkeeper named Laurence Meaney for a bag of meal. Laurence was engaged one day in the unloading of a boat containing goods for himself and other merchants. It chanced that in the course of the work he overbalanced and fell into the water. He was unable to swim and would have been drowned but for the timely aid given by the boatman who owed him the money. Regardless of this Meaney prosecuted him.

Murphys, Ballyneale, Tullogher parish owned a mill at this time where the yellow meal corn was ground for the people of the district. In many cases the poor were unable to pay for the meal. After very short notice, Murphys seized on the pots and pans of the unfortunate people in payment for the meal, thereby leaving them without any means of cooking any food.

Those who were wronged in this manner cursed the Murphy family. The effects of the curse remained for two or three generations. Members of the family were maimed or disfigured in some manner or other.[24]

⁂

Seán Ó Beirne, Malin, Inishowen, Co. Donegal

A man named Bonar in the Culkeeny area who gave out money 'a trush' [on trust] had some money to get from a particular family. His son, the father was dead at the time, went to collect it and found the family making a breakfast of turnips boiled. He did not ask for the money or never tried to collect it afterwards.[25]

⁂

15

'A Terrible Levelling of Houses'

❖

It is difficult to estimate the number of people who were evicted or surrendered their holdings during the Famine or its direct aftermath. It has been estimated that, excluding peaceable surrenders, over a quarter of a million people were evicted between 1849 and 1854. The total number of people who had to leave their holdings in the period is likely to be around half a million and 200,000 smallholdings were obliterated.

After the Quarter Acre or Gregory Clause was introduced in 1847, there was a substantial rise in evictions. This clause meant that no tenant holding more than a quarter acre was eligible for public assistance, either in the poorhouse or outside it. To become eligible, a tenant had to surrender his holding to a landlord. Some Boards of Guardians extended this denial of eligibility to include the wife and children of a tenant who wouldn't surrender. This was not official government policy and neither was the practice of landlords to refuse partial surrender of the land in excess of one rood and to demand the house and all the land.

The £4 rating clause made landlords responsible for all the poor law rates for holdings valued at £4 or less and this was an added incentive to landlords to evict tenants who couldn't pay their rent. In Co. Mayo this accounted for three out of every four holdings. For many landlords to whom large amounts of rent were owed, it became a case of evict or be evicted.

When houses were not surrendered, physical force was used, often illegally, and houses were burnt down by agents or landlords. This prolonged people's suffering and distress, and saw many die from exposure.

The effects of eviction were greatly magnified in those areas which were most severely hit. It is reckoned that the western counties of Clare, Mayo, Galway and Kerry suffered one-third of all recorded evictions, while Tipperary, Limerick, Leitrim and Roscommon were also among those who suffered the most evictions.

❖❖❖

Mrs Peter Reynolds, b.1871, Ballykilcline, Kilglass, Co. Roscommon

Kilglass parish, that is this parish here, and Skibbereen were the two places in Ireland that were the worst hit during the Famine. I always heard the old people say that. There were 800 families in the parish of Kilglass before the Famine. There is not half that number now. In this townland of Ballykilcline, there were 80 families and most of them were evicted. There are only three houses in it now, and about a dozen people.[1]

❖❖❖

Mick Kelly, b.1878 at Streamstown, Co. Westmeath, living at Gartley, Castletown-Geoghan, a shopkeeper and postmaster in Streamstowm P.O. He heard this account from his father, b.1830

Sir Richard Nagle was landlord of Carn but he had to sell all his estates, and the parties coming in made him clear out the tenants. The landlords were all trying to get rid of the small tenants at that time so they insisted on the lands being cleared before they made the purchase. All Donore, 700 acres, was cleared when Sir John Ennis came in. Sir John, or Mister as he was then, took up Sir Richard Nagle's mortgages.

Old Paddy Scally was served with notice of eviction. He came over to Jamestown Court where Sir Richard was at the time and asked for Sr Richard. Sir Richard and some other gentlemen came out to the halldoor steps and Paddy challenged him over the notice. They had some conversation then Paddy said 'You won't evict me', and he stuck his hands in the pockets of his big long black coat and drew out two pistols. He flung them on the ground between them. Says he, 'Take your pick now, Sir Richard,

230

and let us settle it here and now. Let the best man win.' Sir Richard didn't take up the pistol, but the Scallys weren't evicted. The family is there beyond still, his grandson, another Paddy Scally, owns it now.

When my grandfather got the notice of eviction he wrote to Sir Richard stating his case. He got no reply. At this time Sir Richard was in Dublin in very bad health. At last my grandfather said he would go to Dublin to see him. He set out walking. It was 62 statute miles from this place to Dublin. When he got to Kilcock he met Sir Richard's funeral coming to Rosemount.

Shortly after, he got a letter from a neighbour that had been written to my grandfather by Sir Richard six months before that. It was too late then to be of any use. Sir Richard said in the letter that he would save my grandfather from eviction. We were put out in 1853 from our holding in Killeenough.[2]

⁂

Michael Gildea, b.1872, Dromore, Ballintra, Co. Donegal

The year 1849 was chiefly noted for the large number of evictions which took place in the parts of Drumholme parish. Many farmers were from two to three years in arrears, with no immediate hope of clearing them off.

On the Knox estate, which includes the southern half of the village of Ballintra and runs in a north-westerly direction towards the coast, there were dozens of people put out of their homes. There were several families in the townlands of Foyagh and Birrah in 1845 who vanished root and branch before the decade came to a close.

The usual procedure after an eviction was to burn the thatched roof to prevent the tenant from entering the house again after the bailiff and his assistants had left the scene.

A man named Diver who lived in this townland was among those who were evicted out of their homes.

The landlord himself was present on this occasion and he offered the sum of one pound to anybody who would set fire to the house.

Diver, who was standing out on the street with a number of neighbours, stepped forward and said he would earn the money. He thereupon stepped into the kitchen where some turf was still smouldering on the hearth, brought them out on a shovel and placed them among the thatch of the roof. In a few moments it was ablaze, fanned by a strong south-westerly breeze and in a short time his home was gone.

His neighbours were so amazed that they could say nothing, and they made no effort to prevent him when he climbed onto the roof, scooped out a hole, and in a short time had reduced what was once the home of himself, his father and grandfather to nothing but a few fire-scarred walls.

When the landlord tendered Diver the money which he had thus so strangely earned, he coolly put it in his pocket, turned on his heel, nodded to the neighbours and disappeared from the scene.

He lived alone and left nobody to mourn his departure. The few pieces of furniture were left to rot in the ditch, as the rest of the people around said they would not soil their hands by touching them.[3]

❖

Mrs Kate O'Carroll, b.1877, native of Mullingar, Co. Westmeath, living in Bailieboro, Co. Cavan

I heard my grandmother saying that the poor people left their homes and started walking on and on along the roads, from one place to another. They would be seen sitting on the sides of the roads and they would be begging a night's lodgings here and there, and a bit to eat. That left so many poor people on the roads. The homes were taken off some of them because they were unable to pay their rents, and more of them cleared out themselves. That was what caused the custom of poor people calling to houses looking for a night's lodgings.[4]

❖

Seán Ó Duinnshléibhe, Glenville, Fermoy, Co. Cork

Many had to take to the road and a Vagrancy Act was passed to cope with about half of the population of the district. Typhus reduced in number many of the vagrants. Jails and poorhouses were filled. The English government provided alms which the people did not want. They wanted the Repeal of the Union which would end the Famine.

Where the Irish was spoken these people suffered most as the result of the Famine. The cause was that the land was unproductive in mountainy and boggy areas where the greater population lived. They had been driven thither by plantations and evictions. Such was the case in this district and in similar districts throughout Ireland.

Those families who had land on the estate and near the village, and who struggled during the Bad Times, were offered new lands outside the demesne, so that theirs may be enclosed as part of the demesne.

Some others who had not paid up their rents were evicted to make the outlying farm beyond the demesne a complete unit in itself.[5]

❖❖❖

J. O'Kane, Dromore National School, Dromore West, Co. Sligo

There were hoards of poor on the roads every day. The Catholics who could gave some little they had to these, a saucer of oaten-meal, a 'mám' [handful] of potatoes, a drink of milk or a little sweet-milk to carry away with them. It was nothing unusual to see a woman with two, three or four children half-naked, come in begging for alms, and often several of these groups in one day, men too. If the men got work they worked for little or nothing and when they were no longer needed they took to the road again. These wandering groups had no homes and no shelter for the night. They slept in the barns of those who had barns on a 'gabháil' [armful] of straw with a sack or sacks or some such thing to cover them. Generally the wanderers were given shelter in the kitchens of small farmers. A bundle of straw or rushes was brought in at bed-time and spread on the floor of the kitchen in the corner and the wanderers slept on this.[6]

❖❖❖

Mary Daly, b.1874, a farmer, Faughart, Co. Louth, and a native of Creggan Parish, Crossmaglen, Co. Armagh

There was far more people in the country then. I mind them telling it many a time that they got threepence a day to pull down their own houses at Cross and build them into ditches. Old Barny McKenna used to tell it often that there was scores of houses fornint he's door around the time of the Famine, but the people was all thrown out, and got threepence a day to pull down their own houses.[7]

❖❖❖

Pádraig Ó Diomasaigh, b.1854, Lios a Londúin, Cill Conaidhrean, Co. Galway

After the Famine Lord Dunsandle evicted, wasn't he called Lord Leveller? From the cross at Buaicín there was terrible levelling of houses, about 40 houses. Lord Dunsandle. 'They're never tired breeding beggars', he'd say.[8]

❖❖❖

Micheál Mac Phaidín TD, Co. Donegal, in 1945

In 1845 and 1846 the failure of the potato crop, with other causes, principally illness and deaths in households, left the small farmers of Bavin in a perilous position as far as their rents were concerned. They were forced to go into arrears by circumstances over which they had no control. Their plight was welcomed by the landlord, H. Granville Murray Stewart, his agent, Mr Wilson, and his bailiffs. The landlord and his agent coveted this tract of land for its limestone soil and pasture. It would make an admirable grazing ranch.

No time would be given to the unfortunate tenants to pay off their arrears and an order for eviction was given in 1847. Tradition has it that on the day of eviction there was a violent storm, thunder and lightening and rain in torrents, the sea a roaring tempest. All nature seemed in protest. Yet that hoard of bailiffs, with Wilson at their head, descended on the homes of Bavin, threw out the people and their belongings in the storm and set the roof-trees aflame to the skies.

The families evicted were Breslins, Gallaghers, Doogans, Byrnes, Dorrians, Carr, McNelis (20 in all). For some of them the landlord provided farms on the moorland known as the Back of Bavin. Here their descendants live to this day.[9]

❖❖

Sean Crowley, b.1858, Cill Cholmáin, Eniskeane, Co. Cork

But, he said [my father],when one trouble was over they had to face another. The rent warners were out looking for two years rent. The people hadn't it. They sold everything they could sell. Some poor farmers sold even their last cow to pay something. Others couldn't pay anything. My grandfather couldn't pay anything, neither could his next door neighbours, they were Mahonys, pay anything.

They were told they would be evicted but they had hopes for the landlord [Beamish] they knew to be a good man, and he wouldn't have the heart to throw them out. He didn't, but he sold his property to the landlord known as Lord Bandon, a heartless man.

The poor tenants didn't know what was going on until one spring morning the townland was full of redcoat soldiers. From end to the other they put out every tenant in it. He often and often told how the redcoat soldier rode up on his horse to the door and asked for the man of the house. His father went out.

'We want possession of this place. You'd better clear out.'

The old man was like a man would be after getting a blow. He stood looking at the redcoat, unable to speak.

'Get to work and clear out,' was the next quick order.

'O maise, Dia linn,' [God bless us] was all the old man could say as he turned in.

It wasn't like evictions later on when the bailiff and his men would put every article of furniture outside the door and be booed and jeered by a crowd of men on the fences around. No, the soldiers stood by and made the people themselves put out the furniture and there was no one to say boo, for the sight of a redcoat struck terror into the people.

'We want the key,' says the fellow in command when the last article of furniture was out. But, God help us, there was no lock to the door. A hasp on the outside and a bar of iron from wall to wall was used to make it fast on the inside, but it was never used, the door was always unbarred, and a sod always burned on the hearth for the poor carriers to come in to light their pipes when passing, either day or night.

The old man brought out the bar and he said afterwards what he'd like to have done with it was to give the soldier a blow of it, but he didn't, he threw it towards him on the road.

'You damn swine,' muttered the soldier, as he rode off with his men to the next house.

Before the sun was gone down that evening, every tenant in that townland was homeless. It was a sad picture, my father said, to see two or three little families talking between themselves trying to console each other, and trying to plan some way out of their troubles.

The priest came. He had been called to one poor old woman that was dying on the roadside after being put out. She died there too. He went from family to family in the whole townland trying to comfort and console them. He advised them, when night would fall, to take the old people into the houses to rest there for the night, and the young men to remain and watch in case the soldiers would make another visit, and to do this until they had found some other homes.

Their cows the soldiers had driven from the lands. They wandered on the roads and remained there until the May fair in Bandon where they were sold.

'Twas a sad tale. Not one tenant ever went back to till a sod of Lisnacunna. They scattered everywhere.[10]

⁂

William Doudigan (O'Dowd), b.1863, Redbray, Tullaghan, Co. Leitrim

Michael Lorgan, about 70, from near here, told me he heard his father tell of an eviction of a widow named McNulty about 100 years ago from Upper Wardhouse, Tullaghan. His father said the landlord's men went around Wardhouse the evening before warning the people not to appear out and to blind the windows [Windows were very small, only one pane 6 or 8 inches square.] from then until ten o'clock the next morning, anyone disobeying the order to be evicted.

An old woman who had no window on her cabin, but had a small peep-hole in the back side-wall of the kitchen, looked out and saw the crowbar brigade knocking down the widow McNulty's little cabin and destroying her little plot of grain crop. The widow and her couple of children had now no home and so the neighbours gathered and put up a little one-roomed structure for them on the side of the road. It was erected in one day, partly of stone, timber and clay.[11]

⁂

Mrs Concannon, b.1852, Carnagur, Dunmore, Co. Galway

Kathleen Kelly of Carrantrola evicted all Baile Nua and they charged down to the bog in Gorteen. The stones of their houses were used in building Carrantrola 'Big House' which was only pulled down in 1940 or so.

Barrett of near Dunmore evicted a whole village from Belwell. They charged up to Clúid. He was shot, not fatally, soon afterwards by 'a small little man' called Michael Heneghan on whose head was placed £1,000. Even though the people knew it well, they never gave him away.[12]

※※

Martin Manning, b.1875, Carrowholly, Kilmeena, Westport,
Co. Mayo

Now as to evictions, everybody heard of the clearances of Kilmeena and Ruadh, also Cooboreen and Log near the Demesne [Lord Sligo's]. There were few evictions this side [Carrowholly] because 75% of the households had no land at all. They lived by labour at building Westport and laying out the Demesne. When the Famine came they had to leave, some to the emigrant ships which sailed from Pigeon Point [townland nearing Carrowholly] in those days, others locked the old cabin door and took to the road, others went to the Workhouse or to the big stores at the Quay [Westport] which were filled with starving people. Others went to England and Scotland.

The whole parish of Kilmeena was, it may be said, cleared of its peasantry. The O'Donels of Newport and the Brownes [Sligo] of Westport were the landlords. The former cleared the townlands of Kilbride, Carrowmore, Carrickaneady, Lecarow, Shandruim, Knockmoyle, Rossow, Knocknabola, Kiltyroe, while the latter cleared Knockachatton, Kilmena, Ruadh, Knockievan, Ballinlough, Shanvalley, Coolbaineen, Cnoc a Mhanloman, Log, Myra, Rossakeeran, Carrigane.

In the half-parish of Kilmeena-Kilmaclasser things were no better. Lord Lucan was landlord and he cleared with a vengeance. With the O'Donels it is said that the agents were at fault. They held out promises of substantial payments instead of the paltry sums payable to the tenant whose holding consisted only of a few acres. This led to the clearance and the making of the large farms [ranches] and the introduction of Scotch farmers into the area [Newport]: the Ormes, the Sproules, the Aitkens, the Roses, the Dicks, the Nixons. A few of the old people to this day speak to me of those agent named Bridger. When the foreigners failed, and fail they did, they brought O'Donel down with them, and when Bridger in his turn had to leave, Sir Richard O'Donel cursed him that he was the cause of banishing his good tenants.[13]

⁂

Thomas O'Flynn, John Melody, Attymass, Ballina, Co. Mayo

Evictions during the Famine were many. In one townland, Kilgellia, 14 of the 24 families were evicted the same day - O'Donnells, Conlons, Reynolds, Melodys, Folens, Walshs, Hennigans, Gintys, Gallaghers, Loftus etc. The landlord was Moore, related to the great Maurice Moore and George Moore who passed away in recent times. The Knox-Gores laid waste a large tract of the parish along the way and places are pointed out where entire villages once stood. Practically all this land has come back to the adjoining tenants through the Land Commission. The Knox-Gores and McGloinn were the only resident landlords. The McGloinns (Irwins, in Famine times) were charitable, carried out no evictions and fed and clothed the poor as far as their own slender means allowed. The (Perry) Knox-Gores on the other hand were rich, had a huge estate and spared nobody.[14]

⁂

Mrs Hanniffe, b.1867, Cillceascin, Cairbre, Co. Kildare

Fifty families were evicted from this district of Kilkeaskin by a local landlord. The thatch of the roofs were torn off even before the poor people had time to leave.[15]

⁂

Peter Gonoude, b.1865, farmer, Muclach, Screagáin, Tullamore,
Co. Offaly

In the Mucklagh lands Capt. Bernard of Kinnity was the
landlord. He was up for MP about the election of 1850 or '51. He
was opposed by Bland and O'Brien. The clergy opposed Bernard
and he was heavily defeated. He evicted all his tenants in 1852,
except the two who voted for him, Peter Gonoude of Mucklagh
and Larry Conroy of Cloonagh, their sons are now in the
farmsteads, the other 60 tenants had to go. Two farmers went to
the fair of Castlebrick, Killeigh to sell stock. They were Peter
Gounoud, Muckagh, and Larry Conroy, Cloonagh. After they
had sold the stock the mob gathered round them when they saw
all the money they had got.

Peter Gonoud jumped on his mare and told Larry to lead her.
Peter had to fire his pistol in the air, the horse stumbled and
Larry fell. In the mêlée that followed both men would have been
killed, only a family from that place, named McCormack, saved
them. This was about the year 1852.[16]

❧❧

Séamas R. Ó Domhnaill, b.1888, national teacher, Meenbanad,
The Rosses, Co. Donegal

Although the Rosses is of the most barren districts in Ireland,
there are very few stories of any deaths from famine. The whole
district was flooded by bacachs, beggermen or very poor from
Connacht, probably on the principle that the very poor get a
kindlier welcome from their own than from any other stratum of
society. However in those days charity and hospitality were part
and parcel of their religion.[17]

❧❧

Stiofán Mac Philib, Edenmore National School, Emyvale,
Co. Monaghan

An old woman, Anne Curley, went to visit a family who were about to emigrate because of the poverty at home. The women were baking oaten cakes (hard bread) to take with them on the ship. People going abroad brought bread with them for the journey. While they were baking the sheriff came and ordered everyone out. He left all the furniture on the doorstep and took possession of the house. He would not give them time to finish their baking.

There was a large number of homeless people from famine stricken areas in Donegal and Mayo in this district. Many of them became beggarmen and beggarwomen.

An old woman, called McCarron, and her family were evicted. She had no home so she went to an old graveyard – Errigal, and in one corner she built a hut of sods and wattles for herself and her children.

Another poor beggarwoman and two children came to a house in this locality asking alms. When they came to the doorstep they saw the pigs in the sty eating food. The children ran over to the trough and started to eat the pigs' food because they were so hungry.

Homeless individuals abounded. Many of them made rounds of certain districts at intervals for the rest of their lives. They were well treated always. They were known in many cases only by nicknames and no one knew their past history, e.g. Bill the Sheep, Cathrine a Leanbh, Mickey Money, The Grey Lady, Din the Rabbish, Johnny the Baffety, to mention a few.[18]

❧❦❧

Tuosist, Kenmare, Co. Kerry, 1945, from Seán Ó Súilleabháin,
Irish Folklore Commission

Two ships came into Kenmare Bay and took local families to America. One of them was called 'The Furnessy' of the Beaver

Line. She anchored at Blackwater. The other ship anchored further west of the Bay. People from both sides of Kenmare Bay and from Kenmare district went to Ottawa to live. Lord Landsdown was Governor General there at the time. He was landlord of the estate to which these people in Tuosist and were tenants of his.[19]

⚜

Hugh Macken, b.1876, Drumbargy, Co. Fermanagh

I often heard my mother tell that the Tyrone people were worse off at that time than we were. The Tyrone people used to come in batches to this country begging for food. The people round here at that time called them 'the Tyrone Beggars'. One day a batch of them, men, women and children come in the Rossdowney road and fought like dogs over potato skins which were thrown out on James Keenan's 'dochal' [manure pit].[20]

⚜

Michael Kilemade, Ferefad, Longford

Soon after the Great Famine, a large tract of land, upwards of 350 Irish acres, the property of Lord Longford, was completely cleared of tenant-farmers in this locality. The land thus cleared was given to a Protestant who was a bailiff to Lord Longford. The landlord paid the passage money for all who desired to go to the USA. There was no ill feeling felt by the tenants towards the landlord, they seemed anxious to leave the stricken country.[21]

⚜

Liam Ó Danachair, Sunvale, Athea, Co. Limerick

During the worst period of the Famine the local landlord was Wyndham Goold. Like other landlords of his time he exacted excessive rents from his tenants but was otherwise considered a kind landlord, but his rule in Athea was marred by numerous evictions. In Coolaclaur for instance some forty tenants were evicted, as many as thirty in one day.

It was on the latter occasion that six women proceeded to the riverbank bringing the last ashes of the fires of their wrecked homes. These ashes they threw into the flowing water while on their knees they called down dire maledictions on landlord and agent.

Of these thirty families, some dozen were allowed to build hovels in uninhabited parts of the estate, but the majority of the evicted went to America while many went to the Newcastle West workhouse.[22]

16

The Coffin Ships and the Going Away

⁕

The flight from the Famine caused unprecedented levels of emigration. Famine-related emigration equalled Famine-related deaths, each accounting for the loss of one million people, although total emigration from Ireland in the ten years after the blight struck totalled two million people in all. Famine emigration was not the beginning nor the end of large-scale emigration from Ireland, but Famine emigration reached a scale never before seen in the history of international emigration. Before the Famine, emigration had tended to be of the more solvent tenants of the north and east, mainly farmers and tradesmen. With the Famine the poorest western counties were the worst hit. While the very poor were more likely to die at home than find the resources to leave Ireland, many paupers did reach Liverpool which was seen as a staging post for further emigration.

By 1851 there were one million Irish in the United States, three-quarters of a million in Britain, a quarter of a million in Canada, 70,000 in Australia and others in Central and South America.

Up until 1848 mostly single men or families emigrated, but after that, equal numbers of men and women left. After an economic crisis in Britain in 1847 they were increasingly bound for the United States, often via Canada.

Of the two million people who emigrated in those ten years, only a few thousand got official subsidies. Some others got assistance from landlords who were consolidating their estates but these accounted for only about one in twenty. More than three-quarters of the emigrants got the money for their passage from those who had already gone to America. In 1850 those remittances came to about one million pounds.

The speed and scale of the flight from Ireland saw an under-regulated passenger trade, where dirty and dangerous vessels were pressed into service. Lack of medical screening on land and lack of medical care on board, combined with lack of food, and overcrowding, got these early vessels the name of 'coffin ships'. On the worst of these ships sailing to Quebec and during quarantine on Grosse île, in 1847, up to 40,000 passengers died. Legislation soon curbed the use of unsuitable cargo ships and regulated and greatly improved the passenger trade.

Panic-driven emigration and the desire for economic betterment in foreign lands took away from Ireland a third to a half of each rising generation after the Famine.

❦

Mrs Gilmore, b.1867, Moyleroe, Delvin, Co. Westmeath

Lots of people were not able to move or walk from hunger. Some of the poor people used to leave their children at some rich person's house, unknown to them. Others would have them locked in the houses and go off to America and leave the children to die.

Children used to be heard crying with the hunger miles off.[1]

❦

Maggie McKinley, b.1874, Craigmacagan, Rathlin Island,
Co. Antrim

My grandmother minded the Famine. She said there was a boat come into the bay here that took away over a hundred people, whole families. She had five or six sisters and two brothers and they went away. A wild lot died on the boat going over.

From here they went to East Port, Maine, and a lot went to Boston.[2]

❦

Seosamh Ó Dochartaigh, b.1894, a farmer, Ballagh, Cnoc Glas,
Malin, Inishowen, Co. Donegal

That was the time the 'going away' started and they did leave in crowds. Most of the people from the Malin Head side, and indeed from all over Inishowen, went to Boston.

The ships that used to take them away were very bad and a whole lot of them died on the road and were thrown overboard. At that time the ships going to America used to call at Liverpool and when they did, the voyage was so bad up to that, that big crowds of the people got off and stayed there. That is why there are so many of our people in Liverpool.[3]

❧❧

Patrick Redmond, b.1872, a farmer, Forrestalstown, Poulpeesty
Parish, Co. Wexford

There was a gentleman in Dunmaine near Campile. He was something in England. He had a son by his first wife and then married again and his wife and stepson were living in Dunmaine. The stepmother used to treat the young lad very bad, so the young lad ran away to Ross. He was picked up by the English crowd who were shipping to America all the young people who were being sent to the workhouse in Ross. They were selling them into slavery in America at this time. Anyway this young fellow was picked up too. His name was James Annesley, and he was called 'The Wandering Heir'. He was sold into slavery in America. After a while his father began to make inquiries about him. He had come into some money or property and the father tried to find him. He was found, a slave in America. Only then it became known that the English were shipping the young people and selling them into slavery in America.[4]

❧❧

Eamonn Mac Dhuirnín, b.1878, retired national teacher, Creeslough,
Co. Donegal

I have in mind's eye two old men, they were old when I was a youth, who went to America in 1847 but returned again just before the outbreak of the Civil War in 1863. Both men were very interesting, both when telling of their experiences during the Famine years and also of their lives in America. Their names were William McIlhinney and James Morrow. McIlhinney was a big powerful man of 15 or 16 stones in weight, while Morrow was a smaller man but as hardy as steel. Both were newly married. McIlhinney in 1844 and Morrow early in 1845. The Famine came along and since a living could not be made at home, they thought of America. The two did not go off together. One went some months before the other.

McIlhinney went first. He walked to Derry. Being a seafaring man he was interested to find that there was a vacancy on a large American barque called 'The Baltimore' for a sailor. He applied for the position and got it. This man could tell most interesting stories of his voyage to America on the Baltimore, of the times that they had and of the storms they encountered. The voyage must have been pretty rough for it took almost three months to reach Baltimore in Maryland USA. He worked for a time in Maryland, but the greater part of his time in Georgia, where he was a boss over a gang of black slaves. He was very happy there but war began to loom on the horizon, so he cut his stick and came back to old Ireland where he died in 1897, aged well over 80 years.

The second man mentioned, James Morrow, also walked to Derry (people thought nothing of walking 50 miles in those days), got a berth on an American Schooner that came across with a cargo of American meal for the starving people, and thus worked his passage to America. He had a quieter passage than McIlhinney and reached America in less than six weeks. He was out as far as Pittsburgh and worked in a foundry for about 10 years. The same fear of war brought him home to Ireland where he lived well and happy until he was a very old man. He died in 1903, aged about 91.

A few returned, but the majority never returned.[5]

❧❧

Seán Breathnach, b.1891, a labourer and shepherd, Coill Mór,
Cloughane, Co. Kerry

Many of the local families went to America. Often they moved in one night, selling most of their possessions to the neighbours and carrying with them enough to supply them with food during the voyage. They left by night so the landlord could not interfere with their goods.

The voyage usually took from three to nine months. The food was cooked in communal pots. A number of people's food was thrown in together and cooked. The strongest sometimes came out better than the others because of this. Lots died of disease on these voyages. Some of the ships had water oozing in between the planks.

The Poor Law Guardian had the power of getting places for a certain number on these voyages to America. He usually gave them to his friends who needed to go.[6]

❧❧

Terence Clarke, b.1872, Bailieboro, Co. Cavan

The family of General Phil Sheridan, Commander-in-Chief of the United States Army, emigrated from the townland of Beagh to the United States at the time of the Famine. Old Andrew Smith of Beagh, said he remembered the General as a child in his mother's arms, leaving Beagh to go to America.

When whole families died out or left the country, their farms lay on the landlord's hand, and they were anxious to give them to anyone who would take them and pay rent for them.[7]

❧❧

Charles Clarke, b.1873, Tullynaskeagh, Bailieboro, Co. Cavan

There were 52 Heereys living in the townland of Wilton before the Famine, and after the Famine there wasn't one of them in it. They went to Britain.

The people left their farms without being evicted. The rent was £2 an acre at the time, and they wouldn't be able to pay it. They left their farms and it is not known where the most of them went to. The people had so much suffering of their own that they didn't bother about where their neighbours went to.

When a man left his farm the landlord or the agent came to a man that remained, and threatened him that if he didn't take the vacant farm he would lose his own. And in that way local farmers got derelict farms, but they took them against their will. They didn't want to take them because of the high rent and the Bad Times. The landlords were not harsh towards their tenants, but the tenants had to pay their rent or leave.[8]

❧❧

Hugh Clarke, b.1873, Bailieboro, Co. Cavan

One night during the Famine my father remembered two men coming to the house, each of them had a farm of about 10 acres, and they asked my grandfather to give them £10 a piece for the two farms, that they were going off to America. He refused and they pleaded with him, and my grandmother pleaded for them, and in the end he gave them £10 a piece for the farms.[9]

❧❧

Anthony Dwyer, b.1876, a painter and Thomas Magner, b.1860, a blacksmith, Golden, Cashel, Co. Tipperary

Thomas Magner remembers hearing of many people who got their passage to America and Australia from the government. He was told the government packed them into rotten ships, so many of which went down that he heard a neighbour named Kennedy say in years gone by that there were enough Irish bodies gone down in the Atlantic to make a road from Ireland to America.

People were given passage to Australia for 30 shillings. Thomas Magner says that the lands of the people who died or left were taken by Scotch people who were imported at the time.[10]

⁂

John D. O'Leary, Lynedaowne, Rathmore, Kerry

The government took shiploads of paupers, many from Killarney poorhouse, to America and Australia. It is said some were not allowed to land in America and were brought back again. There was free emigration to Canada, but the emigrants had to pay back their passage money to the government when they had it earned.[11]

⁂

Maighréad Ní Dhonnabháin, b.1866, a farmer, Drom Inide, Drimoleague, Co. Cork

As a result of the Famine many families were broken up. This was in a good way due to the tempting offers to emigrate. This was what was called 'Free Emigration'. Everyone who left paid a pound and the English government paid the rest. This was freely accepted for years after the Famine with the result that it was always the young members of the family that left. When they became well off they persuaded the parents to go. It was usually to America or Australia they emigrated. It often happened in the poor mountainous districts of West Cork that only the aged parents were left to keep the little homestead. They were often unable to pay the rent except they got help from across and the result was that evictions were numerous. The most of the landlords were of no help to the suffering people. They oftentimes took from them the solitary cow or goat which was their sole support. If a family was suspected of receiving money from America the rent was sure to be raised, so the poor people got no chance anyway.[12]

❧

Conchubhair and Solomon Ó Néill, b.1860s, farmers, Cratloe, Co. Clare

The principal family in this parish at the time was that of John O'Neill [grand uncle of Con and Solomon] who owned Cratloe Mor Castle and the adjoining lands. As a result of the Famine they were forced to emigrate to Canada in 1846. One daughter married a Surveyor-General and another a Provincial Surveyor. The third [Margaret O'Neill] became a nun in France and did such wonderful work that steps were taken some four or five years ago by the church authorities, to petition for her beatification, but according to my informants, the full particulars necessary were not available.

In the same townland [Cratloe] and within the space of half a mile on the old Wood Road, 33 families cleared out, some to the workhouse, others to Australia or Canada, there was little emigration to America in those days, while some joined the English army and this was considered a great disgrace. It was a common saying for a father or mother that they would rather see their sons in the grave than in the service of England. The idea of facing the workhouse was equally repugnant. They preferred to die in the old home, and it was only as a last resort they went there.

The ships which carried the emigrants were known as 'fever ships' also and were not so called without good cause. Con O'Neill mentioned one such which was driven by gales on to the rocky Newfoundland coast where it was lost with all on board. A memorial commemorating the tragedy was erected on the coast nearby.

Emigrant ships sailed from Arthur's Quay, Limerick, and it was a common practice for relatives to travel as far as Kilrush. Con

O'Neill's father did so on the occasion of his uncle's departure for Canada, and walked home, a distance of 40 miles.

The banks of the Shannon used to be lined with people and the sights witnessed 'would break your heart'.

The sailing boats were usually old hulks, anything but seaworthy, often taking months to reach their destination.[13]

❖

Seán Mac Cuinneagáin, Scoil Mhín an Aodhaire, Carrick, Co. Donegal

A ship which came to Killybegs to take off emigrants sold the provisions which were to be used on the journey. Before the boat reached America there was starvation on board and many deaths resulted.[14]

❖

Conchubhar Mac Suibhne, Aughrim, Co. Wicklow

It was pitiful and heartbreaking the many people tried to get English for their children. Small blame to them. There was America and bread in it. Any dearbhfhaoil English they could give them. In my young days at home in Ballinamona, near Mallow, everyone over 40 knew Irish. No one spoke it. It wasn't lucky.[15]

❖

Cáit Uí Bhraonain, b.1858, Kilbeggan, Co. Westmeath

The Famine compelled thousands from Westmeath to emigrate to South America. Please note South America where they have several connections still. They paid no passage money. The landlords paid it.[16]

❧❧

John Phillips, b.1855, New Inn, Co. Tipperary

The British government tried another plan to get rid of the poor Irish people. They gave them a free ticket to America and packed the poor people like cattle into sailing vessels and badly fed them while at sea.[17]

❧❧

Patrick Clarke, b.1859, Carra, New Inn, Mote, Co. Galway

The potatoes rotted in the pits. The priests said it would be better if some of the people left Ireland. A fleet of ships left Ireland with nine priests on board. They were left in Canada on the banks of a river but four of the priests died of cholera, and when the children were asked their names, they had forgotten them and their parents' names, it was such a long time since they'd seen them. Many people from around here died in Canada.[18]

❧❧

Bean Uí Sheoighe, b.1873, a farmer's wife, Dawrosmore, Letter, Letterfrack, Co. Galway

Some families went to America. They got their money from friends to enable them to travel. They travelled in sailing boats that were covered with canvas. On their way to America they often got short of food and many of them were killed as food for the other people. Once a young man and girl were on a ship on their way to America. They were to be married when they reached there. The people ran short of food and lots were cast to see who should be killed. The lot fell three times on the girl. However the young man said he would die in place of her. The were about to kill him when a ship appeared with food and the young man's life was spared.[19]

❖

Seán Ó Duinnshléibhe, Glenville, Fermoy, Co. Cork

Hence started emigration from here to the USA, chiefly to Boston, New York and Philadelphia. Before 1845 a few had emigrated from here and there, and these informed those at home about their whereabouts in America. Many families sold up what they had to make up a few pounds for their emigration. I think the fare at that time was about £6. Two months at sea had to be spent when weather was unfavourable.

In the Glenville area there was wholesale emigration from the Hudson Estate, about 62 small farmers left for the States. A craze for going came upon the people. One went to the landlord and offered him his holding, in return the landlord gave him the 'handsome gift' of £5. Each in turn followed suit, and in a few years all had left, giving him their livings practically for nothing.

Then commenced the change. The idle houses were razed to the ground. The fences levelled and large regular fields from 50 to 70 acres each took their place. The stones of the houses were used for building. A demesne wall about ten times the size of the original demesne was the result.

Local families who left the district around the Famine times never saw the shores of America. Many died on the way owing to the Famine fever, and those who survived scarcely saw the new land. They died on landing. Of those who survived many had their new homes in Boston and New York. Probably the life in cities did not agree with them and they went further west into the country to take part in the farming industry. After a while they spread to the towns and cities where better wages were available, and when they had spared a little they gladly thought of the homes and families and, as a relief, sent home their savings. Chicago, Montana, San Francisco were the cities having some of the famine-stricken from here.

In the village all the houses were thatched and owned by their occupiers. Those who took to the craze rushed to Hudson offering their homes to him. These too he took. To some he gave

£2, to others £5, until he had possession of the whole village. The people considered him good, as he gave them money.

The Labour Rate Act was passed and the small farmers had to foot this additional burden. The Poor Rate thus sinking them lower, so much so that many of them threw up their lands to join the government labour gang or emigrate.[20]

❧❧

Seán Crowley, b.1858, Cill Cholmáin, Eniskeane, Co. Cork

'Twas a sad tale. Not one tenant ever went back to till a sod of Lisnacunna. They scattered everywhere. Three families, two families of the Mahonys and a McCarthy family, went off to America. The money the made off their few cows paid their passage over. I never heard to what part of America they went, for when the old neighbours they had scattered away, they didn't know where to send a line to, so they were never heard of after.

My own father said that himself, like many more, would have gone too at the time but he couldn't leave his father and mother. They were feeble. If he left them they should go to the poorhouse, and by any chance they could not face to America.

There were many like him. The old people kept them from travelling.[21]

❧❧

J. O'Kane, Dromore National School, Dromore West, Co. Sligo

The depopulation of this district during the years 1845 to 1855 or so, according to what I can gather, is almost unbelievable. The depopulation was caused far more by emigration than by deaths caused by hunger, although hunger took its toll in every district here, and indeed in every townland. A conservative estimate I would say is this, that between two-thirds and four-fifths of the total population, young and old, disappeared in the 10 years 1845–55, through death, mainly starvation, but principally through emigration. Townland of Belville near Mrs Joyce's Public House, a whole village wiped out. You can count the remains of at least ten houses. As a matter of fact the number of ruined houses in this district, when I came here 35 years ago, was the one aspect of the place I thought most extraordinary and most depressing.

The general exodus was to America, USA and Canada after the Famine. Many many families have disappeared from this district after the Famine. The ruined houses are a proof of that. I was told that most people who could muster sufficient money to pay the passage to America went, father, mother, children, young and old. All sailed from Sligo and the voyage, I was told, took sixteen weeks. One voyage to Quebec was given to me very accurately in one instance as sixteen weeks and three days.

When the emigrants landed in Quebec, if there was no one to meet them there, a thing that rarely happened, they wandered round until they could find work. I was told that employers from states in the Middle West who needed help on farms etc. came into Quebec, met emigrants and engaged them and took them home with them. Irish emigrants often had to wander around for weeks before getting employment.

It puzzled me at first to know why emigrants from this district after the Famine settled down in the northern states of the Middle West, with a small percentage in Canada, and this was the explanation I got. All landed in Quebec and were taken into employment by someone who came to engage or hire all the help he required. It would remind one of the hiring fairs in the north of Ireland, with however a difference, the difference not being to the advantage of the emigrants. The emigrants paid their passages without any outside help. Later came the 'Free Emigration' when emigrants were transported free without payment from Sligo to Quebec. The British sponsored and paid the fares of these emigrants.

The emigrants got no food on board ship during the voyage except what they took with them. Now I mean those who paid their own fares on the ship.

Besides their ordinary dress-wearing clothes each emigrant

had to bring bed-clothes, a feather tick, blankets and pillows. The feather tick was often omitted but everybody [had] a pillow and blankets.

In regard to food each person brought a supply of oaten cakes, baked three times, baked in the ordinary way first, then allowed to cool, then baked again until each large cake was hard as a stone. Even bags of potatoes and any other items of food available for which the individual had a taste, but the oat cakes always, potatoes generally and ordinary oat-meal raw. A small bag too.

Then very often emigrants went to Sligo and were often a week, two weeks and three weeks there before the boat sailed. The boat would not leave the dock in Sligo until the wind and weather were favourable.

One boy Flynn who went from here was held up in Sligo for three weeks, and his parents brought down fresh supplies of food to him each weekend. They wanted him to return home, but he would not because, he said, everybody would be laughing at him if he did. He settled down after a time in Nebraska and died there.

I was always told that emigrants left home secretly to go to Sligo when they went on board ship at the dead of night. I asked at last why the middle of the night, why not go in the daytime. They said that if the emigrants went in the daytime and if the landlord knew of their going, he might or would hold them and take from them money and everything else they had, and so their last state would be worse than their first. They would have nothing then at home to live on and then not [have] had the wherewithal to emigrate.

The landlord's men, underlings and tale-bearers, were those to be dreaded. They carried the news to the landlord and he then gave the order to stop the emigrants. So then, the emigrants, were obliged to make preparations secretly in the dead of night.[22]

Peter Sloan, b.1865, a farmer, Glenloughan Upper, Mourne Parish, Kilkeel, Co. Down

My mother and father left here till go to America in the bad year, that was '46. They went till Canada. There was four of us born there, and three born here, and they were left with the old woman, that was my granny, and one down in Ballygowan. Me and another sister were born here after they come home. The ship they sailed on was the Duke of Quebec. Many's a time they used to make a joke of it. 'Aw, you Duked [avoided] it,' they'd say. I mind that well. They were 13 weeks and I mind granny saying, good rest to her, that they took oaten bread with them and it was like a slate there, and it was as good when they got there as it was when they left.[23]

❧❧

William Blake, b.1895, a labourer, Rathnagrew, Co. Carlow

Mr Foley's grandfather drove people to New Ross in a long car or wagon with a big box in the back to carry the belongings of the emigrants. The car was made for that purpose and he did a big trade and brought away many families. It took him a week to go and a week to come back. They simply closed the door after them as they had little to bring and could not sell their farms.[24]

❧❧

Amby Flynn, b.1878, a labourer, Rathbawn, Co. Wicklow

In the last year of the Famine a lot died and a priest Fr Hoare made a plan with the English government and got them out to America and they were never heard tell of afterwards.[25]

❧❧

Martin Donoghue, Ryleen, New Ross, Co. Wexford,
a native of Ballinasloe, Co. Galway

Kilmolaw was a village near Ballinasloe. It contained 60 houses. Every single family emigrated from it in Black '47 to Chicago. Each had someone previously there who sent them their passage, so they all went in batches leaving Kilmolaw a deserted village.[26]

❧❦

Pilib Ó Conaill, national teacher, Main Street, Kilfinane, Kilmallock,
Co. Limerick, b.1878, Wilkinstown, Navan, Co. Meath

Old Pat Quail or Mac Quail told us stories of deaths on board and how the body was sown up in canvas and consigned to the deep. He added horrifying details, for my brother's benefit and mine, which may or may not be true: how the sailor who sewed up the corpses stuck his needle into the dead body to oil it so that the point would pass more easily through the canvas and how a shark always followed the ship when anyone was slipped from a plank over the gunwale into the sea.[27]

❧❦

17

Of Curses, Kindness and Miraculous Food

⚜

The material we have been looking at so far in this review of the folklore of the Great Irish Famine has largely been historical lore of one type or another. We should also cast a cursory glance at the many legends found among the general lore about the disaster which reflect people's attitudes to it.

While a folklorist could devote a complete study to these Famine legends, I will only attempt to give a flavour of their variety. Some are obviously variants of the same type of legend, while others give an idea of the range of legends incorporated into the folklore of the Famine.

From the folklorist's point of view a legend is defined more closely, and somewhat differently, than is the case in the general usage of the word. By legend, in this case, I mean those narratives of occurrences which the teller believes to have happened in fact. There are varieties of legend which folklorists classify and index as, for example, local legends or migratory legends. Although a legend may originally have been associated with a particular place, person or event, some legends captured the popular imagination in such a way that they travelled from their original locality to places near and far. Often the telling, retelling and transmission over time and places leads to changes in the legend from place to place or, indeed, from teller to teller. Nevertheless many of the migratory legends, while differing in certain details and motifs, are obviously versions of the same tale type and have preserved their general narrative structure, although the names of characters and places may have been changed.

Legends tend to be more simple in narrative structure and shorter in length than folktales, but occasionally there are overlaps where a simple folktale can also be regarded as a legend. Perhaps the most important element of a legend is that it is believed to be true and realistic by the person who recounts it and will often feature local and realistic detail which add to its credibility.

Many of the legends which follow can be found in contexts other than the Famine and many of the examples given can be repeated in versions from other parts of the country. In some cases I have given only one version of the legend in question, in other cases I have given a number of versions of the same legend to give an idea of how details may change from place to place while the tale still preserves its narrative structure. To a large extent the legends give us a picture of how people would have liked the world to be, express moral and religious values, and are a mechanism which helped communities deal with the horrors that surrounded them.

DOCTOR KNOWS BEST

Kathleen Hurley, Corlock House, Ballymoe, Co. Galway

The writer when a child remembers seeing a very old man who in his youth was an inmate of the workhouse, Glenamaddy. His name was Patch, and it was Patch's duty to carry the remains of any person after dying to the 'Dead House', where the remains were dressed and prepared for burial. The doctor going his rounds one day through the sick ward told Patch: 'Patch, when Shamus dies carry him to the 'Dead House''. 'Yes, yer honour.' The doctor gone out of sight Patch approached the dying man's bed, caught him by the two wrists and slung him across his shoulders. While poor Shamus shouted 'I'm not dead yet. I'm not dead yet.' Patch in a hurry to have his work done shouted 'Stop you amadán, doesn't the doctor know best.'[1]

James Doyle, b.1875, a mason, Hacketstown, Co. Carlow

An undertaker in Carlow got the contract in Carlow town for burying the dead at the rate of so much a corpse, so they collected people even before they were quite dead. They used tell the story of a person who woke up as he was being carried in a hinge-bottomed coffin for burial. He shouted to know where he was and the undertaker replied, 'We are going to bury you.' 'How'll you bury me when I'm not dead?' The undertaker calmly replied, 'Oh, the drop will kill you anyhow.'[2]

GENEROSITY REWARDED – FOOD REPLENISHED

Pádraig Pléimionn, Killarney, Co. Kerry

Mr Lyne told me a good story about the wife of a farmer named Sheehan who lived near Rathmore in the old Parish of Kilcummin. This man Sheehan was a close-fisted chap who had not much 'bowes' for the starving people near him. The wife on the other hand was very, perhaps too, generous towards them. It is said that she gave nearly all the new milk of her 'bawn' of 20 cows to her starving neighbours. She had complete charge of her dairy and had also the sole management of her dairy produce. Now some local person told her husband about her wastefulness in this respect and he, to find out if there were any truth in the tale, went out to the dairy one day to see his milk-pans. He found them all full to the brim and went away disgusted because of the foolish twaddle of his 'kind' neighbour. Now that same morning Mrs Sheehan had given almost all her new milk to the starving neighbours and the people of the district, on hearing of the visit of the husband to the dairy and what he found there, set down what he saw to a miracle.[3]

262

Pádraig Ó Conchobhair, b.1875, Ard Mór, Belmullet, Co. Mayo

A Paddy Lavelle lived with his wife in Cross. He was called Paddy Major as he must have been working for Major Bingham. They were very poor as they had no money to earn. Next to them lived another very poor couple, and if one of them was without meal the other woman would give her some.

One day the woman next door came to Mrs Paddy Major and asked for some meal as she had no time to grind some that day. Mrs Lavelle had not very much to spare either but she gave her some of it and told her if she could at all to bring the meal over to her in the evening. The woman told her that she would have some ground by that time and that she would bring her some of it.

Evening came and still she did not come with the meal so that Mrs Lavelle said she would scrape the bottom of the chest and try and get as much as would do the husband for the supper. When she went to the chest and opened it she found that it was full to the top and she dropped on her knees and thanked God. She was like that when the other woman came in with the meal and she too went on her knees when she saw that the chest was full of meal. Mrs Lavelle told her to bring the meal home again and to come for some any time she wanted it. That was the time of the Famine and when the neighbours heard about the meal they all flocked around the house and none of them ever went away empty. They came from far and wide to get some of the meal and stirabout and there was always a pot down on that fire.[4]

❖❖

Pádraig Ó h-Arrachtáin, b.1886, a farmer, na h-Insí, Eyeries, Castletownbere, Co. Cork

To the west of Castletownbere there is a place called Drom. In this townland there is a field known to many of the older people as 'The Field of the Crop', and this is how it got its name.

At the time when the Famine was in Ireland, a man of the

Hurleys lived here. He had a small farm and was married to a small charitable woman. This farmer was a hard worker and he always tried to be up to time with his crops and to have everything done blasta [tastefully]. He could not bear to hear anyone say that he was a lazy or untidy man. That was an asachán he could not stand.

Well the Great Famine came in 1848. Times got very bad entirely. The potatoes all blackened and other crops too, especially oats was very bad the same year. This poor man was struck very hard for he had only enough potatoes that would feed a few pigs and he had only two bags of oats, as he thought.

When he had everything gathered in the first thing he did was to fill a firkin of potatoes and put them aside as seed for the coming year. Then he sieved the oats and found that it was all chaff and only a grain here and there. He gathered chaff and grain all into one bag and put that aside also.

That was all right till the winter came, and the hunger and the cold. The place was full of poor people going around looking for something to eat. Again and again they came to the farmer's house. His good wife never left them go empty. She couldn't bear to refuse a thing to anyone who asked it for God's sake. Soon she found that her store was getting very small. Yet in spite of all, the numbers of poor people who came to the house increased daily. In the end she was up against it as she hadn't left but the firkin of seed potatoes and the few bags of chaff. Often and often the husband told her not to meddle with the seed whatever else she would do.

Now the poor people who came to the house had to go away empty-handed. Still they continued to come day after day. The poor woman was very troubled when she had to put them off day after day like this. She thought it very wrong to be refusing it when they asked it for 'God's sake', and when she had a little still left. In the end it came so hard on her that she commenced giving out the potatoes now and again.

When the spring came her husband went to examine the seed one day and when he found that the firkin of seed potatoes was half-empty he became very angry. He abused his wife left and right. He said that they would be shamed for ever by the neighbours when they would have no crop in the fall or in the harvest, a thing that he said never happened in their family before. The only answer the wife made him was to leave it to God, that he was strong and that he had a good mother.

About Patrick's Day when the farmer had the field ready for the sciolâns [seed potatoes] he went again to the firkin to get as much seed as he could out of what remained. He was amazed this time when he saw that the firkin was full of fine potatoes. When he told his wife she was more surprised. They cut them into sciolâns and planted them.

The farmer thought the oats he had was no good and was not going to sow it at all. His wife made him plough the field and made him shake it anyhow.

When the harvest came round again, the talk and wonder of that neighbourhood was the crops that were grown by that farmer. Their like were never before seen or, perhaps, since.[5]

❧

Ned Buckley, Knocknagree, Co. Cork

I often heard that old Mrs Cremin, the grandmother of Fr John Cremin, Lissyconnor, Rathmore, was very good and full of charity to the poor and hungry in the Famine days. She used always boil a lot of potatoes for the meals and she never used the ones left over after dinner for either pig or cows or poultry but collected the best of them and put them near the fire in order to have a few of them for any hungry poor person who might chance to call to the house for some bite to lessen their mad hunger. A few potatoes half-cold and a basin of milk was a great boon to such starving people and often they went away blessing the house and the owners of it. Many were the poor mother and father who came to her for one single head of cabbage she had growing in the field. It was poor fare but it kept many a family from starving in those days. A head or a couple of head of cabbage boiled with a pinch of salt were divided out among the family and if they had enough of that they'd be very thankful. One day her husband seeing as much cabbage being carried away went into the house to blame her for giving away the cabbage and asked her did she want to leave themselves with nothing at all. She denied giving away as much of it and said she only gave away a few heads to a few poor women who were starving. 'Come out now,' said the man of the house, 'and show me what cabbage is left for ourselves.' She went out fearing the worst and hoping he would not blame her too much for helping God's poor. When they reached the cabbage field great was her surprise to find there was not a single head missing out of the whole field. There it was – the whole field of cabbage without the loss of a single head but what was used for their own household.

She was greatly surprised and fell on her knees to give thanks to God for thus miraculously saving her from her husband's censure and for acknowledging her kindness for the poor. Her husband was speechless with surprise as he knew well she had been giving away the cabbage and refusing none of it. He was as impressed by this miracle that he told her to continue on the way she was doing and that he'd never again object to her helping God's poor.[6]

⟡

Miraculous Food – Strange Visitor

Ned Buckley, Knocknagree, Co. Cork

Mick Connor Doon [b.1900] is my authority for the following which he heard from his father [b.1830s] who is dead over thirty years and was 80 when he died.

In the height of the Famine a poor woman lived in Doon. She was a widow with four young children about the house and they were very poor all the time. One winter's morning she was completely out of food and the children were crying from hunger. She had nothing for them but to pacify them she put down the pot over the fire as usual, though there was nothing in it but water. But when the water in the pot was boiling she had no meal and when the children used to say why don't you put meal in the pot, she used to say the old Irish saying '[Is gaire] cabhair Dé ná an doras', the English for which words was that 'God was nearer than the door'.

Out about twelve in the day the children were wild with hunger and the pot of water was still boiling over the fire. At that time a man came to the house saying in Irish 'God save all here'. 'God save you kindly sir and welcome,' said the poor widow. The man sat down on the chair she offered him and talked. After a while he asked the why were the children crying or was it how they were sick. 'Yerra,' said the mother, making an effort to deny the real cause, 'the blackguards, 'tis easy to make them cry and there's nothing ails them.' They talked on and the children started crying. After being again questioned she told him they had plenty cause to cry, poor things, as they had nothing to eat since this time yesterday.

'What have you in the pot?' questioned the visitor.

'Nothing,' she said, 'but water.'

'Are you sure?' said the man.

'I am and very sure,' said she. 'What else could be in? 'Tis long ago today I put it down.'

'Look at it again,' he said. 'Didn't you say that "God was nearer than the door".'

He persuaded her to lift the cover and when she did she was surprised to see it full of big bones of beef and they boiling and simmering away. She was greatly surprised.

'Now,' said he, 'would it not be nice if you put a couple of quarts of oatmeal down on that and you'd have fine porridge for yourself and the children.'

'I have no meal in the house,' said the widow.

'Try your little bin,' said the visitor. 'There may be some grain of meal in it.'

'God help us,' said she, 'there isn't. I cleaned it out well yesterday.'

'Try again,' said he.

She lifted the cover of the bin and lo, it was full to the top with fine oatmeal.

'God be praised and glorified,' said she turning round but the visitor had gone. She went out to see were he was or where he was going to but, though there was nothing round the house to hide him, he had completely disappeared. She made many inquiries among the neighbours, whether anyone had seen such a man, but she never got trace or tidings of him again. She had no doubt, nor had any of the people she told her story to, but that her visitor was sent by God to aid her in answer to her hope that 'God was nearer than the door'.[7]

⁘

Bean Uí Artagáin, b.1878, a farmer, Cnocán Aoibhinn,
Cill Fhionnáin, Co. Cork

There is one outstanding incident still related here about the Famine years. In this district there lived a woman and her husband (their grandson and his children live here now), they were small farmers. One day the husband and his workman were out working not far from the house. Coming on to dinnertime the wife got a meal of porridge ready for the three and put it on plates on the table. She then went out to call the men and when she returned she found a stranger in the kitchen. He was redheaded and of wild hungry appearance. He asked the woman for something to eat as he was starving. She hadn't much in the house besides what was cooked on the plates and she thought of the two men who would be in any moment. She told him he could have a meal. He cleaned one plate and the greater portion of the second, then thanked the woman and left. The husband and workman came in almost immediately and were asked if they saw any stranger passing out. They said they had not. The wife told what had happened and the husband said it was all right as the plate of porridge would do the two of them and they could make up for it at supper. It was said that from that day on everything prospered with that family – stock, crops, milk, undertakings.[8]

❖❖

PRAYER ANSWERED – MIRACULOUS FOOD

Anna Shortt, Stradbally, Co. Laois

I heard my father say that there was a poor widow with five children living outside the town. She and her family were on the verge of starvation and she had no means of securing food. She prayed fervently to almighty God and begged of Him not to let herself and her little ones die of hunger. On looking out one morning she was astonished to see a field at the back of the house white with mushrooms, thought it was not the season of the year when mushrooms would be in the fields. For several mornings she collected the mushrooms and they lived on the food until a farmer came to their assistance with some oatmeal.

The miraculous food was the result of the widow's prayers.[9]

❖❖

GRAIN FROM CHAFF

Tadhg Ó Briain, b.1865, a farmer, Curr a Cóimeád,
Cillmhacumóg Parish, Bantry, Co. Cork

Carraig na Cátha, there was a woman living there in the bad times and she had some oats to plant and she gave all the oats to the poor and she had only the chaff left. When the spring came the boy came in for the oats to plant it and she had only a bag of chaff, and he brought it out and he shook it and it grew fine oats and the place is called Carraig na Cátha since. 'Tis in Inchegella or in the Parish of Kilmurry.[10]

❖❖

Seán Rowley, a storyteller, Rossport, Co. Mayo

There was however a man of a very well-to-do family who lived in Stonefield, by the name of Jack Bán Bournes. He was a gentleman of great benevolence and charity, and succeeded in getting some relief for the people – food, seeds etc. In the exercise of his generosity, often giving away his own private goods, he was excelled by his lady who, they say, was the essence of benevolence and charity to the poor and afflicted. It is on record that the very chaff of grain which she gave to people grew up into a fine crop. This growth of chaff was of course considered miraculous, but coming as it did from a good-natured and affable lady, it was not regarded as so very surprising that God would bless her gift.[11]

❧

FOOD FROM FAIRIES

In the Famine times, in the district of Grantstown, lived a woman with seven children. She had nothing to give them to eat, but a strange woman brought her porridge, butter and milk every day. The woman told her not to look out after her when she would go out. They did as she commanded and the fairy woman continued to bring them food.

After some time this inquisitive woman became anxious to see where the fairy woman lived or where she got the food. One morning her curiosity became too much to bear so she decided to follow the kind fairy. She went after her and she saw her enter a well. Just as the fairy was entering the well she saw the woman following her. She was so startled that she disappeared and forgot to close the lid. The well overflowed and covered the house and the district around it, and it was called Grantstown Lough.[12]

❧

MILK-STEALING WITCH

During the Famine time here lived in Boherard an only widow. Near her house a man who possessed very good cows lived. Every night the widow went to the man's field, in which his cows grazed, and sucked the milk from them. For some time the man was ignorant of what was happening, but as time went on, he noticed that his cows were being milked at night.

One day while the man's wife was churning, she saw an old red-haired witch approaching the house. When she reached the door she asked for a drink of water. The woman handed her a cup of milk. At first she looked at the milk and then told her what was happening. She also commanded her to tell her husband to get two greyhounds and lie in wait for the widow. Immediately the witch went to the widow to give her the form of a hare, and she told her to go from that day on to the man's field as a hare.

The next night the widow took her new form and went to the field to suck the cows. When she reached the field she started to suck the cows. When the man saw this he let loose his hounds which followed the hare through Mrs Thompson's field out into John Carroll's field and home to her own house. Just as she succeeded in entering, the greyhounds injured her but she succeeded in entering. Instantly the man came and he heard the cries of the widow who lay on the floor and among blood. He entered and he found the widow almost dead. She died and the man buried her. The ruins of the widow's house are still to be seen on Boherard road.[13]

❖❖

COME BUTTER COME

Thomas Flynn, b.1860, a farmer, Carntulla, Ballinaglera, Carrick-on-Shannon, Co. Leitrim

The priest got some trouble from people who, by charm or other means, could take their neighbours' butter. So he visited the scene of operations and found out the means and words by which it was done. After restoring peace among the parties, and having got a pledge that such would not occur again, he returned home rhyming to himself the words used in taking the butter, in order that his housekeeper, Nabby, would hear all. He lived in Hollymount townland and kept one cow, so that when Nabby went to churn she could not move the dash. The churn was packed with butter and the priest had to go back and see who lost it.[14]

⊰⊱

MEANNESS CURSED

J. O'Kane, Dromore National School, Dromore West, Co. Sligo

Miss Flynn tells the following. She had a grand-uncle, John Flynn, who lived beside Leharrow chapel. One day he saw a man named Philibín passing with an asscart with his two dead children in it, bringing them to Kilmacshalgan graveyard to bury them. Flynn saw that the man Philibín looked weak and tottering. He thought this man will never be able to dig a grave. He took up a spade and shovel and crossed over the fields to the graveyard. Near the graveyard he met another man, Miss Flynn could not remember his name, but Flynn asked him to come and help him make the grave. He refused, and said to Flynn if he began that work, grave-digging, he would be at it every day and would be able to do nothing else. That evening this man's arms became paralysed, and Miss Flynn could not say if he ever recovered the power of his arms again.[15]

⊰⊱

Micheál Mac Carthaigh, b.1891, a farmer, Cnocán an Mhuilinn, Sneem, Co. Kerry

There is an old ruin to the north of the house here and there is

272

another old ruin in Myles' Matthew's [Ó Súilleabháin] place, a man named 'Blanket' Mac Amhlaoibh lived there.

Myles Matthew told me that he heard old people saying that he [Blanket] went to Cork and bought a blanket, [and as he was on his way home] a snowstorm came and he put on the blanket. That's why he was called Blanket Mac Amhlaoibh.

Blaud owned the cnocán [little hill] that time and he had an agent, Darby Connell, a sort of an agent.

Blaud had turnips and a son of Blanket's used to go down this way and down by the sea, a half-naked creature and the rest of them starving at home. He used to pull the turnips and eat them, and come up this way again and bring some of them home to the rest.

One evening the Darby [Connell] happened to be passing this way, and there was a man of the Connors with him from the village here. They saw this poor half-naked fellow coming up by the river. Darby asked Connor who he was. He told him. 'Oh, by gor, he's the man that's stealing the master's turnips.'

He called him over and he pulled a root of furze and started beating him on the naked limbs until Connor had to tell him to stop.

He went home and took the bed and died, and Connell died too soon afterwards and got a bad death too, he fell off a stairs in a public house in Sneem.

The agency was gone. His wife and children had to go begging and he had three daughters imbeciles. 'Blanket' moved down to the Oyster Bed and he built a little shack there, and the times were improving. Connell's wife and family came begging to him. He wanted to give them a bad send-off but his wife said 'return good for evil' ['maith in aghaidh an oilc']. She gave them a dish of potatoes and sent them off.

The ruins of 'Blanket's' house is still there and there is another old ruin near it.[16]

⚜

Michael Corduff, The Lodge, Westport, Ballina, Co. Mayo

During the time of the Great Famine, a century ago, there lived in the townland of Kilgalligan a landlord's bailiff who was known by the name of Jack Mór a Raighailligh. Like his neighbours, he was a small farmer and used to have some tillage. Like most of the bailiffs of his kind he was an oppressor and with sternness he dominated and exercised his despotism over the community amongst whom he lived. People speak in scathing terms of landlords in the past and not without much justification in many cases, but my opinion is they were not half as bad as the native hirelings in their employment and Jack Mór it appears was one of the worst of his ilk.

There was a widow in the village whose husband had only died recently and she had two little orphan boys. The father had died indirectly of starvation, for in these days the primitive and scanty nature of the people's food was unable to sustain life in numerous cases for long. The two children were one day discovered by the bailiff on his land searching for stray potatoes in the soil called 'prátaí romhair' [digging potatoes]. These were potatoes which having escaped the digger the previous season, grew up again, but they were invariably of very inferior quality and were only fed to animals. Of course, in the time of the Famine people would eat almost anything and these two children were out to procure the makings of a 'cast' to roast in the ashes for themselves, but the merciless bailiff soon put an end to their operations. He seized the two children and brought them to his house, and secured them to the cow's stake at the end of the kitchen, he then returned to his work in the field, having told his wife not to release the children until he would come back to his midday meal. She was making stirabout and it is said she gave some of it to eat to the two children in the absence of the husband. The plight of the two children owing to their cruel captivity and fear was extremely sad. Their mother came to the house of their confinement and begged their release, but the woman of the house who was kind and charitable, and the direct opposite of her haughty and wicked husband, was afraid to incur her husband's displeasure by letting the children go. The mother then went to the field where the bailiff was working and begged for the children's release. Instead of showing any sympathy or mercy for the poor woman in her woe, he merely threatened to do the same to herself and that there was further punishment awaiting the two boys on his return to the house.

She told him to do his wickedest and perhaps he would repent of his cruelty sooner than he expected. On reaching home she went through all of the prescribed formalities of the widow's curse and on her knees she exercised her incantations for evil on her enemy, the bailiff.

Before the appointed time for returning for his dinner Jack Mór was seized with a severe pain in his side, so he had to return to the house and lie on his bed writhing in agony.

In the consternation which followed in the household consequent on the suffering of the man of the house, no attention was paid to the chained boys and one of them managed to release himself and his brother. When leaving the house one of them said to the other 'Now, thank God, we are free, but neither God, man nor devil will ever release you'.

The suffering man sent for the woman whom he had injured and begged her forgiveness, but she merely said she would leave him to God to deal with him, as he was only reaping the fruits of his bad deeds. He died in a few hours.

Many misdeeds could be quoted against him. He even used to intercept the fishermen and compel them hand over to him any quantity of fish which he demanded.[17]

⁕⁕

Mrs Kate O'Carroll, b.1877, native of Mullingar, Co. Westmeath, living in Bailieboro, Co. Cavan.

My grandmother showed me a house outside Mullingar, from which a poor widow was evicted at the time of the Famine. She wasn't able to pay her rent, and one day she was cooking the children's dinner in a pot that was hanging from a pot-hook over the fire. The old bailiff came in and took the pot off the fire.

'Oh,' says she, 'let me boil the children's dinner.'

'No,' says he, and he flung the pot out of the door, and he put the widow and children out as well. My grandmother told me that, after his death, he was seen going about that road with the pot-hooks hanging around his neck.[18]

❧

William Torrens, b.1872, Lisminton, Ballintra, Co. Donegal. He heard it from his father, William Torrens, 1828–1912, in the townland of Rath

The well-to-do class caught the fever as well in trying to bring aid to the stricken. Mr Alexander Hamilton of Coxtown near Ballintra, a local landlord and land agent for many big estates in south-west Donegal, caught the fever in May 1847 and nearly died from it.

This man rose from very commonplace people and in his early years lived in a common thatched country house, but he got on rapidly and well after securing the agency of a small estate. He had a record of stern harshness to poor tenants who could not pay their rent promptly and many evictions took place on his land.

At the time of the Famine many people were evicted from farms surrounding his own homestead and he eventually found himself in possession of between 200 and 300 acres of good land.

This man also attained notoriety by his severity as a local magistrate. There is still a story current in the district regarding a priest from Pettigo who was brought up at a court in Ballintra on some charge of which he was entirely innocent. The attitude of Alexander Hamilton on the bench was so entirely hostile to the priest that it drew comment from many Protestants. The priest eventually was acquitted, and arising out of it, he is said to have made a remark that there would never be an heir for Coxtown which ran in the male line.

Shortly afterwards Hamilton's wife was brought to her

confinement and gave birth to something with a head on it like a dog which vanished under the bed.

It is know for a fact that there has never been an heir for Coxtown in the direct family ever since.[19]

⁂

SAVED FROM THE GRAVE

*Maighréad Ní Dhonnabháin, b.1866, a farmer, Drom Inide,
Drimoleague, Co. Cork*

But the most remarkable of all Famine victims in this district was Tom Gearins. Tom was a young lad the time of the Famine. With many others he was taken and thrown into the Famine Hole in Skibbereen Abbey. He was not dead and somehow or other he was able to raise his hand. He was eventually rescued but it was found that both his legs were broken and badly deformed from the weight that was on him. However he lived, but his legs were all out of joint. He spent the greater part of his time in the district working with the Protestant Minister.

When the poorhouse was built in Skibbereen, Tom used go in there for the winter and then return to Drimoleague for the summer. Whenever he was getting tired of the work he would say to the Minister, 'Would to God sir, 'tis time for Tom Gearins to go to roost'.

On one occasion the Board of Guardians in Skibbereen were providing poor people with boots. Tom thought that a pair would be a great relief to his bórach [misshapen] legs so he applied. He was told however that he had no hope of the boots unless he composed a verse about himself. Whether he is the author of the following or not, this verse is known to all the older stock in Drimoleague.

I arose from the dead in the year '48,
Though a grave in the Abbey had near been my fate,
And since for subsistence I've done all my best,

Though one leg points east and one leg points west.
And never a tax on the ratepayers I've been,
I've roamed o'er the country enjoying each scene,
I only appeal to you now for a pair
Of boots and I'll vanish again into air.[20]

⋯⦿⋯

OUTWITTING THE SOUPERS

Patrick O'Donnell, b.1863, Cam, Mostrim Parish, Co. Longford

The parson gave the grass of a cow to a man if he'd go to church for three Sundays. So the man agreed to the bargain and went to church for three Sundays, but he was going to mass as well and the parson found out about it. So the next time they met the parson says,

'I hear you're going to mass.'

'Why wouldn't I,' says the man, 'I go to you for the grass of me cow, but I go to mass for the good of me sowl.'[21]

⋯⦿⋯

*Thomas Kelly, Rockfleet, Carrowbeg, Westport, Co. Mayo,
b.1855, Rosturk*

There were soup schools in Mulranny and Murrevaugh (just east of Mulranny). Some of the people turned with the soupers and remained with them till they died. A few of these went to Inisbiggle in Ballycroy when driven from home by shame, fear or otherwise.

One man, not a native of this parish, turned. He was passing by the priest's house one day in his native place and raised his hat.

'Ah', says the priest, 'you cannot please God and the devil.'

'Ah father,' said he, 'It's only till the praties grow.' He turned back later. His son was also a Protestant, but only for a time during the Famine.[22]

❦

Mary Daly, b.1874, a farmer, Faughart, native of Creggan Parish, Crossmaglen, Co. Armagh

'Aw, bad luck to you, oul bottle the soup.' Sure I heard that cast up to people at home myself. You'd get so much soup yourself, and so much to take home to your own ones in a bottle.

At that time the courthouse in Cross was where the old barracks was. They had beef and soup and were giving it out. And Minister Ashe, I think it was from Philipstown he was, he was trying to convert the Catholics [to Protestantism].

And fever was awful prevalent, but in them times all men was bled for that. Someone would take so much blood from them. That was common. But when Minister Ashe come he was able to give the people more than the priest.

It was Minister Ashe tried to convert them all. The fever was raging at the time and this man and his family were all bad. This was out at Cross. He hadn't the land or anything tilled. So Minister Ashe come to him and said he'd till it.

'I'll till it,' says he, 'if you come to the church.'

So he said he would and I think some of them died. It's long since I heard them at it. But he got the crop in anyway. And so he was to go to Minister Ashe's church this Sunday, to get the communion I think. So when he didn't come Minister Ashe come to him, but he wouldn't go into the house for fear of the fever. He had him converted up to that to get the communion. So he says 'I though you were to come to my house for the communion?' 'Aw,' says he, 'sure I'm not fit.' So he got a shovel and he put it into him on a shovel. 'I'm not able to lift it,' says he to Minister Ashe. 'Well own up to it and that'll do,' says Minister Ashe.

So anyway he got over the fever and when he was able to go about he went to the chapel and Minister Ashe come to him again.

'You were at your own chapel today,' says he, 'and you were to come to my church. You and your whole family was it. And,' says he, 'I put in your crop and I want the price of it.'

'Aw,' says the man back, 'own up to it and that'll do.'[23]

APPENDIX I

Here are examples of some of the questions about the Famine brought to the attention of collectors by Seán Ó Súilleabháin in *A Handbook of Irish Folklore* (Dublin, 1942). As well as those included here, to give an idea of the wide range of possible questions and answers, there are many other relevant sections under heading such as Acts of Violence, Landlords and Tenants, Land-agents and Middlemen, Sickness, Medical Practitioners in Olden Times, The Care of the Sick, Death, The Funeral, The Graveyard, The Grave.

FAMINE YEARS

By what names was the Famine of 1847 known locally: the Bad Times, An Droch-Shaoghal, An Gorta Mór, Bliain an Ghorta? Did the Famine affect the people of your district very much? Write down all available stories and accounts about it under the following heads: condition of the local community prior to the Famine, density of population, main sources of food supply, how the blight came on the potato crop, attempts to counteract it, quality of potato and grain crops during those years, special foods used by the people (list of herbs, plants, roots, fruits, sea-growths, shellfish, various kinds of flesh, animal blood, meal, and other substitutes used to supplement the ordinary diet). Attempts made by the people to secure food (taking of crops and cattle belonging to others, man traps and warning notices etc.). Give an account of the privations suffered by the local people as a result of the Famine; hunger, cold, sickness, fever, cholera, evictions, death, dissolution of families. Write down accounts of local graves and graveyards which came into being during the Famine. Stories of kindness and generosity shown by the people to one another at that time; accounts of help given by benevolent societies and hospitable individuals (well-to-do farmers, landlords, priests and ministers, shop-keepers etc.).

RELIEF OF THE SUFFERING

What local schemes were adopted either by the people themselves, by the government, or by benevolent societies to relieve distress? Give as much detail as possible with regard to your own district. Distribution of soup and meal ('soup-kitchens', 'tighthe praisce', 'tighthe brochain', 'brot', Indian meal, meal obtained from wrecked ships etc.). By whom was this food distributed locally? How was it cooked and divided? Meal earned in wages or in exchange for land. Work provided as relief schemes: accounts of roads, bridges, piers and harbours built during the Famine; daily wages of men and women (in money or in kind), stewards, stories told by those who worked at such schemes, hardships endured etc. Poorhouses during the Famine. Rent-collection, evictions, kindness of some individual landlords. Migration and movements of population during the Famine (e.g. in some places people went toward the sea-side where food was said to be more plentiful). Miracle-stories of the Famine: mermaid-cow supplied people near the Shannon with milk; stones put to boil in pot became potatoes; food appears on a table mysteriously; chaff sown after distribution of seed among the needy produces good crop (story told to explain placename Ros an Chátha). Are there any local examples of such stories?

PROSELYTISM

Write down accounts of attempts made locally to win over people as a whole or some of them from the Catholic faith. When were some activities most pronounced? Attitude of the people and the clergy towards them. Were any Missions or colonies established locally for the purpose of proselytism? Details. Bible-schools: use to which they were put, attendance, teachers, programme, success or failure. Activities of bible-readers. Distribution of tracts and bibles printed in Irish. Were there any centres set up locally for the distribution of soup or food among the people (soup kitchens)? Give their location. By what names were these centres called? Were they regarded as proselytising centres? Were persons who refused to 'turn' sent away without food? Did some local people give up their faith? Temporarily or permanently? Were priests similarly involved? By what names were perverts known locally (soupers, jumpers, cait bhreaca, Albanaigh, Sasanaigh)? Songs, ballads and stories about persons who gave up their faith through proselytism.

EXTRACTS FROM EMIGRATION

Did people emigrate from your district to other countries? When did this custom begin? What local responses were responsible for it? Did it continue over a period of years. To what countries did the local people emigrate..? Did whole families emigrate in former times? Accounts of this (details of free emigration, 'coffin ships', long hazardous voyages)...Did the local people assemble to bid the emigrant farewell? Give an account of this. By what name was such a gathering known locally? (e.g. American Wake)? From which ports did local emigrants leave?...

EXTRACTS FROM LOCAL EVICTIONS

Give an account of evictions which were carried out in your district at any time. When were evictions most frequent? Were some of the local landlords ill-disposed towards their tenants? Why were people evicted (refusal or inability to pay rent; refusal to vote as the landlord wished;...clearance of families to make way for richer tenants...)...How were evictions carried out locally? Was notice given? When did they usually take place? Stories about 'emergency men', 'grabbers', bailiffs, and battering rams. Was force used to eject the people?...Was the fire quenched and the roof thrown down? What was done with people's furniture and other possessions? Was their livestock taken in lieu of rent? Where did evicted families usually go? Did any of them return to their homes later? Did some go to the workhouse or emigrate?...Stories about the following: evicted man becomes highway robber; curse of evicted family or widow falls on heads of evictors; houses haunted by ghosts of persons implicated in evictions.

Appendix II

Irish Folklore Commission Questionnaire: The Great Famine of 1845–1852

1. Are there any local traditions about the manner in which the blight first appeared? How was the crop affected (while growing, before being dug, or when stored)? Did the blight return on successive years at that time?

2. Please write down any stories or traditions you can find locally about the following: Famine deaths, burials, graves, graveyards, the Cholera in your district; local fever hospitals at the time.

3. Can you give any accounts of the dissolution of individual local families during the Famine (or soon afterwards) by death or migration (to other districts) or emigration (to other countries)? Where did those who left the districts go to? Passage money, emigrant ships.

4. Local evictions during or soon after the Famine. What was the attitude of the local landlords, merchants and shopkeepers, well-to-do families and priests to the people during the Famine; alms, credits, mortgages on land, seizures, evictions etc. Local 'Poorhouses'. Homeless individuals.

5. Food during the Famine: types of food available locally; uses made of special foods (herbs etc.). Food-centres set up by the government and various societies; local soup-kitchens: how run, individuals associated with them; conditions (if any) attached to the receipt of food at some of those centres. Souperism and proselytism in your district during the Famine (it is necessary to distinguish between centres at which proselytism was carried and those at which it was not). Any accounts of the forcible taking of food (crops, cattle etc.) and of means taken to counter it (man-traps etc.).

6. Accounts of local relief schemes during the Famine (road-making, drainage etc.). Financing of these schemes, pay, stewards, choice of workers, value of the work done. Attitudes of the people generally and of the well-to-do farmers to relief schemes.

REFERENCES

CHAPTER 2 BEFORE THE BAD TIMES
(pp 20–33)
1. IFC 1068:27–38
2. IFC 1075:666–680
3. IFC 1071:1a–73
4. IFC 1072:185–230
5. IFC 1075:602–608
6. IFC 1069:351–378
7. IFC 1071:1a–73
8. IFC 1072:376–400
9. IFC 1071:1a–73
10. IFC 1071:77–154
11. IFC 1072:237–309
12. IFC 1072:376–400
13. IFC 1072:185–230
14. IFC 1068:125–134

CHAPTER 3 ABUNDANCE ABUSED
AND THE BLIGHT (pp 34–49)
1. IFC 1075:142–152
2. IFC 1136:299–305
3. IFC 1068:289–298
4. IFC 1069–66–69
5. IFC 1072:1–64
6. IFC 1075:688–694
7. IFC 1075:1–69
8. IFC 1069: 182–190
9. IFC 1429: 143–145
10. IFC 1071:233–241
11. IFC 1075:612–615
12. IFC 1069:323–326
13. IFC 1417:281–285
14. IFC 1071:1a–73
15. IFC 1069:108–114
16. IFC 1069:457–468
17. IFC 1072:237–309
18. IFC 1072:376–400
19. IFC 1069:344–348
20. IFC 1069:383–384

21. IFC 1069:351–378
22. IFC 1072:112–116
23. IFC 1075:1–16
24. IFC 1069:33–40
25. IFC 1072:185–230
26. IFC 1075:67–19
27. IFC 1072:65–73

CHAPTER 4 TURNIPS, BLOOD, HERBS
AND FISH (pp 50–67)
1. IFC 1068:235–239
2. IFC 1070:314–316
3. IFC 1069:351–378
4. IFC 1068:135–141
5. IFC 1072:237–309
6. IFC 1074:441–445
7. IFC 1072:319–322
8. IFC 1071:1a–73
9. IFC 1072:376–400
10. IFC 1072:237–309
11. IFC 1074:1–64
12. IFC 1069:43–47
13. IFC 1069:7–10
14. IFC 1069:108–114
15. IFC 1244:61–78
16. IFC 1069:61–82
17. IFC 1072:237–309
18. IFC 1069:351–378
19. IFC 1069:58–63
20. IFC 1173:256–257
21. IFC 1075:542–549
22. IFC 1075:142–152
23. IFC 1075:200–222
24. IFC 1075:192
25. IFC 1075:196–197
26. IFC 1075:164–165
27. IFC 1072:393–396
28. IFC 1072:65–73
29. IFC 1072:1–64

30. IFC 1069:351–378
31. IFC 1075:520–535
32. IFC 1071:1a–37
33. IFC 1069:351–378
34. IFC 1068:251–269
35. IFC 1075:520–535
36. IFC 1069:61–82
37. IFC 1356:111–116
38. IFC 1072:1–64

CHAPTER 5 'NO SIN AND YOU STARVING' (pp 68–84)
1. IFC 1072:185–230
2. IFC 1071:77–154
3. IFC 1075:164–165
4. IFC 1069:185–230
5. IFC 1068:204–206
6. IFC 1136:299–305
7. IFC 1075:321–412
8. IFC 1075:192–193
9. IFC 1075:179–180
10. IFC 1075:164–165
11. IFC 1075:67–129
12. IFC 1075:142–152
13. IFC 1074:359–376
14. IFC 1075:67–129
15. IFC 1073–376
16. IFC 1072:237–309
17. IFC 1072:65–73
18. IFC 1071:233–241
19. IFC 1069:351–378
20. IFC 1069:404–407
21. IFC 1069:344–348
22. IFC 1069:270–280
23. IFC 1069:191–194
24. IFC 1069:215–221
25. IFC 1069:224–225
26. IFC 1068:278–283
27. IFC 1075:558–564
28. IFC 1174:464–468

29. IFC 1220:390
30. IFC 1395:218–230
31. IFC 1480:383–384
32. IFC 1417:281–285
33. IFC 1075:615–621
34. IFC 1068:197–203
35. IFC 1075:520–535
36. IFC 1069:454–456

CHAPTER 6 MOUTHS STAINED GREEN (pp 85–99)
1. IFC 1075:1–16
2. IFC 1480:383–384
3. IFC 1480:136–142
4. IFC 1429:80–81
5. IFC 1356:111–116
6. IFC 1220:394
7. IFC 1174:464–468
8. IFC 462:8–11
9. IFC 415:92–97
10. IFC 1075:663–666
11. IFC 1075:621–627
12. IFC 1068:50–59
13. IFC 1068:235–239
14. IFC 1068:278–283
15. IFC 1069:33–40
16. IFC 1069:132–140
17. IFC 1069:351–378
18. IFC 1070:273–276
19. IFC 1070:312–314
20. IFC 1070:361–362
21. IFC 1071:77–154
22. IFC 1071:224–265
23. IFC 1072:185–230
24. IFC 1072:378–379
25. IFC 1072:406–408
26. IFC 1074:359–376
27. IFC 1075:179–180
28. IFC 87:312

REFERENCES

CHAPTER 7 'THE FEVER, GOD BLESS
US' (pp 100–115)
1. IFC 1075:615–621
2. IFC 1068:289–298
3. IFC 1344:454–456
4. IFC 1136:299–305
5. IFC 1075:558–564
6. IFC 1068:251–269
7. IFC 1069:17–19
8. IFC 1069:33–40
9. IFC 1069:143–146
10. IFC 1069:215–221
11. IFC 1069:231–234
12. IFC 1069:291–294
13. IFC 1069:351–378
14. IFC 1070:304–308
15. IFC 1071:77–154
16. IFC 1071:266–275
17. IFC 1071:290–306
18. IFC 1072:237–309
19. IFC 1072:319–322
20. IFC 1072:328–332
21. IFC 1072:406–408
22. IFC 1074:441–454
23. IFC 1075:1–61
24. IFC 1075:49–52
25. IFC 1075:67–129
26. IFC 1075:153–158
27. IFC 1075:164–165
28. IFC 1075:200–222
29. IFC 1075:270
30. IFC 1075:321–412

CHAPTER 8 THE PAUPERS AND THE
POORHOUSE (pp 116–31)
1. IFC 1075:67–129
2. IFC 1069:351–378
3. IFC 1069:249–260
4. IFC 1068:272–277
5. IFC 1068:244–250

6. IFC 1068: 50–59
7. IFC 1068:125–134
8. IFC 1069:41–44
9. IFC 1136:284–288
10. IFC 1069:141–142
11. IFC 1068:272–277
12. IFC 1068:207–211
13. IFC 1069:215–221
14. IFC 1480:136–142
15. IFC 1356:111–116
16. IFC 1344:218–222
17. IFC 1220:339
18. IFC 1075:653–659
19. IFC 1075:641–653
20. IFC 1075:627–637
21. IFC 1075:621–627
22. IFC 1075:484–498
23. IFC 1069:61–68
24. IFC 1068:147–151
25. IFC 1068:319–322
26. IFC 485:241–245
27. IFC 1069:249–260
28. IFC 1071:224–265
29. IFC 1072:237–309

CHAPTER 9 BOILERS, STIRABOUT
AND 'YELLOW MALE' (pp 132–49)
1. IFC 1395:218–230
2. IFC 1393:275
3. IFC 1358:178–190
4. IFC 1244:484–486
5. IFC 1075:666–680
6. IFC 1075:637–641
7. IFC 1075:641–653
8. IFC 1075:535–541
9. IFC 1069:108–114
10. IFC 1068:272–277
11. IFC 1068:278–283
12. IFC 1068:319–322
13. IFC 1069:20–25

14. IFC 1069:26–32
15. IFC 1069:33–40
16. IFC 1069:43–47
17. IFC 1069:58–63
18. IFC 1069:168–170
19. IFC 1069:304
20. IFC 1069:351–378
21. IFC 1070:304–308
22. IFC 1071:1a–73
23. IFC 1071:77–154
24. IFC 1071:233–241
25. IFC 1072:323–326
26. IFC 1072:346–353
27. IFC 1072:370–372
28. IFC 1072:393–396
29. IFC 1075:67–129
30. IFC 1075:255
31. IFC 1068:319–322
32. IFC 1072:237–309

CHAPTER 10 NEW LINES AND 'MALE ROADS' (pp 150–65)
1. IFC 1075:464–474
2. IFC 1075:456–457
3. IFC 1075:414–510
4. IFC 1075:67–129
5. IFC 1075:153–158
6. IFC 1075:200–222
7. IFC 1074:359–376
8. IFC 1072:376–400
9. IFC 1072:333–334
10. IFC 1072:167–171
11. IFC 1071:1a–33
12. IFC 1069:351–378
13. IFC 1069:344–348
14. IFC 1069:281–295
15. IFC 1069:33–40
16. IFC 1069:26–32
17. IFC 1069:7–10
18. IFC 1068:278–283

19. IFC 1068:235–239
20. IFC 1068:147–151
21. IFC 1068:27–38
22. IFC 1072:185–230
23. IFC 1072:185–230
24. IFC 1070:304–308

CHAPTER 11 'SOUPERS', 'JUMPERS' AND 'CAT BREACS' (pp 166–81)
1. IFC 143:7
2. IFC 1429:80–81
3. IFC 1344:146–151
4. IFC 1136:293–296
5. IFC 1075:627–637
6. IFC 1075:612–615
7. IFC 1068:27–38
8. IFC 1068:50–59
9. IFC 1068:147–151
10. IFC 1068:207–211
11. IFC 1068:251–269
12. IFC 1068:272–277
13. IFC 1068:300–303
14. IFC 1069:17–19
15. IFC 1069:50–52
16. IFC 1069:164–167
17. IFC 1069:249–260
18. IFC 1069:316
19. IFC 1069:323–326
20. IFC 1069:344–348
21. IFC 1071:1a–73
22. IFC 1071:224–265
23. IFC 1071:261–275
24. IFC 1072:338–340
25. IFC 1072:357–361
26. IFC 1075:1–61
27. IFC 1075:153–158
28. IFC 1072:112–116
29. IFC 1072:312–318

REFERENCES

CHAPTER 12 THE BOTTOMLESS
COFFIN AND THE FAMINE PIT (pp
182–96)
1. IFC 1075:200–222
2. IFC 1075:164–165
3. IFC 1072:167–171
4. IFC1069:167–171
5. IFC 1068:50–59
6. IFC1480:383–384
7. IFC 1413:177
8. IFC 1399:551
9. IFC 1075:627–637
10. IFC 1075:558–564
11. IFC 1068:27–38
12. IFC 1068:50–59
13. IFC 1069:108–114
14. IFC 1068–125–134
15. IFC 1068:135–141
16. IFC 1068:197–203
17. IFC 1068:244–250
18. IFC 1068:272–277
19. IFC 1069:26–32
20. IFC 1069:244–248
21. IFC 1069:266–269
22. IFC 1069:351–378
23. IFC 1070:308–312
24. IFC 1071:1a–73
25. IFC 1072:112–116
26. IFC 1072:237–309
27. IFC 1075:414–510
28. IFC 1075:164–165

CHAPTER 13 LANDLORDS, GRAIN
AND GOVERNMENT (pp 197–212)
1. IFC 1417:281–285
2. IFC 1390:228–232
3. IFC 1069:61–82
4. IFC 1068:289–298
5. IFC 1071:224—265
6. IFC 1072:376–400
7. IFC 1075:306–310
8. IFC 1072:237–309

9. IFC 1074:359–376
10. IFC 1072:1–64
11. IFC 1071:224–265
12. IFC 1071:77–154
13. IFC 1069:339–343
14. IFC 1069:132–140
15. IFC 1068:235–239
16. IFC 1075:484–498
17. IFC 1075:321–412
18. IFC 1344:454–456
19. IFC 1069:344–348
20. IFC 1068:319–322
21. IFC 1071:224–265
22. IFC1071:233–241
23. IFC 1075:535–541
24. IFC 1075:255
25. IFC 1075:663–666

CHAPTER 14 AGENTS, GRABBERS
AND GOMBEEN MEN (pp 213–28)
1. IFC 1071:77–154
2. IFC 1075:464–474
3. IFC 1068:300–303
4. IFC 1069:351–370
5. IFC 1069:182–190
6. IFC 1069:351–378
7. IFC 1075:458–463
8. IFC 1071:77–154
9. IFC 1072:185–230
10. IFC 1068:135–141
11. IFC 1075:67–129
12. IFC 1068:135–400
13. IFC 1072:376–400
14. IFC 1070:301–303
15. IFC 1069:304
16. IFC 1068:319–322
17. IFC 1075:520–535
18. IFC 1068:27–38
19. IFC 1072: 1–64
20. IFC 1244:561–563
21. IFC 1075:688–694
22. IFC 821:484–485

23. IFC 1069:454–456
24. IFC 1075:109–129
25. IFC 1069:43–47

CHAPTER 15 'A TERRIBLE LEVELLING OF HOUSES' (pp 229–43)
1. IFC 1480:383–384
2. IFC 1075:464–474
3. IFC 1074:441–454
4. IFC 1075:688–694
5. IFC 1071:1a–73
6. IFC 1072:237–309
7. IFC 1072:312–318
8. IFC 1073:350–376
9. IFC 1074:83–85
10. IFC 1071:290–306
11. IFC 1072:185–230
12. IFC 1069:304
13. IFC 1069:344–348
14. IFC 1069:351–378
15. IFC 1069:222–223
16. IFC 1069:236–242
17. IFC 1069:66–69
18. IFC 1069:26–32
19. IFC 1069:108–114
20. IFC 1403:26–27
21. IFC 1069:168–170
22. IFC 1069:61–82

CHAPTER 16 THE COFFIN SHIPS AND THE GOING AWAY (pp 244–59)
1. IFC 1075:558–564
2. IFC 1365:86–88
3. IFC 1358:178–190
4. IFC 1344:218–222
5. IFC 1136:299–305
6. IFC 1136:284–288
7. IFC 1075:641–653
8. IFC 1075:627–637
9. IFC 1075:621–627
10. IFC 1069:41–44
11. IFC 1068:235–239

12. IFC 1068:244–250
13. IFC 1068:289–298
14. IFC 1069:58–63
15. IFC 1069:132–140
16. IFC 1069:191–194
17. IFC 1069:291–294
18. IFC 1069:294–329
19. IFC 1069:323–326
20. IFC 1071:1a–33
21. IFC 1071:290–306
22. IFC 1072:237–309
23. IFC 1072:409–410
24. IFC 1075:153–158
25. IFC 1075:160–162
26. IFC 1075:306–310
27. IFC 1075:321–412

CHAPTER 17 OF CURSES, KINDNESS AND MIRACULOUS FOOD (pp 260–79)
1. IFC 1069:249–260
2. IFC 1075:171–172
3. IFC 1068:125–134
4. IFC 1190:289
5. IFC 842:39–42
6. FC 1071:77–154
7. IFC 1071:77–154
8. IFC 1068:204–206
9. IFC 1075:54
10. IFC 778:553
11. IFC 1072:65–73
12. IFC 1069:294
13. IFC 1069:294
14. IFC 1069:454–456
15. IFC 1072:237–309
16. IFC 1070:301–303
17. IFC 1244:561–563
18. IFC 1075:688–694
19. IFC 1072:376–400
20. IFC 1068:244–250
21. IFC 1429:80–81
22. IFC 1072:112–116
23. IFC 1072:312–318

SELECT BIBLIOGRAPHY

Campbell, S.J., *The Great Irish Famine*, Dublin 1994.

Crawford, E.M., *Famine: The Irish Experience 900–1900*, Edinburgh 1989.

Daly, M., *The Famine in Ireland*, Dublin 1986.

Donnelly, J.S., 'The Great Famine' in Vaughan, W.E., *et al* eds., *The New History of Ireland* V, Oxford 1989.

Edwards, R.D. and Williams, T.D. eds., *The Great Famine: Studies in Irish History*, Dublin 1956.

Kinealy, C., *This Great Calamity*, Dublin 1994.

Lee, J., *The Modernisation of Irish Society 1848–1918*, Dublin 1973.

Ó Gráda, C., *An Drochshaol: Béaloideas agus Amhráin*, Dublin 1994.

Ó Gráda, C., *The Great Irish Famine*, Dublin 1989.

Ó Gráda, C., *Ireland Before and After the Famine*, 2nd edition, Manchester 1993.

Ó Tuathaigh, G., *Ireland Before the Famine 1798–1848*, Dublin 1972.

Póirtéir, C., ed., *The Great Irish Famine–Thomas Davis Lectures*, Dublin 1995.

Póirtéir, C., ed., *Gnéithe den Ghorta*, Dublin 1995.

Póirtéir, C., *Glórtha ón Ghorta*, Dublin 1995.

Woodham-Smith, C., *The Great Hunger: Ireland 1845–1849*, London 1962.

INDEX

Conlon family, 239
Connell, Darby, 220–21
Connell, Mr, 225
Connor, Mr, 220–21
Connor Doon, Mick, 69, 266
Connors, Michael, 222
Conroy, Larry, 240
Cootehill, Co. Cavan, 67, 86–7, 124
Corbett, F., 211
Corcoran, Mrs Peter, 123–4
Corduff, Michael, 14
  agents, 223–5
  food, 55, 64, 67
  food distribution, 133, 134–5
  landlords, 205–6
  potato blight, 36–7
  theft, 81
Cormack, James, 56
Cotter, Miss, 90
Craig, Frank, 198
Cratloe, Co. Clare, 35, 101, 199, 251–2
Creeslough, Co. Donegal, 35, 71, 102, 247
Cremin, Mrs, 265–6
crime, 6
  during the Famine, 68–84
Cronin, John B., 207–8
Croom, Co. Limerick, 90, 121, 170, 184, 187
Crossbridge, Co. Wicklow, 61
Crossmaglen, Co. Armagh, 180, 234
Crowley, Seán, 108, 235–6, 255
Curley, Anne, 241
curses, 10
Cusack, Mr, 90

Daly, Mary, 180–81, 234
Danagher family, 101
Dave, Freeman, 209
De Clifford, Baroness, 208
  death, causes of, 6, 85–99
Delaney, James G., 14
Delaney, Richard, 102, 210
Delmedge family, 138

Delvin, Co. Westmeath
  agents, 222
  burials, 185–6
  disease, 102
  emigration, 245
  food, 58, 64–5, 66
  food distribution, 137
  food relief, 211
  meal mongers, 225
  theft, 80, 84
Dempsey, Darby, 76–7
Dennehy, Mick, 95–6
Devoy, John, 73–4
Dick family, 238
disease
  during the Famine, 6–7, 100–115
  nutritional, 85
Diver, Mr, 231–2
Dohallow, Co. Cork, 69
Doherty, Shaun, 135
Dolan, Pat, 104
Donegal, County, 234–5
Donegan family, 167
Donnelly, James, 55, 161
Donoghue, Martin, 201–2, 259
Donoghue family, 162
Doogan family, 235
Dorrian family, 235
Doudigan, William
  agents, 218
  death, 97
  evictions, 237
  potato blight, 48
  pre-Famine, 22, 31–3
  relief works, 165
  theft, 68–9
Dowling, Fr, 137
Downshire, Marquis of, 139
Doyle, James, 262
Doyle, John, 59–60, 114, 155, 182–3
Doyle, Mr, 137
Doyle, Paddy, 193
Drimoleague, Co. Cork, 119–20, 189, 250–51
Drogheda, Co. Louth, 104

food
- distribution of, 7, 132–49
- before the Famine, 30–33
- during the Famine, 5–6, 50–67

Forde, Patrick, 143
Forde family, 176
Forkhill, Co. Armagh, 53, 110, 146
Fox, Arthur, 72
Furlong, Walter, 167–8

Gage, Mr, 198
Gallagher, Tony, 43
Gallagher family (Ballina), 239
Gallagher family (Donegal), 235
Gargan, Barney, 22–3, 83, 101
Garrison, Co. Fermanagh, 164
Gearins, Tom, 119–20
Geoghegan, Brien, 137
Gildea, Michael, 53, 111, 231–2
Gilmore, Mrs, 80, 102, 185–6, 245
Ginty family, 239
Glencolumkille, Co. Donegal, 173
Glenelly, Co. Tyrone, 87
Glenflesk, Co. Kerry, 51
Glenville, Co. Cork, 143–4, 157–8
gombeen men, 9, 213–28
Gonoude, Peter, 240
Goold, Wyndham, 199, 242–3
Gorman, Michael, 157, 183
Gorman family (Inistioge), 112–13
Gorman family (Moule), 144
Granard, Co. Longford, 86, 123–4
Grand Juries, 150–51, 227
Grant, Sarah, 178–9
Grantstown Lough, 270
graveyards, 8–9
Greany, Ellen, 106–7
Green, Hugh, 154, 219
Green, Mr, 72
Gregory Clause, 229
Griott family, 162
Grod, Harry, 227
Guinness, Mr, 105
Gwynn, Mr, 147–8

Hacketstown, Co. Carlow, 262
Hadlock, Tom, 90–91
Hamilton, Alexander, 201
Hamilton, John, 203–5
Hanniffe, Mrs, 239
Hanrahan, John, 154
Hardiman, Fr Tom, 159
Harte, James, 32
Hayes, Joan, 189
Healy, Pat, 68–9
Healy family, 172–3
Heerey family, 249
Heffernan, Mr, 222
Heneghan, Michael, 238
Hennigan family, 239
Henry, Manus, 49
Heuston family, 179
Higgins, James, 110–11
Hilltown, Co. Down, 139
Hoare, Fr, 258
Hollywood, Co. Down, 103, 173
housing, 26–30
Howard, Michael, 41, 82, 198
Howley, Colonel, 202
Hudson, Mr, 158, 254–5
Hume, Minister, 173
Hurley, Kathleen, 88–9, 118–19, 128–30, 174, 261
Hurley, Mr, 264–5
Hussey, Edward, 127

Indian meal, 132–49
Inishowen, Co. Donegal, 55, 134, 141, 228, 246
Inistioge, Co. Kilkenny
- disease, 112–13
- food distribution, 148
- gombeen men, 227–8
- land grabbers, 219
- poorhouse, 117
- potato blight, 48
- relief works, 154
- theft, 72, 73–4
Irish Folklore Commission, 5, 13–16, 17

INDEX

298